T0301399

Tax Policy Design and Behavioural
Microsimulation Modelling

Tax Policy Design and Behavioural Microsimulation Modelling

Hielke Buddelmeyer
Research Fellow
University of Melbourne, Australia

John Creedy
The Truby Williams Professor of Economics
University of Melbourne, Australia

Guyonne Kalb
Associate Professor
University of Melbourne, Australia

Edward Elgar
Cheltenham, UK • Northampton, MA, USA

Published by
Edward Elgar Publishing Limited
Glensanda House
Montpellier Parade
Cheltenham
Glos GL50 1UA
UK

Edward Elgar Publishing, Inc.
William Pratt House
9 Dewey Court
Northampton
Massachusetts 01060
USA

A catalogue record for this book
is available from the British Library

Library of Congress Control Number: 2006940755

ISBN: 978 1 84542 914 0

Printed and bound in Great Britain by MPG Books Ltd, Bodmin, Cornwall

Contents

x   *Contents*

PART IV   FURTHER DEVELOPMENTS

Figures

Tables

Acknowledgments

The work on which chapters 5 to 8 are based was supported by the Australian Department of Family and Community Services. Research projects on which chapters 4, 9, 11 and 12 are based were supported by, respectively, an Australian Research Council SPIRT grant, *The Australian*, the Australian Labor Party and the New Zealand Treasury. We are grateful for this support and the permission to use the results from these research projects. However, the views expressed in this book are those of the authors and do not represent the views of the Minister for Families, Community Services and Indigenous Affairs, the Department of Family and Community Services and Indigenous Affairs, the Commonwealth Government, *The Australian*, the Australian Labor Party or the New Zealand Treasury.

The material in this book is based on work which initially appeared in a number of separate journal papers, reports and discussion papers, although they have undergone substantial revisions. Chapter 3 is based on Creedy and Dawkins (1999). Chapter 4 is based on Creedy, Kalb and Kew (2003). Chapters 5, 6 and 7 are based on Kalb, Kew and Scutella (2002), Creedy, Kalb and Scutella (2006), and Cai, Creedy and Kalb (2006) respectively. Chapter 8 is based on Kalb, Kew and Scutella (2005). Chapters 9, 10 and 11 are based on Buddelmeyer, Dawkins, Freebairn and Kalb (2004b), Buddelmeyer, Dawkins and Kalb (2004), and Buddelmeyer, Dawkins, Duncan, Kalb and Scutella (2004a) respectively. For chapters 9 to 11, the simulations were re-run and some of the results are slightly different from those in the original papers. Chapter 12 is based on Kalb, Cai and Tuckwell (2005). Finally, chapter 13 draws on parts of Creedy and Kalb (2005a).

We are very grateful to our joint authors, Lixin Cai, Peter Dawkins, Alan Duncan, John Freebairn, Hsein Kew, Rosanna Scutella and the late Ivan Tuckwell for their contributions to the papers underlying this book. Finally, we should like to thank the editors of the relevant journals for permission to use the material here.

PART I. INTRODUCTION

1 Microsimulation Modelling

This book is concerned with the ways in which tax policy design can be enhanced by the use of a behavioural tax microsimulation model capable of providing detailed ex ante evaluations of the effects of planned or actual tax reforms. Tax policy questions may relate to specific issues, concerning perhaps the revenue implications of a particular tax, or they may involve an extensive analysis of the cost and redistributive effects of a large number of taxes and transfer payments. The many complexities involved in examining tax issues force economists to produce a framework in which the various inter-relationships become more manageable and transparent. Hence the use of tax models is unavoidable. Small models help to provide useful general lessons and guiding principles for reform. However, specific analyses that can be directly related to practical policy questions and can provide direct inputs into policy debate require the construction of larger tax microsimulation models.

This book gives examples of several practical applications, analysing tax and social security payment policies using a microsimulation model. However, this first chapter provides an introduction to this type of model by explaining in relatively non-technical terms the basic form of a behavioural tax microsimulation model. It also briefly describes the model on which most of the analyses in this book rely, the Melbourne Institute Tax and Transfer Simulator (MITTS).

The distinguishing feature of microsimulation models is the use of a large cross-sectional dataset giving information about the characteristics of individuals and households, including their labour supply, earnings and (possibly) expenditure. Microsimulation models are therefore able to replicate closely the considerable degree of heterogeneity observed in the population.

A behavioural microsimulation model estimating labour supply responses to policy changes consists of three components. The first, discussed in section 1.1, is an accounting or arithmetic microsimulation model, sometimes called a static model. This component imputes net household incomes for a representative sample of households, for both incumbent and counterfactual tax-benefit regimes.

The second component is a quantifiable behavioural model of individual tastes for net income and labour supply (or equivalently, non-work time), with which individuals' preferred labour supply under a given set of economic circumstances may be simulated. The third component is a mechanism to allocate to each individual a preferred supply of hours in the face of any tax-benefit system. Analysing simulated changes in this allocation of labour supply, between some base tax system and a counterfactual regime, forms the essence of behavioural microsimulation. These two components are described in section 1.2.

The MITTS model is then described briefly in section 1.3, where emphasis is placed on giving an informal explanation of the way in which labour supply variations are modelled in the behavioural component of MITTS. Although microsimulation models deal with a wide range of types of individual and household, it is useful to compare some aggregated measures regarding labour supply variations with those available from independent studies. Such comparisons are made in section 1.4.

Thinking in terms of models forces analysts, as far as possible, to be explicit about the simplifications used. Hence the inevitable limitations of models can be clearly recognised – all models have their limitations though some are less transparent than others. In using microsimulation models it should be borne in mind that they are supply-side partial equilibrium models. Behavioural components concentrate on examining the effects on variations in the hours of work that individuals wish to supply of changes in the tax structure. No allowance is made for the demand for labour. Hence, depending on what happens to the demand for labour, individuals may in reality not be able to work their desired number of hours. Large changes in the tax structure, designed for example to increase the labour force participation of benefit recipients, may themselves have effects on the demand for labour. In partial equilibrium models, there is an additional assumption that changes in the tax and transfer system have no effect on individuals' wage rates. Microsimulation models also typically provide a static overview of one point in time and do not allow for life cycle dynamics. Decisions on labour force participation could be different when only short-term implications are taken into account compared with decisions based on a longer time horizon.

1.1 Non-behavioural Microsimulation

The majority of large-scale tax simulation models are non-behavioural or arithmetic. That is, no allowance is made for the possible effects on individuals' consumption plans or labour supplies of tax changes. It is sometimes said that they provide information about the effects of tax changes on the 'morning after' the change. This section describes a typical arithmetic microsimulation model in subsection 1.1.1, followed by a discussion of the data required to build this type of model in subsection 1.1.2. This is followed in subsection 1.1.3 by discussion of an important component of any tax policy microsimulation model, the tax and transfer system.

1.1.1 A Typical Arithmetic Model

Advantages of non-behavioural models include the fact that they do not involve the need for estimation of econometric relationships, such as labour supply or commodity demand functions. They are relatively easy to use and quick to run. They can therefore be accessed by a wide range of users. Furthermore, in view of the fact that no econometric estimation is required, they retain the full extent of the heterogeneity contained in the survey data used.

When examining the effects of policy changes, these models generally rely on tabulations and associated graphs, for demographic groups, of the amounts of tax paid (and changes in tax) at various percentile income levels. The more sophisticated models have extensive 'back end' facilities allowing computation of a range of distributional analyses and tax progressivity measures, along with social welfare function evaluations in terms of incomes.

Arithmetic models are typically used to generate profiles, again for various household types, of net income at a range of gross income levels. These profiles are useful for highlighting certain discontinuities, and are helpful when trying to redesign tax and transfer systems in order to overcome discontinuities and excessively high marginal tax rates over some income ranges.

1.1.2 The Data

Reference has already been made to the data requirements of tax models. This raises special problems for modellers in Australia. The two large-scale household surveys that are potentially useful are the Household Expenditure Survey (HES) and the Survey of Income and Housing Costs (SIHC). The former does not contain sufficient information about hours worked by individuals while the latter does not contain information about expenditure patterns. The SIHC is a representative sample of the Australian population, containing detailed information on labour supply and income from different sources, in addition to a variety of background characteristics of individuals and households. The measurement of income in the HES is known to be unreliable, so that in developing models for the analysis of direct taxes and transfer payments, it is not surprising that reliance has been placed on the SIHC. This means that it is not straightforward to include indirect tax in Australian direct tax models.[1] The extension of models to cover consumption taxes would require some elaborate data merging.

When analysing actual or proposed policy changes, it is preferred to use data which are as close to the relevant time period as possible to avoid having a starting point that is too different from reality. Given the delays in the release of data by the Australian Bureau of Statistics (ABS) and the occasional changes in surveying frequency of the SIHC, this can be difficult to achieve. For example, when simulating the effect of the tax and social security changes of July 2000, only 1997/1998 data were available. MITTS updates all financial information to the relevant year; that is, the amounts of income in 1997/1998 were increased to reflect the corresponding July 2000 amounts. To update incomes, the Consumer Price Index is used, and to update wage rates, the average male and female wage indices are used. However, if the tax and social security system is substantially different in the year for which the data are obtained from the year for which a change needs to be simulated, the different incentives arising from the different

---

[1] Indirect tax models for Australia include the Demand and Welfare Effects Simulator (DAWES) developed in Creedy (1999).

systems in the two years might well have caused labour supply changes. To take this possibility into account, MITTS can also update labour supply in the base dataset if required.

An alternative approach to deal with this issue is to run two simulations instead of one simulation and compare the pre-reform and post-reform systems via a common third system, which is to be used as the base system in both simulation runs. This third system has to be the system in place at the time the data were obtained. This approach was used in Buddelmeyer *et al.* (2004a, b) and in Buddelmeyer, Dawkins and Kalb (2004), where data from 2000/2001 were used to evaluate the 2004 system against alternative systems.

1.1.3 The Tax and Transfer System

Detailed knowledge of the tax and social security system is required to build a microsimulation model. This sometimes involves several government departments and the full details are rarely codified in accessible forms. Actual tax and transfer systems are typically extremely complex and contain a large number of taxes and benefits which, being designed and administered by different government departments, are usually difficult to integrate fully. The complexity increases where several means-tested benefits are available, because of the existence of numerous eligibility requirements. It is only when a great deal of detailed information about individuals is available that it becomes possible to include the complexities of actual tax and transfer systems in a simulation model.

However, it is unlikely that household surveys contain sufficient information to replicate realistic tax systems fully. In some cases, for example where asset values are required in the administration of means tests, it may be necessary to impute values, which may not always be possible. Furthermore, regulations regarding the administration of taxes and transfers often leave room for some flexibility in interpretation. In particular, the administration of means tests or other benefits may allow a degree of discretion to be exercised by benefit officers who deal directly with claimants. Changes in the interpretation of (possibly ambiguous) rules, or the degree to which some rules are fully enforced, can take place over time. Furthermore, there may be changes in people's awareness of the benefits available, and the eligibility rules, thereby affecting the degree of take-up.

In view of these limitations, even large-scale models may not be able to replicate actual systems entirely. Thus they may not accurately reproduce aggregate expenditure and tax levels. Similarly, the same problems may give rise to distortions in measuring the extent to which redistribution occurs. Another difficulty is that household surveys may contain non-representative numbers of some types of household and benefit recipient. It is usually necessary to apply a set of grossing-up factors, or sample weights, to enable aggregation of results to the population level.

1.2   Behavioural Microsimulation

Behavioural models are often needed when assessing proposed policy changes, because many tax policy changes are designed with the aim of altering the behaviour of individuals. In the context of consumption, environmental taxes such as carbon taxes, or sumptuary taxes, are used to reduce the demand for harmful goods. For example, some policies are designed to induce more individuals to participate in paid employment or, for those already working, to increase their hours of work. The production of behavioural microsimulation tax models, allowing for labour supply variations, represents a considerable challenge and has involved substantial innovations in labour supply modelling. On labour supply modelling in the context of tax simulation models, see, for example, Apps and Savage (1989), Banks, Blundell and Lewbel (1996), Blundell *et al.* (1986), Creedy and Duncan (2002), Creedy and Kalb (2005b), Duncan (1993), Duncan and Giles (1996) and Moffitt (2000). On behavioural responses in EUROMOD (a European microsimulation model including tax and transfer systems of a number of European countries), see Klevmarken (1997).

Even where labour supply is not the main focus of a policy, there may be unintended consequences which affect other outcomes. Measures of the welfare losses, for example resulting from increases in taxes, are also overstated by non-behavioural models which rely on 'morning after' changes in tax paid, rather than allowing for substitution away from activities whose relative prices increase. In addition, estimates of the distributional implications of tax changes may be misleading unless behavioural adjustments are modelled. Estimates of tax rates required to achieve specified revenue levels are likely to be understated.

1.2.1 A Typical Behavioural Microsimulation Model

Existing behavioural microsimulation models are restricted in the types of behaviour that are endogenous. At most, individuals' labour supplies and household demands are modelled. Variables such as household formation, marriage and births, along with retirement, labour training and higher education decisions, are considered to be exogenous and independent of the tax changes examined. Independence between commodities and leisure is also assumed. Allowing also for consumption demands essentially involves a two-stage procedure in which a decision is made regarding labour supply and hence income, and then the allocation of the resulting net income over commodities is made. Typically, labour supply in just one job is examined, so that the possibility of working additional hours at a different wage rate is ignored. Indeed, the wage rate is typically calculated by dividing total earnings by the total number of reported hours worked.

A component which evaluates the net income corresponding to any given number of hours worked by each individual is a fundamental component of a behavioural model. This produces, for each individual, the precise budget constraint relating net income to hours worked. The behavioural part of the model can then evaluate which part of each individual's constraint is optimal. This component is in effect an associated non-behavioural model. However, it does not mean that any existing non-behavioural model can be augmented by just adding a behavioural component. The complex architecture of microsimulation models requires the kind of integration that can most conveniently be achieved by simultaneously planning and producing all the components. For example, non-behavioural models are not usually concerned with the production of net incomes corresponding to various hours worked by each individual, but with the relationship between net and gross income at observed labour supply for well-defined demographic types. Therefore, in addition to creating the behavioural component, the non-behavioural component needs to be adjusted as well.

Behavioural microsimulation models have, to some extent, a lower degree of population heterogeneity than non-behavioural models. This is because econometric estimation of the important relationships must involve the use of a limited range of categories. For example, in estimating labour supply behaviour, individuals may be divided into groups such as couples, single males and single females, and single-parent households. The number of groups is limited by the sample size, but many variables, such as age, location, occupation and education level, are used to estimate the relevant functions. In addition, individual-specific variability may be re-introduced to ensure that the optimum labour supply in the face of current taxes actually corresponds, for each individual, to the level that is observed in the current period.

Some households may be fixed at their observed labour supply in the base sample if, following econometric estimation, individuals in the household do not conform to the assumptions of the underlying economic model. For example, implied indifference curves must display decreasing marginal rates of substitution over the relevant range. Problems with the assumptions of the economic model could be reflected by a difficulty of ensuring for each individual that the predicted labour supply under the base tax and transfer system is equal to observed labour supply.

1.2.2 Simulating Changes in Labour Force Participation

An important policy issue relates to the nature of tax and transfer changes designed to encourage more people to participate in the labour market. Hence this is likely to provide a focus for behavioural microsimulation studies, but this is also precisely the area that raises the greatest difficulty for modellers. There are several reasons for this. First, there is less information about nonparticipants in survey data. For example, it is necessary to impute a wage rate for non-workers, using estimated wage equations and allowing for selectivity issues. In addition, variables such as industry or occupation, which are often important in wage equations, are not available for non-workers. A second problem is that there are fixed costs associated with working, irrespective of the number of hours worked. These are usually difficult to estimate in view of data limitations. Finally, labour supply models typically treat nonparticipation as a voluntary decision, giving rise to a corner solution. However, demand-side factors may be important and there may be a discouraged worker effect of unemployment, which is difficult to model.

An important choice must be made between continuous and discrete hours labour supply estimation and simulation. Earlier studies of labour supply used continuous hours models, involving the estimation of labour supply functions. In this case, it is important that the results are such that hours worked can be regarded as the outcome of utility maximisation. In other words, it must be possible to recover the indirect utility function by integration.[2] This contrasts with discrete hours estimation and microsimulation, where net incomes, before and after a policy reform, are required only for a finite set of hours points. The discrete hours approach has substantial advantages from the point of view of estimation, since it allows for the complexity of the tax and transfer system and avoids the problems with endogeneity between the net wage and hours worked which are present when a standard labour supply function is estimated. Furthermore, estimation involves direct utility functions, which can be allowed to depend on many individual characteristics. The determination of optimal labour supply is easier, since utility at each of a limited number of hours levels can readily be obtained and compared. The use of direct utility functions also means that integration from estimated supply functions is avoided in simulation. In addition, modelling the move in and out of the labour market is more straightforward in the discrete than in the continuous model. The discrete hours approach is used in the MITTS model, which is described in the following section.

1.3   The MITTS Model

The Melbourne Institute Tax and Transfer Simulator (MITTS) is a behavioural microsimulation model of direct taxes and transfers in Australia. MITTS was designed to examine tax policy reforms which capture labour supply responses to changes in budget constraints, and is the first full-scale simulation model of its kind in Australia. The results reflect only the supply side of the labour market, and a discrete hours framework is used in which individuals can move between specified discrete hours levels, rather than being able to vary hours continuously.

---

[2] On the integrability condition in labour supply models, see Stern (1986).

Since the first version was completed in 2000, and described in detail in Creedy *et al.* (2002), it has undergone a range of substantial developments. Indeed, any large-scale model requires constant maintenance involving, for example, re-estimation of econometric relationships when new data and methods become available, or the introduction of new ways to make simulations more efficient. Furthermore, enhancements such as the extension of 'front end' and 'back end' facilities need to be made.

In the present version of MITTS, SIHC data from 1994/1995, 1995/1996, 1996/1997, 1997/1998, 1999/2000 and 2000/2001 can be used. The econometric estimates of preferences underlying the behavioural responses are based on data observed between 1994 and 1998. Details of the current wage and labour supply parameters used in MITTS can be found in Kalb and Scutella (2002) and Kalb (2002a, b). All results are aggregated to population levels using the household weights provided with the SIHC. Recently, data from the Household, Income and Labour Dynamics Australia (HILDA) Survey have been transformed so they could be used as the base data for MITTS; see Kalb, Cai and Vu (2004). However, the disadvantage of using the HILDA is that it is not straightforward to aggregate results up to the population level.

1.3.1 MITTS-A: The Arithmetic Model

In MITTS, the arithmetic tax and benefit modelling component is called MITTS-A. This component also provides, using the wage rate of each individual, the information needed for the construction of the budget constraints that are crucial for the analysis of behavioural responses to tax changes.

The tax system component of MITTS contains the procedures for applying each type of tax and benefit. Each tax structure has a data file containing the required tax and benefit rates, benefit levels and income thresholds used in means testing. As mentioned before in subsection 1.1.3, in view of the data limitations of the SIHC, it is not possible to include within MITTS all the complexity of the tax and transfer system. However, all major social security payments and income taxes are included in

MITTS.[3] Pre-reform net incomes at the alternative hours levels are based on the MITTS calculation of entitlements, not the actual receipt. Hence in the calculation of net income it is assumed either that take-up rates are 100 per cent, or a simple rule is used whereby a benefit is not claimed if it is less than a specified amount.

Changes to the tax and benefit structure, including the introduction of additional taxes, can be modelled by editing the programmes in this component. MITTS stores several previous Australian tax and transfer systems, which can be used as base systems for the analysis of policy changes. Alternatively, it is often possible to generate a new tax system by introducing various types of policy change interactively within MITTS by making use of the 'front end' menus. This enables a wide range of new tax structures to be generated without the need for additional programming.

The various components of the tax and benefit structure are assembled in the required way in order to work out the transformation between hours worked and net income for each individual under each tax system. For example, some benefits are taxable while others are not, so the order in which taxes and transfers are calculated is important.

MITTS-A contains the facility to examine each household, income unit and individual in the selected base dataset in turn and generate net incomes, at the given hourly wage rates, for variations in the number of hours worked. Thus the changes in effective marginal tax rates (EMTRs) and labour supply incentives faced by households at various levels of the wage distribution can be compared, in addition to calculating the aggregate costs of different reform packages. Furthermore, distributions of effective marginal tax rates, for a variety of demographic groups, can be produced for pre-reform and post-reform tax systems, as well as distributions of gainers and losers, for various demographic characteristics. Hypothetical households can also be constructed and examined.

---

[3] For details of the different payments, see Payment Guides published by the Commonwealth Department of Family and Community Services (of several years), DVA Facts and the annual report published by the Department of Veterans' Affairs (of several years).

1.3.2 Eligibility for Benefits

The information in the SIHC is used to calculate eligibility for the different social security payments. Detailed information on the different sources of income is available, helping to determine this eligibility. However, not all requirements for eligibility can be checked with the available data. For example, information on assets is not available and the amount of assets may also influence eligibility. Fortunately, the group of households who would not be eligible based on their level of assets (which excludes the home), but would be deemed eligible based on their level of income, is relatively small. In particular, because the SIHC records income from investments (such as dividends or interest) and superannuation income, which are incorporated in the calculations, the absence of asset data is unlikely to be a major problem. Other requirements for eligibility, which cannot be checked, are whether someone has been a resident for at least two years and is actively looking for work. One of the requirements for this may be that the unemployment benefit recipient is not working more than a certain number of hours. The number of hours of work may preclude individuals from unemployment-related benefit receipt, if this level of labour supply precludes effective job search. However, there seems no particular hours level available that could be seen as the cut-off point above which no one would receive benefit payments.

The version of MITTS used in these chapters usually does not allow for individuals who decide not to take-up the benefits for which they are eligible. This is likely to cause overestimation of expenditure on the different payments. Although the receipt of benefits as recorded in the SIHC could be used to get an amount closer to the actual amount, this cannot help us to decide whether after a reform someone will take-up a benefit. To simulate changes, we would need to make assumptions or estimate a model that accounts for take-up of benefits. Thus, a 100 per cent take-up is assumed and it is argued that when interest is in the change in expenditure as a result of the reform, this approach is reasonably satisfactory. Both the amounts before and after the reform will be overestimated, and because the changes are not expected to expand eligibility to a large extent, the predicted percentage changes are expected to be reasonably informative.

1.3.3 MITTS-B and Labour Supply

The behavioural component of MITTS is called MITTS-B. It examines the effects of a specified tax reform, allowing individuals to adjust their labour supply behaviour where appropriate. The behavioural responses generated by MITTS-B are based on the use of quadratic preference functions whereby the parameters are allowed to vary with individuals' characteristics. These parameters were estimated for five demographic groups, which include married or partnered men and women, single men and women, and sole parents; see Kalb (2002a, b). The joint labour supply of couples is estimated simultaneously, unlike a common approach in which female labour supply is estimated with the spouse's labour supply taken as exogenous.

The framework is one in which individuals are considered as being constrained to select from a discrete set of hours levels, rather than being able to vary labour supply continuously. Other studies using this approach include Van Soest (1995), Duncan, Giles and MacCrae (1999) and Keane and Moffitt (1998).

Some individuals are observed to be working a number of hours such that they are facing very high effective marginal rates. One explanation for this is that in practice people may not be claiming all the benefits to which they are entitled, especially if the benefits are small, so that their actual EMTR is not as large as it seems from the calculations. An alternative explanation is that people are in practice restricted in their labour supply choice. If people are actually at hours levels that give them marginal rates of 100 per cent or more, this cannot be explained in a continuous hours labour supply framework. Such points could not be the optimal points in the model, since the indifference curves cannot be flat. However, in a discrete hours approach such labour supply points can be optimal, because if people are not free to vary their hours continuously they have to pick the best discrete choice available. In MITTS-B, individuals are constrained to select from a discrete set of hours levels, rather than being able to vary labour supply continuously.

Different sets of discrete hours points may be used for each demographic group. Different sets of discrete hours points are used for married men and all other groups. Given that the married male's hours distribution is much less spread over part-time and full-time hours than the other distributions, but is mostly divided between nonparticipation and full-time work, men's labour supply is represented by just 6 points, whereas women's labour supply is divided into 11 discrete points. For couples, labour supply is estimated simultaneously for the 2 members, contrary to an approach in which female labour supply is estimated with the spouse's labour supply taken as exogenous.

Given the aim of simulating policy changes with regard to the tax and transfer system and assessing its effect on labour supply, priority is given to incorporating all possible detail on taxes and transfers. Utility is maximised conditional on the restricted total amount of time available to each adult and the restricted amount of total household income. It is expected that utility increases with an increase in leisure, or home production time, and income. Usually more income means less leisure time for one of the adults, except when more income is obtained through social security benefits. It is assumed that everyone who is eligible for benefits takes them up. Maximising a household's utility involves balancing the amount of leisure and income. It is assumed that all nonparticipants are voluntarily not working and that participants are at their preferred labour supply points. Wage rates, non-labour income and household composition are exogenous in this model.

Restricting the number of possible working hours to a limited set of discrete values means that complex tax and transfer details can be incorporated. The economic model, assuming there are two adults in the household, is specified as follows. The utility function, $U(x, \ell_1, \ell_2)$, is maximised subject to a time restriction for each adult. Let ℓ_i and h_i denote the weekly aggregate of leisure and home production time, and hours of work of partner i, with $\ell_1 + h_1 = T$ and $\ell_2 + h_2 = T$. The hs, the time spent in employment, are chosen from discrete hours sets. Let x indicate total net income per week, which is assumed equal to household consumption. The gross wage rates of male and female partners are denoted w_1 and w_2 respectively and y_i are the non-labour incomes. Let C refer to household composition, and $B(\ )$ is the amount of benefit for which a household is eligible, given household composition and household income. The tax function indicating the amount of tax to be paid is $\tau(\ )$. The budget constraint is given by:

$$x = w_1 h_1 + w_2 h_2 + y_1 + y_2 + B(C, w_1 h_1 + w_2 h_2 + y_1 + y_2)$$
$$- \tau(B, w_1 h_1 + y_1, w_2 h_2 + y_2, C) \tag{1.1}$$

The discrete hours choices are given by the sets $[0, h_{11}, h_{12}, ..., h_{1m}]$ and $[0, h_{21}, h_{22}, ..., h_{2,k}]$ for partners 1 and 2 respectively. Using these sets, net income can be calculated for all $(m+1)(k+1)$ combinations of h_1 and h_2. For this limited set of hours, the utility each possible combination of hours would generate, according to the specified utility function, can be computed.

The choice of labour supply is simultaneously determined for both adult members of the household. Depending on the form of the utility function, different interactions between household income and labour supply of both adults can be modelled. For one-adult households, the model is simplified by excluding everything related to the second adult.

Utility is assumed to consist of a deterministic and a random component. Choosing an extreme value specification for the random component results in a multinomial logit model; see Maddala (1983) and Creedy and Kalb (2005b).

The utility function used in the MITTS model is a quadratic specification, following Keane and Moffitt (1998), which is simple but flexible in that it allows for the leisure of each person and income to be substitutes or complements. A fixed cost of working parameter, γ, is included in the income variable x to indicate the cost of working versus nonparticipation, following Callan and Van Soest (1996). As a result of the inclusion in x, this cost of working parameter is measured in dollars per week. The deterministic component of utility is specified as follows:

$$U(x, h_1, h_2) = \beta_x (x - \gamma_1 - \gamma_2) + \beta_1 h_1 + \beta_2 h_2 + \alpha_{xx} (x - \gamma_1 - \gamma_2)^2 + \alpha_{11} (h_1)^2$$
$$+ \alpha_{22} (h_2)^2 + \alpha_{x1} (x - \gamma_1 - \gamma_2) h_1 + \alpha_{x2} (x - \gamma_1 - \gamma_2) h_2 + \alpha_{12} h_1 h_2 \tag{1.2}$$

where the α s and β s are preference parameters and γ_1 and γ_2 are the fixed cost of working parameters to be estimated, where the indices 1 and 2 denote the husband and wife respectively. The fixed cost is zero when the relevant person is not working. For single adult households, all terms related to h_2 drop out of the utility function and γ_2 is set to zero.

Observed heterogeneity is included by allowing β_1, β_2, β_x, γ_1 and γ_2 to depend on personal and household characteristics. Unobserved heterogeneity may be added to β_1, β_2, β_x, and γ_2, in the form of a normally distributed error term with zero mean and unknown variance. In estimation, the unobserved heterogeneity parameters were found to be insignificant while the other parameter values remained unchanged. Parameter estimates for all four demographic groups are in Kalb (2002a).

For those individuals in the dataset who are not working, and who therefore do not report a wage rate, an imputed wage is obtained. This imputed wage is based on estimated wage functions, which allow for possible selectivity bias, by first estimating probit equations for labour market participation, as described in Kalb and Scutella (2002, 2004). However, some individuals are fixed at their observed labour supply if their imputed wage or their observed wage, obtained by dividing total earnings by the number of hours worked, is unrealistic.[4] Furthermore, some individuals such as the self-employed, the disabled, students and those over 65 have their labour supply fixed at their observed hours.

Simulation is essentially probabilistic, as utility at each discrete hours level is specified as the sum of a deterministic component (depending on the hours worked and net income) and a random component (here, an extreme value type I distribution, which is associated with the multinomial logit model). Hence MITTS does not identify a particular level of hours worked for each individual after the policy change, but generates a probability distribution over the discrete hours levels used. Net incomes are calculated at all possible labour supply points. Given a random set of draws from the error term distribution, along with the computed deterministic component of utility at each of the labour supply points, the optimal choice for each draw can be determined conditional on the relevant set of error terms.

A behavioural simulation for each individual begins by setting reported hours equal to the nearest discrete hours level. Then, given the parameter estimates of the quadratic preference function, which vary according to a range of characteristics, a set of random draws is taken from the distribution of the error term for each hours level. The utility-maximising hours level is found by adding the random to the deterministic component of utility for each discrete hours level. This set of draws is rejected if it results in an

---

[4] The rejection range is less than 4 and more than 100 dollars per hour. In total, 121 observations are discarded from the behavioural simulations for this reason.

optimal hours level that differs from the discretised value observed. A user-specified total number of 'successful draws' are produced. These are drawings which generate the observed hours as the optimal value under the base system for the individual. This process is described as 'calibration'.

For the post-reform analysis, the new net incomes cause the deterministic component of utility at each hours level to change, so using the set of successful draws from the calibration stage, a new set of optimal hours of work is produced. This gives rise to a probability distribution over the set of discrete hours for each individual under the new tax and transfer structure. For example, in computing the transition matrices showing probabilities of movement between hours levels, the labour supply of each individual before the policy change is fixed at the discretised value, and a number of transitions are produced for each individual, equal to the number of successful draws specified. Some individuals, such as the self-employed, the disabled, students and those over 65 have their labour supply fixed at their observed hours. For the other individuals, the transition matrices showing probabilities of movement between hours levels are computed using these transitions.

When examining average hours in MITTS-B, the labour supply after the change for each individual is based on the average value over the successful draws, for which the error term leads to the correct predicted hours before the change. This is equivalent to calculating the expected hours of labour supply after the change, conditional on starting from the observed hours before the change. In computing the tax and revenue levels, an expected value is also obtained after the policy change. That is, the tax and revenue for each of the accepted draws are computed for each individual, and the average of these is obtained using the computed probability distribution of hours worked.

In some cases, the required number of successful random draws producing observed hours as the optimal hours cannot be generated from the model within a reasonable number of total drawings. The number of sets of random variables tried per draw, like the number of successful draws required, is specified by the user. If after the total number of tries from the error term distribution, the model fails to predict the observed labour supply for a draw, the individual is fixed at the observed labour supply for that draw. In a few extreme cases, labour supply is fixed for all draws of an individual. The use of this probabilistic approach means that the run-time of MITTS-B is substantially longer than that of MITTS-A.

1.3.4 Combining Different Years of Data

The simulation procedure often involves data from several years of the Survey of Income and Housing Cost and information on the taxation and social security regimes of several years. A few transformation steps are needed to combine these years in the analysis.

First, the behavioural part of the simulation procedure is based on labour supply models. These models are estimated using the Survey of Income and Housing Cost from 1994/95, 1995/96, 1996/97 and 1997/98 with the corresponding taxation and social security rules. Combining several years of data actually helps to identify the model, since slightly different tax regimes were operational in the four years. This provides more variation in net incomes at different hours of labour supply than would otherwise be the case. To estimate one model combining the four years, the net incomes calculated over a range of different possible hours have to be made comparable over the four years. This can be achieved by expressing the calculated net incomes in each of the years in the dollar value of one year. That is, it is necessary to account for the change in the real value of the dollar. All net incomes are expressed in 1997/1998 dollars and the Consumer Price Index is used to inflate the other years' net incomes to the corresponding 1997/1998 level, before using them in the labour supply model.

Second, when simulating labour supply responses, pre-reform and post-reform values also need to be expressed in 1997/1998 dollars, before they can be used as arguments in the labour supply model.

Third, in the simulation all income and wage information is first expressed in dollar values of the pre-reform situation and then in dollar values of the post-reform situation, to calculate net income under the different policies. If required by the user, costings in the tables and differences between pre-reform and post-reform systems can be expressed in dollar values of another period. However, the default is to express costings and differences in pre-reform dollars.

1.4   Labour Supply Elasticities

In constructing any microsimulation model it is important to ensure that, using the base system, it can generate revenue and expenditure totals for various categories that are close to independently produced aggregates, for example from administrative data. For a behavioural model, it is also useful to see how summary information about labour supply behaviour compares with results from other studies. Such comparisons are examined in this section.

It is common in studies of labour supply to provide wage elasticities for various groups, often computed at average values of wages. However, the discrete hours labour supply model used in MITTS simulations of behavioural responses to policy changes does not provide straightforward wage elasticities with regard to labour supply. Indeed, for any individual, there are large variations in the elasticity over the range of hours available. However, elasticities can be calculated by comparing the expected labour supply for an individual after a 1 per cent wage increase with the expected labour supply under the original wage. The resulting percentage change in labour supply can be regarded as a form of wage elasticity. By doing this for each individual in the sample, the average elasticity across the sample, or population when making use of the weights, can be computed. Different concepts are used in the literature. For example, the elasticity could be calculated for a hypothetical person with average values for each of the relevant characteristics. Hence it cannot be expected that the same values will be obtained, but comparisons of orders of magnitude are useful.

Table 1.1 presents uncompensated wage elasticities for those in the population who are allowed to change labour supply in MITTS. For the self-employed, full-time students, disabled individuals and people over 65 this elasticity is assumed to be zero, and those individuals are excluded when calculating the average elasticity. In addition to using predicted labour supply alone, calibration can be used to calculate the elasticity starting from the observed labour supply for those already in work. For non-workers, the elasticity cannot be computed because a percentage change starting from zero hours is not defined. The two final columns in Table 1.1 present the predicted participation rate changes resulting from a 1 per cent wage increase.

The range of elasticities published in the literature is fairly wide, with large differences between studies using different data and approaches; see overviews by Killingsworth (1983), Killingsworth and Heckman (1986), Pencavel (1986) or more recently by Blundell and MaCurdy (1999) or Hotz and Scholz (2003). The implicit labour supply elasticities in MITTS are similar to those generally found within the international literature. The results for married and single men and women are well within the range of results usually found.

Table 1.1 Average wage elasticities for individuals for whom labour supply is simulated in MITTS

	Elasticity derived from		Percentage point change in participation derived from	
	Expected labour supply	Calibrated labour supply (for positive hours only)	Expected labour supply	Calibrated labour supply
Married men	0.24	0.06	0.15	0.15
Married women	0.56	0.37	0.20	0.15
Single men	0.22	0.04	0.16	0.17
Single women	0.38	0.07	0.19	0.16
Single parents	1.48	0.78	0.41	0.24

The elasticity for single parents is often found to be larger than for other groups and this is also found in MITTS. The elasticity implicit in MITTS is in the higher end of this range internationally, although other evidence of a high labour supply responsiveness for single parents in Australia has been found by Murray (1996), Duncan and Harris (2002) and Doiron (2004). Murray (1996) found values between 0.13 and 1.64, depending on the exact specification, for part-time working single mothers. The elasticities for full-time workers and single parents out of the labour force are much smaller, at most 0.30. Murray used 1986 data, where only 13 per cent of all single mothers worked part time and about 23 per cent worked full time. In the 2001 data used here, around 50 per cent of single parents work, and about half of the workers are employed between 1 and 35 hours per week.

Duncan and Harris (2002) analysed the effect of four hypothetical reforms, using a previous version of the labour supply models underlying the behavioural responses in MITTS. Two of these reforms are close to being a 10 per cent increase and 10 per cent decrease in single parents' wage rates. The first is to decrease the withdrawal rate for single parents by 10 per cent, which increases their marginal wage rate while they are on lower levels of income. Duncan and Harris report that this is expected to increase labour force participation by 2.5 percentage points and increase average hours by 0.55 hours. The second reform increases the lowest income tax rate from 20 to 30 per cent. This is expected to decrease participation by 2.8 percentage points and decrease average hours by 1.2 hours. Comparing this with the effect of a 10 per cent wage increase using recent labour supply parameters and data from 2000/2001, effects of a similar magnitude are found. That is, participation is expected to increase by 2.2 percentage points and the average hours are expected to increase by 1.0 hours.

Finally, Doiron (2004) evaluated a policy reform affecting single parents in the late 1980s and found large labour supply effects. Doiron compared the effect obtained through the natural experiment approach with predicted effects of policy changes from the MITTS model, as found in Duncan and Harris (2002) or Creedy, Kalb and Kew (2003). Based on the results from her evaluation, Doiron argued that observed shifts in labour supply of single parents can equal or even surpass the predictions based on behavioural microsimulation.

These results suggest that single parents' labour supply elasticities may be substantial. This is perhaps not surprising, given the low participation rate of single parents and the tendency to work low part-time hours. An increase in labour supply by one hour is a larger percentage increase compared with the same increase for a married man. For the other demographic groups, elasticities of those working few hours are also generally higher than for those in the same group who work greater hours. The single parent group is the smallest demographic group in the population. Thus, a change in their labour supply responsiveness would have a relatively small effect on the overall result.

Another way of validating results is by comparing the predicted effects of a policy change obtained through a simulation with the estimated effects of the policy change after it has been introduced. The problem with this approach is that it is often difficult to find policy changes that can be evaluated accurately. It can be difficult to find a control group with which to compare a treatment group (those affected by the policy change).

Blundell *et al.* (2004) evaluated a range of labour market reforms in the UK by a difference-in-difference approach at the same time as simulating the effects of these reforms. They found similar results for sole parents and married women, but for married men the estimated effects were opposite. They suggested that this could be due to a number of reasons related to the analyses, such as differences in sample selection rules, not accounting for other changes that occurred at the same time as the reforms or not accounting for general equilibrium effects changing the distribution of wages.

It has been difficult to find policy changes in Australia which could be used to test MITTS in a similar way. Some results comparing, for sole parents, the effect of the Australian New Tax System introduced in July 2000 calculated by MITTS with the effect calculated using a difference-in-difference evaluation approach are available; see Cai *et al.* (2005). The results indicate that, if anything, the simulation results appear to be lower than the effect of the policy change as estimated through an evaluation approach.

2 Outline of the Book

The analyses involving the use of microsimulation modelling in this book are grouped into three separate Parts. Chapter 3, the final chapter in Part I, is concerned with some general aspects relevant to considering means-tested transfer systems, using a concrete example. This assists in introducing those issues which are relevant when using a microsimulation model and illustrates the potential importance of behavioural modelling. Part II is concerned with hypothetical policy reforms. Part III examines actual or proposed reforms. Finally, Part IV discusses examples of further modelling developments.

2.1 Chapters in Part II

This group of chapters illustrates the sort of output that can be obtained from a microsimulation model, by examining simple hypothetical tax changes. The Australian tax and transfer system has a large number of means-tested benefits. The hypothetical policy change analysed in chapter 4 reduces the benefit taper or abatement rates in the 1998 tax and transfer structure to 30 per cent. All taper rates of 50 per cent and 70 per cent are reduced to 30 per cent, while leaving all basic benefit levels unchanged. The exception is the withdrawal rate on parental income for people receiving Youth Allowance or AUSTUDY, which remains at 25 per cent. A 30 per cent taper rate means that for every dollar of additional income in the household, the benefit payment is reduced by 30 cents. An important feature of the example is that behavioural modelling is shown to make a difference when examining the effects of policy changes. Given the importance of work incentives in contemporary policy making, where proposed policies often have as one of the aims improved work incentives, these different implications are relevant when analysing the effect of policy changes. Chapter 5 examines the effects of reducing the taper rate of Family Payment, another means-tested payment.

The use of a discrete hours framework, which generates a frequency distribution of income for each individual after a tax change conditional on being at the observed hours in the base, presents a problem for distributional analyses. Inequality and poverty measures are based on knowing the exact hours of work (and thus income) for each individual and/or household. Creedy, Kalb and Scutella (2004) proposed an alternative approach to deal with this difficulty and compared this approach with other possible approaches. The preferred method, as shown by extensive Monte Carlo experiments, is such that all outcomes for every individual (that is, the combination of hours level and associated income) are used as if they were separate observations. The outcomes are weighted by the individual probabilities of labour supply to produce a pseudo distribution. This approach is computationally efficient and replicates the results of taking extremely large samples to approximate the real underlying distribution.

The hypothetical reform in chapter 6 uses this approach to look at the impact of the extreme example of cutting all payments for sole parents, and compares it with the results from the other approaches. Naturally, this reform would have large effects on sole parents' poverty levels. Even when allowing for labour supply responses, the expected effect on poverty levels and the decrease in net income available to sole parent families remain severe. Although the results from simulating such an extreme policy change are not thought to be as reliable as the results for more subtle changes, this result indicates that the belief held by some commentators that social security payments stand in the way of families gaining independence from benefit payments is likely to be false.

It is sometimes required to reweight the SIHC, that is produce a new set of grossing-up weights such that a specified set of population aggregates (in this case the number of individuals in various age groups) are equal to specified totals that are obtained from extraneous sources (such as Australian Bureau of Statistics (ABS) population projections). This kind of reweighting may be required in a straightforward situation, for example when it is not obvious that the sample weights provided with the SIHC result in the best match of MITTS totals to a range of expenditure and tax aggregates (obtained, say, from administrative records). One situation where reweighting is valuable is where it is required to carry out a policy analysis using a dataset that is several years old, and for which the sample weights provided may have become outdated. Another situation where reweighting is of use is when the effect of policy changes on a future population, where some information on the expected demographic composition is available, are required.

Chapter 7 gives an example of an application in this latter case where reweighting is of use. It examines the implications of changes in the age distribution of the population. This combines MITTS with alternative population projections for 2050 provided by the ABS. A 'pure' change in the age distribution is examined by keeping the aggregate population size fixed and changing only the relative frequencies in different age-gender groups. Not surprisingly, this example of an ageing population shows that the cost of social security is expected to increase and the revenue from income tax is expected to decrease. The effects of a policy change to benefit taper rates in Australia are compared using 2001 and 2050 population weights respectively. Assuming that the labour force participation rates by age groups do not change between 2001 and 2050, this shows that the cost of such a policy is expected to be slightly less in absolute terms and considerably less in relative terms (as a proportion of the expenditure before the policy change) for the 2050 population. The larger proportion of the population out of the labour force (due to an aged population) means that fewer people benefit from the taper rate reduction. As a result, a taper rate reduction is expected to be less costly in the older population. It is suggested that this kind of reweighting approach provides scope for providing insights into the implications of changes to the population composition, indicating likely pressures for policy changes.

2.2 Chapters in Part III

One advantage of microsimulation is that it is straightforward to look at components of policy changes in isolation. Chapter 8 uses MITTS to decompose the effect of the tax and transfer changes introduced in July 2000. First the whole set of changes was studied and then some of its components were analysed separately. The change in income tax rates and thresholds was found to have the largest effect, because it affected a large proportion of the population, whereas the changes to the benefit system were only relevant to smaller groups. This tax change also increased labour supply for all groups, in particular for sole parents, making up part of the loss in tax revenue. Compared with the change in revenue resulting from the complete reform, the increase in expenditure on social security payments is quite small.

Families with children benefited on average most from the changes, first through the changes in income taxes and second through the changes in Family Payments. However, families with children were more likely to experience a loss, indicating a wider range of positive and negative outcomes for this group. For sole parents, the changed structure and rates of Family Payments were also shown to be important. Other components of the reform provided several positive incentives for sole parents but the Family Payment reforms seemed to counteract this at least partly, resulting in a small positive overall effect only. The simulation results also show that the introduction of the gradual withdrawal of the minimum rate of Family Payment rather than the previous 'sudden death' cut-out had a negligible effect as the reform only involved a small amount of income at a relatively high level of family income.

The analysis further shows that the reduction in pension taper rates had little effect on government expenditure, given that a large proportion of pensioners do not work because of disability or retirement, and are not affected by a change in the taper rate. The reduction in the taper rate had a small positive labour supply effect for sole parents. The effect of an increase in the threshold of the Parenting Payment Partnered is even smaller both in expenditure and in labour supply effects. This is not surprising given that the reform only had a minor effect on net incomes of a small proportion of the population.

Looking at the combined effect of all changes, families with children experienced the largest increase in net government expenditure, mainly caused by increased Family Payments. However, from a comparison of the proportion of households experiencing a loss, this proportion is also higher for households with children. This indicates a wider variety in both positive and negative effects for these families than for others resulting from the reform. Single person households had the lowest average increase in average income. Due to the large effect of the income tax reform, it was also found that families in higher income deciles had larger average income gains.

Although expenditure on benefit payments increased following the reform of July 2000, this increase is lower after taking into account labour supply behaviour. For single men and women, the expectation is that the increase in expenditure may even turn into a saving on expenditure after the behavioural changes are taken into account. Similarly, the decrease in revenue is lower after taking into account the increased labour supply (which increases government revenue from income tax) among all groups. Thus, the expected changes in labour supply should help to reduce the cost of the reform. Net expenditure (tax revenue and expenditure on benefit payments and rebates taken together) is also increased by a lower amount after accounting for behavioural changes.

MITTS can also be used to examine the effect of a lack of change. The absence of a mechanism to update the income tax thresholds for inflation between July 2000 and March 2004 is examined in chapter 9. This chapter focuses on the extent of bracket creep since the Australian New Tax System (ANTS) package and the distribution of effective marginal tax rates. It is estimated how much extra tax is paid per year due to bracket creep, that is, the relative increase in tax burden when nominal incomes increase and income tax thresholds remain the same. Thus at the same level of real income the average tax paid increases.

A range of possible tax cut proposals and other proposals increasing households' net incomes is then examined, where the costs (before taking into account behavioural changes) are roughly equal to the dollar amount of bracket creep resulting from increases in prices not having been matched by the raising of thresholds. The effects of these different policies were simulated using MITTS. Components of these reforms include: indexing tax thresholds for inflation; increasing the threshold at which the top marginal tax rate applies; lowering the second-highest marginal tax rate from 42 to 40 per cent; introducing an Earned Income Tax Credit; reducing taper rates on benefits; and combinations of these measures.

The labour supply responses are clearly different for the different packages. Two of the eight reform proposals are compared in detail: one that only involves indexation of all tax thresholds with Consumer Price Index (CPI) increases and one that introduces an earned income tax credit for low-income households and indexes only the top two thresholds. The expected labour supply effects of the tax credit proposal are nearly twice as large as for the other proposal. The resulting subsequent increase in tax revenues and reduction in benefit payments means that the long-run cost of the tax credit proposal drops considerably compared with the indexation proposal.

Chapter 10 examines the changes announced by the Coalition in the 2004 Federal Budget, concentrating on the effects of the Family Tax Benefit package and the income tax cuts, the two central features of the budget. Labour supply and distributional effects are explored using MITTS. While all families with children benefited from the changes, the benefits tended to go mostly to individuals and families with high incomes.

Examining the labour supply effects of separate components, the effect of the increase in Family Tax Benefit Part A by $600 per child was estimated to reduce labour supply by about 19,000. The largest reduction was for sole parents, a high proportion of sole parents in work before the change are expected to leave the labour force. This effect is almost exactly offset by a positive labour supply effect from reducing the withdrawal rate of Family Tax Benefit Part A.

The most surprising finding from the modelling is that changes to Family Tax Benefit Part B are expected to cause around 20,000 people to withdraw from the labour market. Those affected are partnered men and women. This is a result of the additional eligibility of non-working families with full Parenting Payments for Family Tax Benefit Part B. This raises net incomes at zero and low hours of work of the primary earner relative to net incomes at higher levels of labour supply. This seems to be an unintended consequence of this policy change, and its discovery through the analysis provides a further illustration of the usefulness of behavioural microsimulation.

Modelling the effect of raising the top two income tax thresholds reveals that it raises labour supply by about the same amount as the Family Tax Benefit changes reduce labour supply. However, a different type of worker is involved in these two opposite effects. Finally, suggested alternative reforms show that better results with regard to work incentives could have been obtained at the same price as the policy changes in the budget.

Chapter 11 considers the Australian Labor Party's Tax and Family Package, and examines the potential labour supply effects associated with some of the policy changes announced in the package. It calculates the effect of these labour supply changes on the budgetary cost of the proposed policy. The package analysed has four components. These are the Consolidation of Family Tax Benefit Part A and Part B into one payment (and some changes to rates and tapers); a Single Income Tax Offset (which provides a tax rebate for single-earner families); the Low and Middle Income Tax Offset, which provides a tax cut of up to $8 per week to tax-payers with an income between $7382 and $56,160 per annum (with those below $8453 not paying any tax) and incorporates the existing Low Income Tax Offset; and an increase in the top income tax threshold to $85,000. Although some of these changes restructured the 2004 system considerably, these changes could be simulated in MITTS after some programming.

A feature of chapter 11 is the inclusion of a time path for the predicted employment changes using evidence from previous policy changes. Due to labour market frictions and displacement effects, not all the labour supply effects estimated in MITTS may be converted into an actual increase in employment and thus into the predicted budget savings resulting from these responses. In addition, the projected savings may not all be achieved in the short term, but may take a number of years to take full effect. On the other hand, when the increase in labour supply is converted into employment, those entering or re-entering employment may experience increases in their wages over time. This would further increase income taxes paid by these employees and lower government benefits received by them, thus increasing the budget savings above that estimated by the MITTS model, which does not account for such wage progression. Evidence is presented that the employment effect can be expected to take about four years to be realised, with the biggest incremental effect in the second year. The results are calculated using different scenarios. The central estimate of the time path of the employment effect, taking into account labour market frictions, displacement effects and the time lags involved, assumes that at the end of four years 85 per cent of the projected increase in labour supply is converted into increased employment.

The final chapter of Part III, chapter 12, analyses a New Zealand tax and transfer reform which has been and still is being introduced over the period 2004-08. This analysis makes use of an alternative microsimulation model, TaxMod-B, which was built specifically for New Zealand using the same approach as MITTS, the model used in the other chapters of this book.

The simulated effects of recent policy changes on labour supply and government revenue and expenditure in New Zealand are presented. The policy change concerned reforms of Family Assistance and the Accommodation Supplement (AS) as they have been introduced recently, in addition to proposed future reforms as they will be implemented between 2004 and 2008. The simulation compares the labour supply responses resulting from going from the tax and social security system as it was in 2001 to the full reform as it will be in 2008. The recent development of TaxMod-B, a behavioural microsimulation model for New Zealand, has made such an analysis possible.

The changes involved decreased benefit rates; increased Family Assistance, which is partly made to depend on labour supply; and an increased AS. The effects of the changes on average hours worked, participation rates, government expenditure on different payments, government revenue from direct income taxes, and the implied effect on poverty and inequality in New Zealand are calculated.

The effect of changes to the AS appears to be small. Although the effect is likely to be underestimated in the calculations presented here, they are not expected to increase to a large amount if they could be calculated more accurately. The changes to Family Assistance have had a positive effect on sole parents' labour supply and a small negative effect on married men and women's labour supply. For sole parents, independent of the number of children the simulated effects are on average positive and the positive effects were generally largest for those with one child. However, the sample size is relatively small for this group when the number of children is three or more. For couple families, independent of the number of children the simulated effect is negative, but similar to what is observed for sole parents, the negative effect is smaller for those with only one dependent child.

2.3 Part IV

Chapter 13, in Part IV, discusses areas in microsimulation which would benefit from further development. Areas that are discussed in this chapter are welfare measurement; take-up of social security payments, which should ideally be modelled jointly with household labour supply; general equilibrium effects of policy changes; feedback effects of changed labour supply on wage levels; household consumption and associated indirect taxes; and life cycle and population dynamics.

2.4 Conclusions

Comparing the different outcomes of the range of studies discussed in this book, a few patterns can be observed with regard to the effects of tax and transfer policy changes. The analyses are not strictly comparable, because they have not been designed to be ex-post revenue neutral. Therefore, we cannot generalise the results. However, some broad observations can be made based on the simulation analyses.

First, it appears that financial incentives are most effective in terms of increasing labour supply for single parents. That is, applying the same policy change to different groups, we often observe the largest effect for single parents. This is observed in analyses by other researchers as well (see for example, Eissa and Hoynes, 1999; Blundell *et al.*, 2000; Blundell and Hoynes, 2004). Given the low starting point of labour force participation for this group, the relatively large responses are perhaps not surprising. However, it is also shown that despite the relatively large size of responses to policy changes, the resulting income increases cannot compensate sufficiently for extremely large cuts in income support.

Second, decreasing withdrawal rates of social security payments or income tax rates tends to have a negative effect on the labour supply of married or de facto women. This indicates that the income effect dominates the substitution effect in these cases. This result is also often found in other studies (see for example, Scholz, 1996; Blundell *et al.*, 2000; Blundell and Hoynes, 2004). This effect is observed even more strongly when introducing additional withdrawal rates through a Tax Credit scheme. Although initially effective marginal tax rates are reduced for households, at middle-level incomes effective marginal tax rates are increased because the additional payment is withdrawn. This withdrawal is more likely to affect women than men, given that women are more likely to be the secondary earners in a household. The income effect and the substitution effect in this case work in the same direction, discouraging labour supply. However, for singles and married men, this type of policy change encourages additional labour supply and labour force participation. In part the problem lies in the assessment of these payments on household income rather than individual income. Unfortunately, using the alternative of income testing individual income only would increase the cost of this type of policy and considerably reduce the level of targeting to the households most in need.

Third, as expected, increasing net income for everyone independent of labour market status is predicted to have a negative effect on labour supply. Providing additional rebates to low-income households instead of additional payments across the board stimulate labour supply. However, low-income households who for some reason cannot participate in the labour market would of course miss out on this type of additional income.

One of the useful features of microsimulation modelling is that different policies can be compared in a straightforward manner. Complex sets of policy changes can be decomposed into their separate components and the effects can be analysed for separate subgroups of individuals or households. Using these features, a fourth observation can be made regarding the effectiveness of different types of change. Focusing incentive changes on low-income households results in larger labour supply responses. For those with middle and higher incomes, a reduction in tax or benefit withdrawal rates is in fact more likely to result in a negative labour supply response than for those with lower incomes due to the income effect of this change being larger than the substitution effect.

The way in which additional payments are provided can be important for the effect these payments have on labour supply. For example, the New Zealand policy changes analysed in chapter 12 showed that imposing a twenty-hour work requirement for receipt of additional payments to families with children worked reasonably well for single parent families, resulting in an increase of predicted labour supply. However, the combined thirty-hour work requirement for the two adults in couple families turned out to make the additional payment ineffective with regard to increasing labour supply. For most families no increased effort was required to attain that level of labour supply, given the large proportion of partnered men already working (close to) full time. In fact, some families are expected to reduce labour supply due to the additional income provided compared with the situation before the policy change. To them, the policy represented a disincentive to labour supply.

3 Flattening the Rate Structure

This chapter is concerned with some general aspects relevant to considering means-tested transfer systems, using the concrete example of a 'basic income and flat tax' system (BI/FT) versus a 'means-tested with graduated tax' scheme (MT/GT). In the debate about the efficiency and equity effects of alternative tax-transfer systems, a major feature is the argument between universal and means-tested systems. A variety of terms has been used to describe tax systems; these include the negative income tax, minimum income guarantee, tax credits and linear income tax. However, the meaning attached to these terms is not consistent in the literature, so it seems useful to describe the main alternatives in terms of BI/FT and MT/GT schemes. This concrete example assists in introducing those issues which are relevant when using a microsimulation model and illustrates the potential importance of behavioural modelling.

Those on the two sides of the debate typically have in mind different value judgements as well as different frameworks of analysis. For this reason discussion can sometimes be at cross-purposes. Advocates of means testing typically argue that the primary concern of a transfer system should be to alleviate poverty. Hence, schemes are compared using measures of 'target efficiency' which reflect the extent to which transfer payments are concentrated on the poor; see Beckerman (1979) and Mitchell (1991). Target efficiency measures are not concerned with the extent to which poverty is actually reduced by a tax and transfer system and, despite the terminology, have nothing to do with economic efficiency. For further discussion of target efficiency measures, see Creedy (1995).

The framework of reference used by proponents of means testing is one in which the distribution of income before taxes and transfers is assumed to be fixed and labour supplies do not change as the tax and transfer system changes. In criticising a BI/FT scheme there is a tendency to focus on the high level of the constant marginal tax rate required to finance the basic

35

income; in a pure transfer system the tax rate is equal to the ratio of the basic income to arithmetic mean income.

The proponents of universal benefits argue that taxes and transfers have a wider redistributive role than simply alleviate poverty, and that an emphasis on the gross level of government revenue is not appropriate in a tax and transfer system. Hence more emphasis is placed on the distribution of average tax rates. Stress is placed on the incentive effects arising from the high marginal tax rates involved in means testing. In an MT/GT system it is the lower income groups who face much higher marginal tax rates than the higher income groups, creating a strong disincentive to participate in paid employment. Atkinson (1995, p. 296) argued that 'Even if the poverty trap no longer involves marginal tax rates in excess of 100 per cent, the marginal rates are still higher than those levied on the rest of the population.'

In discussing these aspects, Atkinson (1995, p. 224) suggested that 'the case for greater targeting is typically based on the assumption of a fixed total budget for the social security ministry ... Account has to be taken of changes in the behaviour of recipients, and the limits to targeting may arise from the adverse incentives created.'

The later chapters in this book examine alternative reforms using a behavioural microsimulation model. However, this chapter limits itself to examining in broad terms the types of behavioural effect that a stylised version of the BI/FT system might have, compared with a stylised version of an MT/GT structure. The motivation for such a comparison is to be able to understand the way in which labour supply effects may modify the outcome of comparisons between the alternative tax systems. The results emphasise the need to develop a behavioural microsimulation model of tax-transfer systems for meaningful policy analysis and the need to undertake empirical examination of the labour supply parameters to be included in such a model. Using this type of model, a more detailed study of specific policy proposals along these lines can be undertaken.

The framework of analysis is described in section 3.1. This describes a simple but flexible tax and transfer system and the resulting labour supply behaviour. Comparisons of alternative systems are made in section 3.2. Such simple models can provide a useful aid to thinking about the possible forms of labour supply response to tax changes, and highlight the complexities that need to be faced in examining practical policy changes.

3.1   A Framework of Analysis

3.1.1   The Tax and Transfer System

This section describes a simple specification of a tax and transfer system that is able to model alternative MT/GT structures and contains the BI/FT system as a special case. Despite its simplicity the system is able to highlight some important implications for labour supply of the existence of nonlinear budget constraints facing individuals. Consider a tax and transfer system which has a single threshold and two marginal tax rates. One of the marginal rates is the taper which applies to means-tested transfer payments. If y represents gross earnings, the benefit received is $s(a-y)$ for $y \le a$. The tax paid is $t(y-a)$ for $y > a$.

Hence for those who pay tax, the system is just like an income tax function having a single marginal rate of t applied to income measured in excess of a tax-free threshold of a. If $y = 0$ the individual receives the full amount of the transfer payment, equal to sa, and the benefit is withdrawn at a marginal rate of s for each additional unit of income. In means-tested systems, it is often the case that higher marginal rates are faced by those with lower incomes, which in the above system implies that $s > t$.

Although this tax structure is very simple and involves just three parameters, it is able to provide a reasonable approximation to the net result of many existing tax and benefit schemes. It is extremely flexible. For example, it allows for the extreme where $s = 1$, providing a stylised version of means-tested systems with 100 per cent effective marginal tax rates imposed on benefit recipients. At the other extreme, the BI/FT structure arises when $s = t$.

The relationship between gross earnings and net income, z, is given by $z = as + y(1-s)$ for $y \le a$, and $z = at + y(1-t)$ for $y > a$. These define a piecewise-linear tax function.

3.1.2   The Budget Constraint and Labour Supply

The nonlinear tax function defined above has important implications for labour supply behaviour. This is most easily seen in terms of the associated budget constraint. Suppose an individual faces a wage rate of w, has no non-wage income other than transfer payments, and is endowed with a unit of time. The individual is assumed to choose the consumption of goods, c, and leisure, l, in order to maximise utility, subject to the budget constraint. Suppose that the price of consumption goods is normalised to 1, so that consumption and net income are synonymous. In this type of static model there is no role for savings.

Figure 3.1 The budget constraint

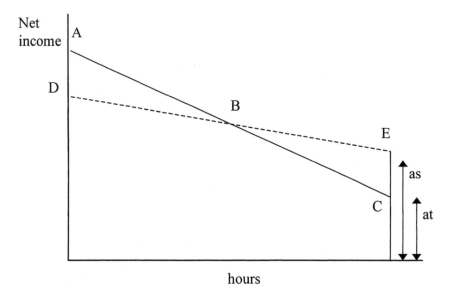

hours

The budget constraint for a typical MT/GT structure is shown in Figure 3.1 as the line ABE. This is made up of the linear section, EB, with a slope of $w(1 - s)$ that applies when transfer payments are received, and the linear section AB which has a slope of $w(1 - t)$. This budget constraint defines a non-convex budget set due to the assumption that $s > t$. At point B, net income and gross earnings are both equal to the tax threshold, a, as no taxes are paid and no benefits are received. The maximum value of the transfer payment is obtained when the individual has no earnings, and is equal to as. When $s = t$ the two lines AC and DE coincide and the resulting linear budget line describes a BI/FT structure; the basic income under such a scheme is equal to $as = at$. Under the assumption of decreasing marginal utility, indifference curves in Figure 3.1 slope downwards from left to right and are convex to the origin (where $c = h = 0$).

It is necessary to consider how labour supply varies as the individual's wage rate increases, causing the budget constraint to pivot about the fixed point E. For very low values of w the budget constraint is relatively flat and it is likely that the highest indifference curve produces a corner solution at E where no labour is supplied. This corresponds to voluntary nonparticipation in the labour force. Initially, further increases in the wage rate from a very low level have no effect on the participation decision, as the corner solution remains optimal.

As the wage is further increased, two alternatives arise. One alternative, which can occur for high values of s, is that at some wage rate, say $w = w_m$, the individual jumps directly to a tangency position on the section AB of the budget constraint. The wage rate $w = w_m$ is such that an indifference curve is simultaneously tangential to the section AB and touches the corner, E, of the budget constraint. In this case, the individual never simultaneously works and receives transfer payments. Further increases in the wage rate are likely initially to produce an increase in labour supply, though a point may be reached when the income effect arising from the higher wage produces an increase in the demand for leisure, despite its higher price, resulting in a 'backward bending' section of the supply curve.

The second alternative is such that as the wage increases from a very low level, it reaches a value, $w = w_L$, when the individual is induced to move away from the corner, E, and to a tangency position of an indifference curve at a point on the section BE of the constraint. At this point, the individual combines earning some wage income with receiving means-tested transfer payments. Such individuals are often called the 'working poor'. As the wage rate increases further, it reaches a value, say $w = w_s$, when the individual jumps from a tangency along BE to one that is on the section AB. This switch or jump occurs where $w = w_s$ gives rise to a budget constraint such that there is an indifference curve that is simultaneously tangential to both sections AB and BE. The value of $w = w_s$ can be solved explicitly under the assumption of Cobb-Douglas preferences (Creedy, 1994). Lambert (1985, 1988) used this type of modified minimum income guarantee with Cobb-Douglas preferences, but did not consider the possibility of the first alternative.

Hence the point B (along with a range either side of it) is never chosen in practice if the individual is free to vary the supply of labour (hours) continuously. The wage elasticity of hours supplied can therefore vary considerably over the range of wage rates. This shows that for such budget constraints it is not sensible to specify a labour supply function in terms of a fixed wage elasticity of hours, or simply to report an implied elasticity at say the average wage.

Although the budget constraint in the present framework is very simple compared with the actual complexities of tax and benefit systems, it can be used to illustrate the complicated types of labour supply behaviour that are observed in practice.

The government is also faced with a budget constraint, since the tax revenue obtained from those with $y > a$ must be sufficient to finance the transfers paid to those below a, as well as non-transfer expenditure. Although there are three parameters of the tax system, there are therefore only two degrees of freedom in the government's choice.

3.2   Some General Comparisons

It has been mentioned that a shift from means testing towards universal benefits is likely to increase the labour force participation among those facing relatively low wages, as a result of the substantial reduction in the marginal tax rate faced. However, the associated increase in the constant marginal tax rate facing tax payers is likely to produce a reduction in the number of hours of labour supplied by the majority of higher wage earners. The net effect on labour supply and the tax base of these opposite changes is an important determinant of the effect of flattening the rate structure. This section describes the general relationships produced by the above tax and transfer scheme and labour supply model. The comparisons are considered to be neutral in terms of net revenue or deficit.

3.2.1   Labour Supply and Earnings

The influence on labour force participation of the taper, s, in the MT/GT system is shown in Figure 3.2, which illustrates the relationship between the proportion of people who do not work and the marginal tax rate, t. The voluntary nonparticipants receive the maximum value of the transfer payment. The lower line applies to the BI/FT system, and $s_1 > s_2 > s_3$. As t approaches s, each profile approaches its corresponding value under a BI/FT scheme. This diagram illustrates the way in which a high taper s can affect the participation decision. In this case there are very few working poor. A small reduction from a high value of s can have a large (decreasing) effect on the proportion who decide not to work.

A feature of the profiles for the high values of the taper is that they turn downwards for high marginal income tax rates. This is because the increase in t over the relevant range is associated with a reduction in the value of the threshold, a, that can be financed from the tax revenue, and thus in the maximum transfer payment. The increase in the tax rate is outweighed by the reduction in the tax base. Since the tax rate does not have a direct effect on the labour supply decision of those below the threshold, a, the value of the wage threshold $w = w_L$ falls, so that participation increases at these high values of t. For values of the taper approaching 1.0, the profile does not turn downwards for very high values of the tax rate, since the proportion not working approaches 1.0 as both rates approach 1.0.

The total labour supply per capita, in terms of hours worked, is illustrated in Figure 3.3, for variations in the tax and taper rates. The differences between profiles are not expected to be as dramatic as in Figure 3.3. Gross earnings per capita under alternative schemes are likely to display the same kind of pattern as labour supply in Figure 3.3. Under the BI/FT scheme, there is likely to be a higher tax base for a given marginal tax rate. In considering a shift from an MT/GT scheme to a BI/FT structure, or a flattening of the rate structure in a means-tested scheme, it is unlikely that the marginal income tax rate would be left unchanged. Hence a vertical shift from one profile to another in Figure 3.3 is unlikely. Such a shift, involving a reduction in s, would probably be accompanied by an increase in the income tax rate. This is likely to produce a reduction in the hours worked by many relatively high-wage individuals. It is important in practice to know whether there is likely to be a net increase in total hours worked per capita and the tax base. In the context of the simple model used here, this would be expected in view of the strong effect on labour force participation of a reduction in the taper rate.

3.2.2 Transfer Payments

The maximum transfer payment received by those who do not work is shown in Figure 3.4 for alternative systems. The figure displays the expected forms of the variation in the maximum transfer, *sa*, as the marginal income tax rate increases. For a given marginal tax rate, the basic income provided by the BI/FT scheme is lower than in any of the MT/GT systems in view of the fact that the basic income is available to everyone. However, at very high tax rates, the basic income may well exceed *sa* for the highest value of the taper rate.

A reduction in the value of the taper from a very high value is likely to have little effect on the transfer payment that can be financed with any given marginal tax rate. It is even possible in principle for the transfer to increase, if labour force participation would increase substantially. This possibility is important when considering a reform involving a small reduction in the taper rate used in means testing. If there is a similar, or even very small increase in the maximum transfer (resulting from the combination of a drop in the taper and an increase in the tax rate), a reform may be carried out without anyone becoming worse off. Hence a Pareto improvement may be possible starting from a high taper rate.

3.2.3 Average Tax Rates

From the point of view of the distributional impact of a tax and transfer system, what matters is the distribution of average tax rates faced by individuals. In the BI/FT system, only those at the very top of the earnings distribution face average tax rates that are anywhere near to the fixed marginal rate. Furthermore, the average tax rates experienced by those with lower earnings are lower than under an MT/GT scheme, offering a maximum transfer payment that is similar to the universal benefit available in a BI/FT scheme. The variation in average tax rates at different income levels and under alternative schemes is illustrated in Figure 3.5.

Figure 3.2 Proportion not working

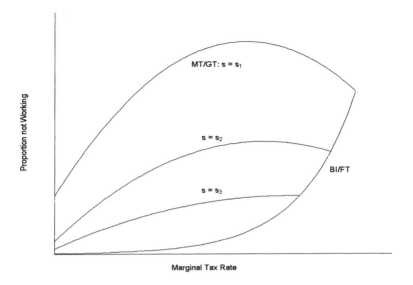

Figure 3.3 Labour supply per capita

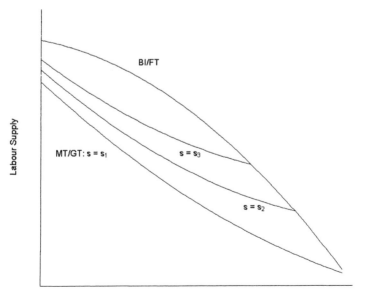

Figure 3.4 Maximum transfer payment

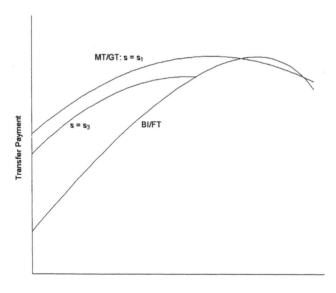

Marginal Tax Rate

Figure 3.5 Average tax rates

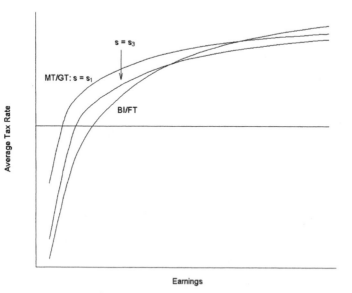

Earnings

A flattening of the rate structure is associated with reductions in marginal and average tax rates faced by low-income groups, although the differences in the average tax rates for the relatively high income groups are much smaller. In a BI/FT scheme, individuals would have to earn substantially more than average earnings before they face an average tax rate approaching the marginal rate.

The evaluation of alternative tax and transfer systems cannot avoid the use of value judgements. As suggested in the introduction, disputes about the appropriate system have often involved the use of quite different fundamental values. The role of rational policy analysis is therefore to examine the implications of adopting alternative views. For example, comparisons using different types of social welfare function are given in Creedy (1997a, b). Debate in this area often focuses on the extent to which the lower income groups, those considered most at risk, are likely to be affected by a hypothetical change in the tax structure. A detailed behavioural microsimulation model would be able to identify the types of individual and household, according to a range of characteristics, that are likely to experience losses (both financial and non-financial, in the form of reduced time for leisure and home production) from a tax reform.

3.3 Conclusions

This chapter has examined the role of labour supply variations in considering alternative tax and transfer systems. One argument used by those people who are in favour of means testing is that a universal system would require a higher marginal tax rate to be imposed, thereby creating a negative incentive effect. Following the introduction of a BI/FT scheme, reductions in the labour supply of those who were previously not receiving benefits would indeed be expected. However, the largest changes in marginal tax rates would in fact be those imposed on the poor. The reduction in the high effective marginal rates imposed on benefit recipients is likely to lead to a substantial increase in labour force participation.

Reductions in the degree of means testing, by reducing the value of the taper applied to benefits, may have potentially large effects on the labour force participation of benefit recipients. Under such a favourable outcome, these effects may outweigh the likely reductions in hours worked by taxpayers, so that the net effect could be an increase in aggregate labour supply and income. If a move from an MT/GT system to a BI/FT structure in one single step is regarded as too large a shift, marginal changes may also have large labour supply (participation) effects.

The model is of course highly simplified. Nevertheless, it is able to capture some of the complexity in labour supply behaviour arising from non-convex budget sets and, in addition, allows for the government's budget constraint to be imposed at all times. The analysis suggests that potential labour supply effects arising from tax reform can be important. The debate cannot of course be settled by the use of such simplified and theoretical models, although they can help in thinking about the types of relationship involved in comparisons. More realistic policy analysis clearly requires the construction of a full-scale behavioural microsimulation model that is able to deal with the considerable population heterogeneity and enormous complexity of the budget constraints facing individuals.

PART II. HYPOTHETICAL POLICY REFORMS

4 Reducing Taper Rates

The tax and transfer system in Australia is highly targeted, with most benefits being means-tested. This leads to high effective marginal rates for many low-income families, which may be a disincentive to participate in the labour market. Some commentators, including the Reference Group on Welfare Reform (2000), advocated the reduction of tapers, or benefit withdrawal rates, as part of a movement towards a flatter rate structure. Such a move decreases the marginal rates facing lower-income groups but is likely to raise the marginal rates facing some higher-income groups. The overall effect on labour supply depends on the extent to which the labour force participation of the lower-income groups increases relative to the likely labour supply reduction of some of the higher-income groups.

This chapter examines simulation results on the effects of reducing the Australian means-tested benefit taper rates to 30 per cent. All taper rates of 50 per cent and 70 per cent are reduced to 30 per cent, while leaving all basic benefit levels unchanged.[1] The only exception is the withdrawal rate on parental income for people receiving Youth Allowance or AUSTUDY, which remains at 25 per cent. Examples are provided of the implications for aggregate tax revenue and expenditure, and the effects on individuals and households, of changes to the system operating in March 1998. The results were produced using the Melbourne Institute Tax and Transfer Simulator (MITTS). It is of interest to compare results where all individuals are assumed to have fixed labour supplies with simulations in which the majority of individuals are free to adjust the number of hours worked. These results reflect only the supply side of the labour market and, as discussed in chapter 1, a discrete hours framework is used in which individuals can move

---

[1] Using a simple labour supply model, the previous chapter showed that revenue-neutral reductions in tapers may achieve widespread welfare gains, though the abolition of tapers involves substantial increases in income tax rates. The MITTS simulations reported here are not revenue neutral.

between specified discrete hours levels, rather than being able to vary hours continuously.

The 1998 tax and transfer system was used because at the time of this analysis the most recent Survey of Income and Housing Costs (SIHC) available was collected in 1997/1998. Weekly incomes in this survey are based on the financial year 1997/1998. The econometric estimates of preferences underlying the behavioural responses were estimated based on 1994/95 and 1995/96 SIHC data.[2] Pre-reform benefits and taxes are based on the MITTS calculation of entitlements, not the actual receipt. Hence it is assumed that the take-up rates of payments are 100 per cent. Furthermore, MITTS only applies income tests, as there is at present no asset imputation in the model. In practice, asset tests affect very few individuals, largely because the value of the home is not counted for means-tested purposes. Revenues and expenditures are expressed in 1998 dollars. All results are weighted using the weights provided with the SIHC to represent the population level effects.

Section 4.1 presents the results of the policy change, assuming no changes in labour supply. The potential changes in labour supply behaviour and its effects on government expenditure and revenue are presented in section 4.2. The final section presents some brief conclusions.

4.1   Non-behavioural Simulation Results

This section examines the effects of the taper reductions assuming that the labour supply behaviour of individuals is unchanged. The effects on income for different groups, and aggregate effects on government income and expenditure are examined in turn.

4.1.1   Income Effects for Different Groups

It is expected that a change in the benefit withdrawal rate has the largest effect on people who are working and earning a low-to-medium income. Weighted distributions of weekly equivalised net household income changes (using Whiteford equivalence scales) of individuals are shown in Table 4.1 for various groups.

---

[2] The current (2006) version of MITTS uses an updated set of preference parameters, based on more years of data and allowing for more heterogeneity of individuals and households.

Table 4.1 Income gainers and losers

	Increase in net income ($)				
	None	0-5	5-10	>10	Average
Number of children					
None	59.4	3.0	3.3	34.3	17.40
One	63.2	1.2	0.6	35.0	27.82
Two	62.8	1.1	1.8	34.3	33.51
Three	60.7	1.4	1.5	36.4	40.65
Four	65.4	2.5	0.6	31.5	32.25
Five	67.8	-	3.0	29.2	36.38
Six	59.8	-	-	40.2	38.97
Age					
15 to 19	84.5	1.0	1.0	13.5	5.76
20 to 24	49.6	2.5	3.5	44.4	20.61
25 to 29	55.9	2.6	2.6	39.0	25.74
30 to 34	58.5	1.8	1.8	38.0	32.75
35 to 39	57.2	1.9	2.3	38.6	36.19
40 to 44	59.3	2.0	1.8	37.0	32.37
45 to 49	56.4	2.4	3.2	38.1	28.01
50 to 54	58.9	1.9	2.0	37.3	24.79
55 to 59	56.2	2.2	2.2	39.4	25.68
60 to 64	55.0	3.9	3.5	37.6	22.96
65 plus	68.8	3.3	3.5	24.4	9.15
Employment status					
Employed	52.8	2.5	2.8	41.9	28.71
Nonparticipation	70.7	2.1	2.3	24.9	16.12
Unemployed	81.9	1.5	0.1	16.5	14.23
Income unit type					
Couple (no dependent child)	57.4	2.9	2.8	36.9	22.48
Couple with dependent child	52.9	1.5	1.4	44.3	43.57
Dependent child	99.0	0.3	0.3	0.5	0.13
Single	61.4	3.1	3.8	31.7	12.17
Sole parent	70.6	1.2	2.5	25.8	10.77
Total	60.69	2.32	2.49	34.5	23.45

In this and subsequent tables, a '-' denotes empty cells, whereas '0' denotes cells with less than 0.5 per cent of the observations for the relevant category. In all categories, over 50 per cent of people experience no change. A change in taper rates typically affects people on low wage rates and/or on low hours of labour supply. People of prime working age have the largest average change, and people aged 15-19 and over 65 have on average the smallest changes in weekly equivalised net household income. The results indicate that there is either no change (in the majority of cases) or there is a greater than $10 increase in weekly equivalised net household income of individuals. The income gain is highest for those who are employed and for couples with dependent children. In view of the large proportion who experience no change in net income, the effect on inequality is small. The Lorenz curve is found to cross, showing more equality in the middle to higher income groups, but the Gini measure falls very slightly in all but the oldest age group.

4.1.2   Effects on Government Revenue and Expenditure

Tables 4.2 and 4.3 present the net increase in costs resulting from the policy change, by main payment type. These values are weighted to represent the values for the Australian population. Comparing some of the most important expenditures in Tables 4.2 and 4.3 to the actual 1997/1998 values (ABS, 2000, p. 157), the actual expenditures on Age Pension ($13.4 billion), Parenting Payments ($5.2 billion) and Family Payments plus Family Tax Payments or Family Tax Benefits (FTP/FTB) ($6.9 billion) are close to the estimated values in MITTS. However, payments on Partner Allowance ($0.5 billion), Sickness Allowance ($92.7 million) and Special Benefit ($95.9 million) are overestimated whereas NewStart Allowance ($5.8 billion) and Disability Support Pension ($4.6 billion) seem to be underestimated by MITTS. The latter may be partly caused by the fact that these numbers include Rent Assistance whereas Rent Assistance is listed separately in Table 4.2. However, it indicates that the assumption of 100 per cent take-up has no major effect on the simulated expenditure.

Government revenue is expected to increase but not enough to compensate for the increased payments. A large proportion of the increased cost is due to allowances. This is partly because they are the largest group of payments and partly because allowance recipients are more likely to work than pension recipients are, which means they are most likely to benefit from a reduction in the taper rate. This group consists of around 4 million individual recipients, which is an overestimation of the true number, for reasons explained earlier. However, notwithstanding the overestimation, the number in this group remains substantial. The group includes basic Parenting Payment recipients, which covers all women with children under 16 years of age who do not work or work few hours only. Finally, if one member of a couple receives a payment, the partner is counted as a recipient as well. In addition, people who are currently working without receiving benefits and who would become eligible for payments after the change as a result of the higher cut-out income would most probably become eligible for an allowance rather than a pension. This would result in an expected increase in the number of people on allowances by 2.8 million recipients, if all newly eligible individuals take-up the benefit.

Table 4.2 Main government revenues and expenditures

Tax or transfer	Cost (million $)		Numbers (×1000)	
	Pre-reform	Change	Pre-reform	Change
Revenue				
Income tax	71910.3	1872.4	13125	2
Medicare levy	4505.8	208.7	8366	629
Total revenue	76416.1	2081.1		
Expenditure				
Tax rebates	4372.8	-593.1	9762	-235
Family Payment	6218.3	1779.3	3214	0
FTP/FTB	631.2	180.4	1641	748
Allowances	17917.7	8828.7	4022	2843
Pensions	21625.5	1190.8	3046	168
Pharmaceutical Allowance	342.4	23.1	3439	284
Rent Allowance	1699.4	975.5	1567	874
Total expenditure	52807.3	12384.7		
Net expenditure	-23608.7	10303.5		

Table 4.3 presents a further decomposition of the different payment types and shows that NewStart Allowance, Partner Allowance and Parenting Payments contribute most to the increase in expenditure. This is because these three groups are most likely to be in work and those benefit recipients who work or whose partners work are more likely to benefit from a reduction in the taper rate. Overall, the payments associated with unemployment seem to be relatively more affected by the change than the

Table 4.3 Detailed costs and revenues

Tax rebate or transfer	Cost (million $)		Numbers (×1000)	
	Pre-reform	Change	Pre-reform	Change
Allowance costs				
Parenting Payment (Single)	2685.9	244.6	336	42
Parenting Payment (Couple)	2525.8	2344.2	793	331
Sickness Allowance	363.6	10.6	46	3
Widow's Allowance	680.9	291.9	103	90
AUSTUDY/ABSTUDY	3618.4	98.3	561	19
NewStart Allowance	5371.2	4593.9	901	1814
Mature Age Allowance	166.8	200.8	38	54
Youth Allowance	251.8	50.6	37	8
Special Benefit	997.8	94.1	136	18
Partner Allowance	1255.5	899.8	199	162
Pension costs				
Age Pension	13605.4	985.8	1844	138
Disability Support Pension	3900.8	83.6	483	1
Wife's Pension	723.1	30.6	103	2
Widow B Pension	366.9	3.2	41	0
Carer's Payment	190.3	1.3	23	0
Veteran Pension	1387.6	86.3	195	5
Veterans' Disability Pension	471.1	0.0	75	0
War Widows' Pension	980.3	0.0	98	0
Rebate costs				
Beneficiary Rebate	685.9	125.6	1604	512
Pension Rebate	2004.0	-54.9	2087	-21
Sole Parent Rebate	642.6	0.0	517	0
Sole Parent Pension Rebate	251.8	-15.0	335	-22
Low Income Rebate	1309.7	-53.1	9160	-319
Dependent Spouse Rebate	1469.5	-614.7	1375	-249
Total rebate cost	6363.5	-612.0		

other payments. This is supported by the fact that the relative increase in the costs of Mature Age Allowance and Youth Allowance is large. However, in absolute terms the latter two payments contribute a small amount because the number of recipients is low for both these payments.

Table 4.2 shows that pensions constitute a small part of the change in costs. Although Age Pensioners form the largest subgroup in the pension payments, labour force participation among people who are potentially eligible for the Age Pension is quite low. As a result, there is little change after the reform.

Finally, Table 4.2 shows an increase of $2.1 billion of government revenue from income taxes and Medicare levy. Rebates have decreased since the reform. The difference in the amount of total rebate, presented in Tables 4.2 and 4.3, is caused by the fact that the amount in Table 4.3 is the potential amount of rebate that people are eligible for, without taking into account the amount of tax paid by each individual. As a rule, the amount of rebate received can never be more than the amount of tax paid. The actual amount of rebate received can only be calculated for the sum of rebates and cannot be decomposed into the separate components. Table 4.3 examines the components of the potential amount of decrease in tax rebates. This shows that, in particular, the dependent spouse rebate decreases considerably after the reform.

4.2 Behavioural Simulation Results

This section reports the effects of allowing for possible labour supply responses. After discussing work-incentive effects, labour supply and revenue and expenditure effects are examined in turn. A description of the way in which behavioural simulations are carried out using MITTS-B is provided in subsection 1.3.3 in chapter 1.

4.2.1 Work Incentives

The decrease in the withdrawal rate has a large effect on the cut-off point below which people are eligible for benefit payments. For example, the cut-off weekly income for Age Pensioners before the change is $410 for singles and $685 for couples. With the decrease in the taper rate, these increase to $650 and $1083. The change in cut-off points is even larger for people on

unemployment benefits like NewStart Allowance, who face taper rates of 70
per cent for incomes over $70 per week before the change, instead of the 50
per cent withdrawal rate pensioners face. The result of the increased cut-off
points is that people on higher incomes also become eligible for benefits.
Under the assumption of full take-up, the number of welfare participants
increases.

Consider a single person, paying $70 in rent and having a wage of $28.39
per hour; the average wage rate in May 1998 was $17.60 (ABS, 1999, p.
26). The net income of this person is graphed in Figure 4.1 for all hours of
labour supply between 0 and 50 hours per week. This shows that the
decrease in the taper rate substantially increases the net income in the part-
time hours range. The reform results in higher net income when the
individual works between about 1 and 23 hours per week. For people on
lower wage rates this hours range is wider.

Figure 4.1 Single person's budget constraint pre- and post-reform

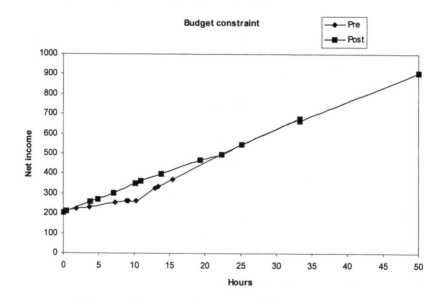

Comparing the effective marginal tax rates (EMTRs) in the two systems,
from about 1 to 11 hours of labour supply the effective marginal tax rates

are lower than in the March 1998 system, possibly providing positive work incentives depending on the increase in the level of the budget constraint at that point (that is, the substitution versus the income effect). However, the EMTRs are higher from about 11 to 23 hours of employment, resulting from the extended eligibility for benefits with the reduced withdrawal rate, making work less attractive in this hours range. Thus, low part-time working hours are expected to become more appealing and the higher levels of part-time working hours may become relatively less attractive. In cases where wage rates are very low, the change in the constraint is dominated by reductions in effective marginal tax rates.

The effect of the taper reductions is that the average EMTR at the respondent's observed labour supply increases slightly as a result of the change, largely arising from an increase in the number of individuals facing rates between 50 and 60 per cent. Indeed, the proportion in this group increases from less than 1 per cent of the population to 20 per cent. Those with EMTRs in the range 30 to 40 per cent fall from 23 to 8 per cent of the population. The youngest and the older age groups have lower EMTRs, reflecting the lower labour force participation and perhaps the lower average wage rates in these categories. In both the pre- and post-reform systems, people aged 30 to 49 have the highest EMTR, reflecting the higher average earnings in this age group. Employed people have higher EMTRs than unemployed individuals or nonparticipants; whereas dependent children have low EMTRs compared with other income unit types, such as couples, singles and sole parents. There is a substantial fall in the number of individuals facing rates in excess of 70 per cent.

4.2.2 Work Probability and Hours

The potential effect on labour supply of the reduction in the taper rates is equivocal because it does not automatically mean a reduction in effective marginal tax rates for all individuals. This is an inevitable consequence of flattening the marginal rate structure while keeping basic benefit levels unchanged. The changes in the probability of working, over all individuals for a range of categories, are presented in Table 4.4. Some individuals, such as the self-employed, the disabled, students and those over 65 have their

Hypothetical Policy Reforms

Table 4.4 Percentage point changes in work probability

	Decrease			Increase			Average
Age	10-50	2-10	none	2-10	10-50	> 50	
15 to 19	-	2	97	1	1	-	0.11
20 to 24	1	12	79	3	6	-	0.65
25 to 29	2	15	69	7	8	-	0.89
30 to 34	4	13	65	11	7	-	0.67
35 to 39	5	16	64	9	7	-	0.43
40 to 44	5	20	61	8	7	0	0.26
45 to 49	4	22	63	6	4	0	-0.37
50 to 54	3	20	66	7	5	-	0.06
55 to 59	2	12	75	8	4	0	0.54
60 to 64	0	7	77	7	8	0	1.81
65 plus	-	-	100	-	-	-	0.00
Income unit type							
Couple	2	18	72	5	3	-	-0.37
Couple + dep. child	6	19	55	12	8	-	0.60
Dependent child	-	-	100	-	-	-	0.00
Single	0	3	96	1	0	0	0.09
Sole parent	0	0	46	12	41	-	8.27
Number of children							
None	1	11	84	3	1	0	-0.14
One	4	17	59	9	12	-	1.46
Two	4	14	64	10	8	-	0.85
Three	4	10	67	10	8	-	1.05
Four	4	6	65	12	12	-	2.15
Five	-	3	64	8	25	-	5.48
Six	-	2	79	9	9	-	1.54
Employment status							
Employed	4	20	75	0	0	-	-1.47
Nonparticipation	-	-	78	13	9	0	2.44
Unemployed	-	-	59	13	28	-	7.28
All	2.25	11.9	75.58	5.47	4.74	0.07	0.39
Count	301	1592	10115	732	634	9	13383

labour supply fixed at their observed hours. The numbers of individuals in these categories are 885, 5.18, 640 and 1625 respectively.[3]

Since actual labour supply points are rounded to the nearest discrete labour supply point, the definition of nonparticipation depends on the number of discrete labour supply points used. For women it is working less than 3 hours and for men it is working less than 10 hours. The oldest and youngest age groups do not have large changes. This is because labour supply is fixed at the observed hours for people over 65 years of age and for full-time students, who probably form a large proportion of the 15 to 19 year old group. However, about one third of people aged between 25 and 54 are expected to have a change in work probability.

Most changes lie between 2 and 10 percentage points and reductions are more frequent than increases. However, on average there is an increase in the work probability. The largest number of reductions in probability is found for the age groups between 40 and 54 years. The largest positive effect is found for the 60 to 64 year olds caused by the relatively large proportion of people who experience an increase.

Most notable among the other characteristics in Table 4.4 is the result that sole parents are predicted to have a larger increase in the probability of working as a result of reduced taper rates than other groups. This sensitivity to work incentives is found in several other studies as well (Blundell *et al.*, 2000; Blundell and Hoynes, 2004). Unemployed people and people with a large family are also more likely to participate in the labour market after the reform. Employed people experience a reduction in work probability on average.

Table 4.5 reports the effects of the reform on changes in preferred hours of labour supply. The same groups who are more likely to have changes in the probability of working are also more likely to wish to change the number of hours they work. Most changes are small, between 1 and 5 hours, and reductions are most prevalent.

---

[3] In some cases, 100 successful random draws producing observed hours as the optimal hours cannot be generated from the model within a reasonable number of total drawings. In the simulations of this chapter, if after 5000 draws from the error term distribution, the model fails to predict the observed labour supply 100 times, the individual is dropped from the simulation. This occurs 521 times, which in addition to the 121 cases rejected because of unrealistic wages represents 6.5 per cent of all individuals in the database. This approach is different from the current approach as described in subsection 1.3.2 above.

Table 4.5 Changes in average predicted hours

	Decrease				Increase			Average
Age	> 10	5-10	1-5	none	1-5	5-10	> 10	
15 to 19	-	-	2	96	2	1	0	0.09
20 to 24	0	1	11	76	7	4	1	0.23
25 to 29	0	2	19	66	9	4	1	0.03
30 to 34	0	3	21	62	10	3	1	-0.12
35 to 39	1	3	24	59	10	3	1	-0.36
40 to 44	0	4	25	56	9	3	1	-0.40
45 to 49	0	3	28	61	4	2	1	-0.54
50 to 54	0	2	24	66	5	3	1	-0.31
55 to 59	-	2	15	76	5	2	1	-0.03
60 to 64	-	0	7	80	8	5	1	0.49
65 plus	-	-	-	100	-	-	-	0.00
Income unit type								
Couple	0	2	21	72	4	1	0	-0.44
Couple + dep. child	1	4	28	52	10	3	2	-0.42
Dependent child	-	-	-	100	0	-	-	0.01
Single	-	0	2	94	2	1	0	0.13
Sole parent	-	1	11	27	34	23	5	2.88
Number of children								
None	0	1	12	83	3	1	0	-0.15
One	1	3	24	54	10	6	2	0.05
Two	1	3	22	59	11	4	1	-0.16
Three	1	3	18	64	11	2	2	-0.04
Four	1	2	13	66	11	4	3	0.29
Five	-	-	2	66	21	5	7	1.55
Six	-	-	7	79	13	-	-	0.17
Employment status								
Employed	0	3	26	68	1	1	0	-0.82
Nonparticipation	-	-	-	84	12	4	1	0.73
Unemployed	-	-	-	63	16	13	7	2.29
All groups	0.26	1.71	15.23	73.64	5.94	2.46	0.76	-0.10
Count	35	228	2039	9855	795	329	102	13383

On average, there is a reduction in hours for most age groups (and indeed for the total population) except for the youngest and oldest groups. The largest reductions are seen for people aged between 35 and 54 years. The younger age groups from 25 to 35 years old and the 60 to 64 age group, for which the increase in work probability is large as well, display smaller percentages experiencing a decrease in predicted hours than other groups.

4.2.3   Labour Supply Transition Matrices

Transition matrices showing the probabilities of movement between discrete hours levels, for each of the five demographic groups, provide further information about changes in labour supply behaviour. For both single and married males, only three hours levels are used, reflecting the observed distribution of hours of work by men.[4] For the female groups and sole parents, 11 discrete hours levels are used. Separate transition matrices for married men and women, single men, single women and sole parents are presented in Tables 4.6 to 4.10.

Table 4.6 shows that some married men are increasing their labour supply as a result of the reform, whereas others are decreasing their labour supply. This indicates that married men's labour supply is spread over the hours and wage range where the budget constraint is affected by the reduction in the withdrawal rate, resulting in both positive and negative effects on labour supply. The net effect is a slight decrease in the number of nonparticipants (by 0.56 per cent) and full-time workers, who move into part-time work. Overall 2.6 per cent of married men reduce their working hours and the average number of hours worked decreases by 0.37 hours.

Table 4.6 Married men's labour supply transitions (rows to columns)

Hours	0	20	40	Total
0	97.0	1.1	1.9	43.07
20	1.3	95.1	3.6	2.24
40	1.3	4.8	94.0	54.70
Total	42.51	5.19	52.30	100.00

---

[4] The estimated preference parameters in the current version of MITTS are based on 6 discrete labour supply points for married men and 11 labour supply points for single men. The simulation in this chapter is based on a different (previous) specification of the labour supply model than the simulations in the current version of MITTS would be.

On average, the change in the hours worked for married women is somewhat larger than for married men, with a decrease by nearly half an hour. Similar to married men, women are more likely to reduce their labour supply than to increase labour supply as a result of the reform. The reform seems to have the smallest effect on married women who work 10 hours or less; see Table 4.7. Most women in this group remain at the same labour supply. At each labour supply level, the largest off-diagonal proportions are for moves from work to zero hours. However, looking at hours before and after the reform, there is little change in the distribution of hours worked. There is a slight shift from full-time to part-time work and nonparticipation.

Kalb and Kew (2002) simulate the same policy change for couple families using updated labour supply parameters in MITTS. Although the exact sizes of the effects are somewhat different, the results for couple families are very similar to those presented in this chapter.

Table 4.7 Married women's labour supply transitions (rows to columns)

Hours	0	5	10	15	20	25	30	35	40	45	50	Total
0	97.1	0.3	0.4	0.4	0.4	0.4	0.4	0.3	0.2	0.2	0.1	59.4
5	1.0	97.7	0.2	0.4	0.2	0.2	0.2	0.0	0.1	0.0	-	0.6
10	3.4	0.3	95.0	0.2	0.2	0.4	0.1	0.1	0.1	0.1	0.1	1.8
15	4.7	0.4	0.3	93.2	0.3	0.3	0.2	0.3	0.1	0.1	0.0	3.2
20	5.2	0.6	0.6	0.7	91.3	0.4	0.4	0.3	0.2	0.2	0.1	4.8
25	4.7	0.4	0.6	0.6	0.5	92.0	0.4	0.3	0.2	0.2	0.1	4.0
30	5.3	0.5	0.6	0.6	0.9	0.6	90.3	0.4	0.4	0.2	0.2	3.7
35	5.9	0.5	0.8	0.7	0.9	0.8	0.8	88.5	0.5	0.4	0.2	4.8
40	5.9	0.6	0.6	0.8	0.8	0.8	0.8	0.6	88.6	0.4	0.2	12.6
45	5.6	0.6	0.6	0.9	1.0	1.0	0.8	0.6	0.5	88.2	0.2	1.9
50	3.6	0.3	0.3	0.5	0.6	0.7	0.6	0.5	0.4	0.3	92.1	3.4
Total	59.8	0.9	2.1	3.4	4.8	4.1	3.8	4.6	11.4	1.8	3.3	100

In the transition matrices for single men and women (see Tables 4.8 and 4.9), both increases and decreases in labour supply can be observed, although the majority of singles remain at their old labour supply. Part-time male workers are most likely to change and are more likely to increase than decrease their labour supply (about 1 per cent of single men increase their labour supply). Few of the nonparticipants are encouraged by the reform to enter the labour market (about 0.25 per cent). The overall effect is a slight increase in full-time work and a slight decrease in nonparticipation for single men. For single women, a slight increase in the two highest categories of full-time work and a tiny decrease in participation are observed. Of all demographic groups, single women seem to be least affected by the reform. Their average number of hours worked decreases by 0.10 hours only and the percentage of women increasing their labour supply is similar to the percentage of women decreasing their labour supply (both are small at around 0.40 per cent).

Table 4.8 Single men's labour supply transitions (rows to columns)

Hours	0	20	40	Total
0	99.30	0.10	0.60	47.71
20	0.70	83.40	15.90	6.69
40	0.00	0.00	100.00	45.60
Total	47.45	5.60	46.95	100.00

Table 4.9 Single women's labour supply transitions (rows to columns)

Hours	0	5	10	15	20	25	30	35	40	45	50	Total
0	99.9	0.0	0.0	0.0	0.0	0.0	0.0	0.0	0.0	0.0	0.0	56.4
5	-	100	-	-	0.0	-	-	-	-	-	-	3.2
10	0.2	0.0	99.5	0.1	0.0	0.0	0.0	0.0	0.0	0.0	0.1	3.7
15	0.4	0.2	0.1	98.4	0.0	0.0	0.0	0.1	0.2	0.3	0.3	2.9
20	0.3	0.3	0.1	0.1	96.7	0.1	0.2	0.1	0.3	0.5	1.3	1.3
25	0.4	0.6	0.3	0.1	0.2	97.0	0.0	0.1	0.4	0.3	0.7	1.4
30	0.8	0.6	0.3	0.2	0.1	0.0	95.4	0.3	0.4	0.3	1.5	2.2
35	0.7	0.6	0.3	0.3	0.1	0.1	0.1	96.5	0.2	0.4	0.8	5.5
40	0.6	0.6	0.3	0.3	0.2	0.1	0.0	0.0	96.7	0.3	0.9	16.0
45	0.2	0.3	0.2	0.2	0.1	0.1	0.1	0.0	-	98.4	0.4	3.1
50	0.1	0.1	0.1	0.0	0.1	0.1	-	0.0	0.0	-	99.4	4.3
Total	56.6	3.4	3.8	2.9	1.3	1.4	2.1	5.3	15.5	3.1	4.6	100

Sole parents also experience both increases and decreases in labour supply; see Table 4.10. However, compared with singles and couples they are more likely to change labour supply, particularly at the lower and upper end of the hours range. Sole parents working fewer than 25 hours seem most likely to increase their hours whereas sole parents working 35 hours or more are more likely to reduce their hours.

After the reform, more sole parents are expected to participate in the labour market since very few women move from work to nonparticipation, whereas a substantial proportion moves into work from nonparticipation. The net effect is more than 8 per cent. As a result, their average weekly hours are increased by nearly 3 hours, showing that the overall effect is positive. However, there is a relatively small negative effect for a subgroup caused by the 1.8 per cent of sole parents who decrease their labour supply, which is partly counteracted by the 1.3 per cent of sole parents who increase their working hours after the reform.

Table 4.10 Sole parents' labour supply transitions (rows to columns)

Hours	0	5	10	15	20	25	30	35	40	45	50	Total
0	85.9	0.0	0.3	0.8	1.0	1.9	1.8	1.7	2.1	2.2	2.5	58.7
5	-	89.2	0.3	0.4	1.0	0.7	1.7	1.9	1.6	2.3	0.8	2.9
10	-	-	86.3	0.6	0.5	1.4	1.5	2.7	2.1	2.4	2.5	2.2
15	-	0.1	0.1	91.7	0.3	0.7	1.4	1.1	1.7	1.4	1.6	2.8
20	-	-	-	0.1	95.0	0.2	1.1	0.9	0.8	1.3	0.7	3.9
25	0.0	-	-	-	-	97.8	0.0	0.3	0.4	0.6	0.9	3.6
30	-	0.4	0.3	0.3	0.5	1.1	95.2	0.2	0.7	0.8	0.4	3.4
35	-	0.2	0.3	0.7	1.0	1.6	0.5	94.7	0.2	0.6	0.3	4.0
40	0.2	0.3	0.6	1.6	1.7	2.5	1.7	0.3	90.8	0.2	0.2	12.3
45	0.4	0.3	0.4	1.0	1.9	1.8	2.0	1.9	1.1	87.9	1.3	1.0
50	0.1	0.3	0.4	0.8	1.1	1.0	1.1	1.3	0.9	0.4	92.5	5.2
Total	50.5	2.7	2.2	3.3	4.6	5.2	4.7	5.1	12.7	2.5	6.5	100.0

4.2.4 Government Revenue and Expenditure

Summary information about the revenue and expenditure implications of the reform, for the weighted sample used in the simulations, is given in Table 4.11. The revenue and expenditure changes for fixed labour supply do not correspond exactly to those under MITTS-A. This is because in the case of MITTS-B the costs and revenues are evaluated at the fixed discrete hours nearest to the actual hours, rather than the actual hours themselves. In addition, about 6.5 per cent of individuals are dropped from the simulations in MITTS-B for reasons explained in section 4.2.2. However, the pre-reform results for MITTS-A and MITTS-B are reasonably close.

Table 4.11 Behavioural responses: tax and transfer costs of reform

	Pre-reform ($m)	Allowing for labour supply responses		Keeping labour supply fixed	
		Abs. change ($m)	Rel. change (%)	Abs. change ($m)	Rel. change (%)
Couples					
Government revenue					
Income tax	40884.9	-206.0	-0.5	900.3	2.2
Medicare	2516.2	56.9	2.3	114.9	4.6
Total revenue	43401.1	-149.1	-0.3	1015.2	2.3
Government expenditure					
Tax rebates	2340.8	-555.2	-23.7	-567.6	-24.2
Family Payment	3815.8	1923.6	50.4	1531.4	40.1
FTP/FTB	394.0	202.7	51.4	164.4	41.7
Allowances	6484.6	5852.4	90.3	5222.4	80.5
Pensions	11019.7	784.7	7.1	805.0	7.3
Pharmaceutical Allowance	116.6	10.0	8.6	10.0	8.6
Rent Allowance	525.8	264.5	50.3	208.6	39.7
Total expenditure	24697.3	8482.7	34.3	7374.2	29.9
Net expenditure	-18703.8	8631.8	-46.1	6359.0	-34.0
Single men					
Government revenue					
Income tax	10928.0	523.3	4.8	373.0	3.4
Medicare	754.0	48.0	6.4	40.0	5.3
Total revenue	11682.0	571.3	4.9	413.0	3.5
Government expenditure					
Tax rebates	426.2	-16.8	-3.9	-12.2	-2.9
Family Payment	0.0	0.0	0.0	0.0	0.0
FTP/FTB	0.0	0.0	0.0	0.0	0.0
Allowances	3317.7	1227.7	37.0	1357.1	40.9
Pensions	3204.2	145.7	4.5	145.7	4.5
Pharmaceutical Allowance	54.4	2.4	4.4	2.4	4.4
Rent Allowance	297.5	402.3	135.2	410.9	138.1
Total expenditure	7300.0	1761.3	24.1	1903.9	26.1
Net expenditure	-4382.0	1190.0	-27.2	1490.9	-34.0

Table 4.11 Continued

	Pre-reform ($m)	Allowing for labour supply responses		Keeping labour supply fixed	
		Abs. change ($m)	Rel. change (%)	Abs. change ($m)	Rel. change (%)
Single women					
Government revenue					
Income tax	7398.7	321.0	4.3	334.9	4.5
Medicare	486.2	29.4	6.0	32.4	6.7
Total revenue	7884.9	350.4	4.4	367.3	4.7
Government expenditure					
Tax rebates	793.8	-13.9	-1.8	-19.5	-2.5
Family Payment	0.0	0.0	0.0	0.0	0.0
FTP/FTB	0.0	0.0	0.0	0.0	0.0
Allowances	3297.7	1119.1	33.9	1070.4	32.5
Pensions	7048.2	230.9	3.3	231.6	3.3
Pharmaceutical Allowance	118.4	3.3	2.8	3.3	2.8
Rent Allowance	334.1	309.5	92.6	313.1	93.7
Total expenditure	11592.2	1648.9	14.2	1598.9	13.8
Net expenditure	3707.3	1298.5	35.0	1231.6	33.2
Sole parents					
Government revenue					
Income tax	1643.3	174.5	10.6	74.5	4.5
Medicare	68.9	7.9	11.5	4.9	7.1
Total revenue	1712.2	182.4	10.7	79.4	4.6
Government expenditure					
Tax rebates	533.0	13.7	2.6	-12.0	-2.2
Family Payment	2086.2	116.6	5.6	89.0	4.3
FTP/FTB	224.0	0.0	0.0	0.0	0.0
Allowances	2938.1	77.7	2.6	260.8	8.9
Pensions	155.0	-4.3	-2.7	1.1	0.7
Pharmaceutical Allowance	48.4	6.9	14.2	5.9	12.2
Rent Allowance	398.8	11.8	3.0	5.4	1.3
Total expenditure	6383.5	222.4	3.5	350.2	5.5
Net expenditure	4671.3	40.0	0.9	270.8	5.8

The changes in MITTS-B allowing for labour supply effects are based on averages for each individual, over the distribution of discrete hours levels. An important general result arising from Table 4.11 is that when allowance is made for behavioural responses, in some cases there can be substantial effects on the expenditure simulations. Changes can move in opposite directions for some payment types in the different subgroups, depending on whether labour supply is allowed to vary or is fixed. For example, income tax paid by couples decreases after taking into account behavioural changes, whereas under fixed labour supply, an increase was expected.

The potential importance of including such labour supply effects for tax policy microsimulation is clear from a comparison of the results in the fixed labour supply column with the results in the column where labour supply is allowed to respond to the reform. The net difference in expenditure for couples is about 2.3 billion dollars more after accounting for behavioural changes. This net difference only includes direct taxes and Medicare, and expenditure on social security. Indirect taxes and types of government expenditure other than those mentioned in Table 4.11 are not included. The relative difference in expenditure and revenue between fixed and varying labour supply is largest for sole parents, which is as expected given the predicted effects on labour supply, discussed in the previous subsection. However, given the small size of the group, the absolute effect on total net expenditure is not large. The effect after the reform was small in the fixed labour supply simulation, given that additional expenditure only occurs for individuals with other income (mostly from work) and that the proportion of individuals with other income is small in the sole parent group. According to the model, the increase in revenue from taxes would more than double and the increase in expenditure would decrease by more than a third after allowing for a behavioural response. The combined effect of these two changes brings the cost of this reform down to 40 million from 271 million dollars per year.

4.3 Conclusions

This chapter has examined the effects of a partial flattening of the effective marginal tax rate structure in Australia. Simulations in which all individuals have an unchanged labour supply were compared with behavioural simulations in which the majority of individuals are free to adjust the number of hours worked. The results reflect only the supply side of the labour market, so that no general equilibrium effects on wage rates were considered. Furthermore, a discrete hours framework was used, in which individuals move between pre-specified discrete hours levels, rather than being able to vary hours continuously.

Examples were provided of the implications for aggregate tax revenue and expenditure, and the effects on individuals and households, of a hypothetical change to the tax and transfer system operating in March 1998. The hypothetical reform involved a reduction in the means-tested benefit taper rates to 30 per cent. Thus, all taper rates of 50 per cent and 70 per cent in the 1998 system were reduced to 30 per cent, while leaving all basic benefit levels unchanged. Revenues and expenditures before and after the reform were expressed in 1998 dollars.

This reform flattens the tax structure to some extent by reducing the high marginal tax rates applying to those with relatively low incomes, and this has the anticipated effect of raising the probability of working and of increasing hours worked. For others (those on medium incomes), there is a range of hours for which marginal rates increase, producing reductions in average hours worked.

The results, comparing the simulation where labour supply is fixed with a simulation allowing labour supply to vary, show clear differences in the predicted costs involved in the reform. For example, for couples the overall effect is to reduce labour supply and the expected cost of reducing the taper rate would be higher than expected when labour supply changes were not taken into account. However, for sole parents the opposite effect is observed. The expected cost of this reform is substantially reduced to a fraction of the cost expected when no account is taken of possible changes in labour supply. Hence behavioural changes are likely to be important in assessing policy reforms and the effects of a policy reform can be different for different subgroups in the population.

5 Reducing Family Payment Taper Rate

This chapter examines the impact on total government expenditure, the choice of hours worked and the labour force participation rates among couples with dependent children of a hypothetical policy change to Family Payments in the March 1998 tax and transfer system. The simulation is carried out, using MITTS, for the subgroup of couples, including those without children. In the behavioural simulations, men and women over 65 are assumed to remain at the same labour supply as before the change. Changes are simulated only for people of working age, who are not full-time students, on a disability payment or self-employed. The latter three groups all remain at the labour supply level observed before the change.

Two separate simulations, referred to as Policy I and Policy II, are carried out with the details of the pre-reform system based on the March 1998 tax and transfer system. Policy I reduces the taper rate for the maximum rate of Family Payments from 50 to 30 per cent for household income over $23,400 per annum. Policy II involves two changes to parameters in the social security system. The first replaces the 'sudden death' income test with a 30 per cent withdrawal rate for the minimum rate of Family Payment. The second change increases the income threshold where the minimum rate of Family Payment starts to be withdrawn for families from $65,941 per annum to $73,000 per annum. Policies I and II are designed to provide more generous support for families facing the costs of bringing up children. The difference between the two policies is that Policy I affects families on low-to-medium incomes whereas Policy II affects families on medium-to-high incomes. Low-income couples with children are not affected by the reforms since their incomes are below the minimum income threshold of $23,400 per annum where no Family Payments are withdrawn.

The database used as the basis for the simulations is the 1997/1998 Survey of Income and Housing Cost (SIHC) confidentialised unit record file released by the Australian Bureau of Statistics. Thus, weekly incomes are based on the financial year 1997-98. All tables use weighted results to represent the population, unless otherwise indicated, and simulated revenue and expenditure are expressed in 1998 dollars.

Expenditure and revenue in the pre-reform situation are calculated using MITTS, rather than being based on observed benefit payments in the SIHC. The following section discusses some assumptions that are made in the MITTS model, which result in the base case in the simulations having a higher level of expenditure than was observed in the actual pre-reform situation.

Section 5.1 briefly discusses some background information on the simulations. Section 5.2 discusses the results from MITTS-A and the findings from MITTS-B are presented in section 5.3. Section 5.4 concludes.

5.1   MITTS Assumptions

The estimation of the expected labour supply changes is based on the labour supply model described in chapter 1. MITTS uses a discrete hours specification with a relatively large number of labour supply points. Households are assumed to choose from 0, 5, 10, 15,..., 50 hours of labour supply. However, fewer points are allowed for married men given the low number of married men working part-time hours (which can be caused by factors on both the supply and the demand side). They are assumed to choose from 0, 10, 20, 30, 40 or 50 hours. However, given the probability approach of simulating changes, small changes in labour supply can still be captured even in a ten-hour interval labour supply specification. A small change in labour supply means they may have a small probability of moving from 30 to 40 hours, for example.

The starting point of the behavioural simulations is based on the actual working hours in the data, using the calibration method described earlier, where draws are taken from the error term distributions and only those draws which place the individual at the observed discretised labour supply in the pre-reform situation are used in calculating the expected labour supply.

In 517 cases the labour supply model could not generate 100 draws at the observed labour supply within a total of 5000 tries. This indicates that for these cases the predicted level of labour supply is far from the observed level of labour supply. For these households, labour supply after the reform is kept at the same level as before the reform, thus possibly underestimating the total number of changes as a result of the reform.

The calibration approach ensures that the results before the reform from MITTS-A and from MITTS-B are similar. The difference between the two is the rounding to discrete hours in MITTS-B and the dropping of a few observations that have wages under $4.00 or over $100 per hour (only 69 out of about 5900 observations drop out because of this selection).

Labour supply is kept constant for some groups who are expected to be different in their responses compared with the average working-age individuals. These groups are the self-employed (644 cases), those on disability payments (235 cases), full-time students (67 cases) and people over 65 years of age (715 cases). This leaves 3618 households for whom the effect of the policy reform on labour supply is simulated.

5.2   The Non-behavioural Simulation Results

This section presents the 'morning after' effects of making a series of reforms to withdrawal rates and thresholds associated with Family Payment, a child-related payment available to families satisfying various eligibility criteria. The pre-reform system in MITTS relies on the information provided by the SIHC in terms of population characteristics and all non-benefit income. However, receipt of benefits in the base system is computed using observable characteristics rather than relying on the reported information on benefit income in the data.[1] Thus it is assumed that any individual in the labour force (either employed or unemployed) is eligible for unemployment-related benefits subject only to the means test (see chapter 1 for more discussion). For these reasons, expenditure on payments, particularly on unemployment benefits, is likely to be overestimated in the model.

Eligibility for Family Payment is based on the income unit's total income and the presence of dependent children. Income-unit income is subject to

---

[1] Certain payments such as Disability Support Pension, Sickness Allowance, Carer Payment and the Department of Veterans' Affairs pensions do rely on observed receipt in the base data, as no other information is available to help identify eligible recipients.

two income limits or thresholds, one for the minimum payment rate and another for the maximum payment rate. Families with a level of income below the minimum income limit receive the maximum rate of Family Payment. For each dollar of income above the minimum income limit, the payment is withdrawn at 50 per cent until a minimum rate of Family Payment is reached. This minimum rate of Family Payment is received until the family's income reaches the maximum threshold after which the payment is completely stopped.

Policy I reduces the taper rate on the maximum rate of Family Payment for each dollar of income above the minimum income limit. Thus it does not affect the number of couples eligible for Family Payment overall. However, it does affect the level of payment paid to a section of the population already relying on Family Payment as it increases the number of couples receiving more than the minimum amount of Family Payment. Hence a reduction in the taper rate has the effect of reducing the number of couples receiving the minimum rate of Family Payment. In addition, it increases the level of payment for another group receiving in between the maximum and minimum rate.

Policy II increases the maximum income limit from $65,941 to $73,000 per annum in combination with replacing the 'sudden death' income test with a 30-cent reduction of the payment for every dollar of family income above $73,000 per annum. It therefore has the effect of increasing the Family Payment cut-out point from $65,941 to $75,037 per annum for couples with one child. A higher cut-out income draws a larger number of formerly ineligible couples into Family Payment recipience.

Figures 5.1 and 5.2 show the effects of the combined policy reforms on the net income and effective marginal tax rate schedules for a hypothetical couple with 1 child aged between 5 and 12 years. The couple is paying $130 a week in private rental accommodation and is thus in principle entitled to Rent Assistance. To illustrate the impact of both reforms, it is assumed that the reference person in this family earns a relatively high wage of $30 per hour. Figures 5.1 and 5.2 are created conditional on the partner not working.

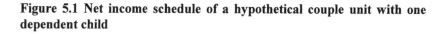

Figure 5.1 Net income schedule of a hypothetical couple unit with one dependent child

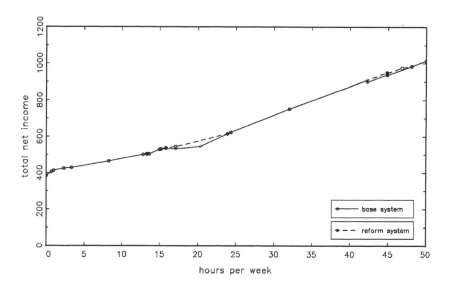

The reduction in the withdrawal rate for the maximum rate of Family Payment flattens the budget constraint and reduces effective marginal tax rates (EMTRs) at low to middle ranges of income. In this example, EMTRs are reduced between about 15 and 20 hours of work and increased between about 20 to 25 hours of work, when the original maximum Family Payment would have been completely tapered out. The high wage rate in this example means that the relevant policy change affects this household at a relatively low number of hours of work. Families on lower wages would see a similar flattening of their budget constraint at higher, possibly full-time, hours of work and the effect may be over a wider range of hours. The introduction of a taper rate for the minimum rate may not affect low-wage families at all, in any reasonable hours range. The replacement of the 'sudden death' income test with a more gradual withdrawal of the minimum rate of Family Payment removes the discontinuity in the budget constraint at a high level of income. Before the reform, this occurred at about 42 hours, at the light dot on the line in Figure 5.2. The EMTR is increased while the payment is withdrawn over a short range of income until the minimum payment is completely tapered out again. The increased income threshold means that withdrawal in the reform case only starts at just over 45 hours of labour supply. The minimum rate of Family Payment is withdrawn in about 2 hours.

Figure 5.2 Effective marginal tax rate schedule of a hypothetical couple unit with one dependent child

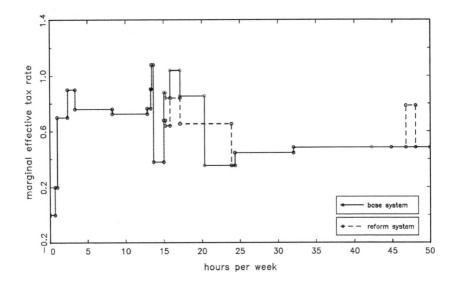

5.2.1 Effects on Government Revenue and Expenditure

Table 5.1 presents the amount of various components of government revenue and expenditure before and after the reform under the assumption that individuals do not vary their number of hours worked. The first column under the heading 'pre-reform' in Table 5.1 shows the amount of government revenue and expenditure based on the March 1998 tax system.

As expected with an increased generosity in benefit payments, the overall net expenditure of the government increases for both policies. Family Payments are expected to increase by $229.4 million after the implementation of Policy I. As mentioned earlier, more couples are expected to receive Family Payment at a rate exceeding the minimum Family Payment rate after the reform. The increase in the number of couples receiving more than the minimum Family Payment means that some recipients who formerly received Family Tax Assistance will receive payments through Family Tax Payment (FTP) after the change. This is a result of the rule that dictates that households who receive more than the minimum Family Payment are entitled to receive assistance through the social security system in the form of Family Tax Payment rather than receiving a similar payment through the tax system in the form of Family Tax Assistance. Therefore, after the reform, more couples are entitled to receive assistance through the social security system, rather than through the tax system. This increases the amount of FTP paid out but at the same time increases the level of income tax paid, to give a neutral effect overall in terms of net income.

Table 5.1 Main revenue and expenditure

Tax or transfer	Pre-reform Cost ($m)	Pre-reform Number (x1000)	Net change (Policy I) Cost ($m)	Net change (Policy I) Number (x1000)	Net change (Policy II) Cost ($m)	Net change (Policy II) Number (x1000)
Government revenue						
Income tax	50177.4	7014	80.1	0	0.0	0
Medicare levy	3087.4	4482	0.0	0	0.0	0
Total	53264.8		80.1		0.0	
Government expenditure						
Tax rebates	2497.4	4397	0.0	0	0.0	0
Family Payment	4065.6	1380	229.4	0	119.4	98
FTP/FTB	398.4	591	80.1	121	0.0	0
Allowances	6823.6	1531	0.0	0	0.0	0
Pensions	10881.8	1617	0.0	0	0.0	0
Pharmaceutical Allowance	117.8	1678	0.0	0	0.0	0
Rent Allowance	531.2	407	56.4	30	0.0	0
Total	25315.9		365.9		119.4	
Net expenditure	-27949.0		285.8		119.4	

Table 5.1 shows that both FTP and income tax increase by 80.1 million dollars. An additional 121,000 couples are expected to receive the Family Tax Payment. To be eligible for Family Tax Payment, families with

dependent children must be receiving more than the minimum Family Payment rate. The estimated number of couples receiving Family Payment is 1,380,000, which after the implementation of Policy II increases by 98,000. The increasing number of couples eligible for Family Payment is a consequence of the higher income cut-out in Policy II.

5.2.2 Changes in the Individual's Income-Unit Income

Table 5.2 presents the distribution of changes in weekly net income-unit income experienced by individuals resulting from Policies I and II. First, individuals are categorised in terms of income deciles, then by the age of their youngest child, their number of children and their own age. The income measure is net weekly non-equivalised income-unit income. This means that each person in the couple is assigned the total income of the income unit to which they belong, without taking into account the number of adults and children in the income unit who have to share this income. For example in Table 5.2, 4.8 per cent of the 840 individuals in decile 4 experience an increase in their income-unit income of between $1 and $5 per week after the reform under Policy I.

Table 5.2 Income gainers/losers by household income deciles (unweighted individual level per capita non-equivalised income-unit income)

	Policy I					Policy II			
		Increase in $					Increase in $		
Decile	None	1-5	5-10	> 10	Average	None	> 10	Average	Count
1	100.0	-	-	-	0.0	100.0	-	0.0	844
2	100.0	-	-	-	0.0	100.0	-	0.0	838
3	99.3	0.2	0.2	0.2	0.1	100.0	-	0.0	842
4	79.8	4.8	3.6	11.9	2.5	100.0	-	0.0	840
5	69.8	3.8	3.8	22.6	6.1	100.0	-	0.0	840
6	84.3	2.1	2.4	11.2	3.7	100.0	-	0.0	842
7	96.4	0.2	0.7	2.6	1.0	100.0	-	0.0	840
8	99.5	-	-	0.5	0.1	90.0	10.0	2.0	842
9	100.0	-	-	-	0.0	86.4	13.6	3.5	840
10	100.0	-	-	-	0.0	100.0	-	0.0	840
Total	92.9	1.1	1.1	4.9	1.3	97.7	2.4	0.6	8408

No one is expected to experience a fall in net income after the reforms, as any family affected by the reform will experience a net increase in income. This is confirmed in Table 5.2. This reflects the generosity of both policy reforms relative to the March 1998 tax and transfer system. Table 5.2 shows that the largest gains in welfare benefits under Policy I go to those who are in deciles 3 to 7. This is expected since Policy I has the largest effect on working couples whose family incomes are above the minimum income limit. Contrary to Policy I, the largest gainers from the Policy II reforms are in deciles 8 and 9. This is consistent with expectations since Policy II draws couples with dependent children who are working and earning income above the pre-reform maximum income limit (which was $65,941 per annum) into receiving Family Payment. The effect is large since people who previously received nothing will receive a relatively large amount as a result of the newly introduced taper rate replacing the 'sudden death' of the minimum Family Payment.

Table 5.3 shows that the income gain under Policy I is highest for those who have a youngest child aged between one and eleven years old. The majority of increases is greater than $10 per week. The largest average increases are observed for those who have three or more children. The latter is at least partly due to the higher payment rates for the fourth and subsequent children and to the higher cut-out incomes for households with more children. Couples aged over 45 have on average the smallest income gain, which is most likely related to the fact that they no longer have dependent children. Table 5.3 also shows that every couple affected by policy reform II experiences an increase in family income of greater than $10 per week. The results indicate that Policy II has the largest impact on those aged between 30 and 44 and those who have between one and four children. The number of households with five or six children is relatively small. The zero effect under Policy II in Table 5.3 indicates that this group of households in the sample has incomes below the relevant income range.

Hypothetical Policy Reforms

Table 5.3 Income gainers/losers by respondent's age, number of children and age of youngest child (unweighted individual level per capita non-equivalised income-unit income)

	Policy I					Policy II			
	None	1-5	5-10	>10	Avg.	None	>10	Avg.	Count
		Increase in $				Increase in $			
Age of youngest child									
No dependants	99.9	-	0.0	0.1	0.0	99.9	0.1	0.0	5153
<1	83.0	2.5	4.1	10.5	3.3	95.9	4.1	0.7	465
1	84.3	3.2	1.6	11.0	2.9	95.2	4.8	2.0	388
2	75.9	3.3	3.5	17.3	4.3	95.0	5.0	0.9	372
3	80.7	0.9	2.5	15.9	4.6	96.6	3.4	1.1	251
4	84.7	1.4	2.4	11.6	2.9	92.5	7.5	1.7	222
5	79.2	6.1	1.2	13.4	3.3	90.0	10.0	2.4	207
6 to 9	82.9	2.2	2.4	12.4	3.6	93.8	6.2	1.7	644
10	83.3	-	1.1	15.6	3.0	96.6	3.4	1.0	158
11	80.3	2.2	1.4	16.2	4.1	97.4	2.6	0.4	140
12	86.2	2.6	4.6	6.6	2.1	94.2	5.8	1.0	233
13	90.5	2.5	2.6	4.4	1.2	92.9	7.1	1.2	164
14	92.2	2.4	1.3	4.1	1.0	88.2	11.8	1.4	173
Number of children									
None	100.0	-	-	-	0.0	100.0	-	0.0	4433
One	94.2	1.1	0.8	4.0	0.9	96.4	3.6	0.5	1417
Two	86.1	2.5	2.0	9.4	2.4	93.7	6.3	1.4	1708
Three	73.1	2.9	4.4	19.7	5.6	95.7	4.3	1.6	747
Four	80.5	3.0	3.4	13.0	4.6	94.1	5.9	2.1	190
Five	71.2	-	5.6	23.2	6.5	100.0	-	0.0	46
Six	50.1	4.7	8.1	37.1	11.4	100.0	-	0.0	27
Age									
15 to 19	91.2	-	-	8.8	2.8	100.0	-	0.0	20
20 to 24	91.8	0.2	0.6	7.4	1.8	98.7	1.3	0.2	298
25 to 29	90.6	1.6	1.5	6.4	1.8	97.7	2.3	0.5	693
30 to 34	84.8	2.5	2.7	10.0	2.8	95.8	4.2	1.2	977
35 to 39	84.1	2.3	2.1	11.5	3.2	94.3	5.7	1.4	1116
40 to 44	88.2	1.2	2.4	8.2	2.2	95.9	4.1	0.8	1086
45 to 49	97.0	0.8	0.1	2.0	0.4	97.2	2.8	0.5	1030
50 to 54	99.1	0.2	0.2	0.5	0.1	99.6	0.4	0.1	907
55 to 59	99.9	0.1	-	-	0.0	100.0	-	0.0	676
60 to 64	99.9	0.1	-	-	0.0	100.0	-	0.0	542
65 plus	100.0	-	-	-	0.0	100.0	-	0.0	1225
Total	93.2	1.0	1.1	4.8	1.3	97.7	2.4	0.5	-
Count	7984	86	90	409	-	8367	202	-	8568

5.2.3 Effect on Effective Marginal Tax Rates

Table 5.4 presents the EMTRs before and after the welfare reform for couples with children, ranging from 0 per cent to over 100 per cent. In this table, only the EMTRs of income unit heads are represented. The pre-reform is shown in the first row and the post-reform is shown in the second and third rows. For example, in the first row, 12 per cent of 2068 couples with dependants face an EMTR of 0 per cent. High EMTR levels can create employment disincentives. For couples with dependent children, the modal EMTR is in the range 40-50 per cent.

Table 5.4 Distribution of EMTRs for couples with dependants (row percentages)

Lower bound	0	0	10	20	30	40	50	60	70	80	90	100			
Upper bound	0	10	20	30	40	50	60	70	80	90	100	∞	Mean	Count
Pre-reform	12	0	1	4	26	41	0	1	6	6	0	2	45.2	2068
Policy I	12	0	1	4	23	40	2	9	7	2	0	1	45.4	2068
Policy II	12	0	1	4	26	41	0	1	6	6	0	2	43.6	2068

The average EMTRs before and after the reform are roughly similar for Policy I, although there are some changes in the distribution. From Figure 5.2, it can be seen that for some households the EMTR increases whereas for other households the EMTR decreases after the reform. These shifts are revealed in Table 5.4.

The average EMTR after implementation of Policy II decreases, but the changes must be within the categories. Figure 5.2 shows that this policy change affects only households in the higher-income range over a relatively small range. The EMTR decreases for some individuals because a withdrawal rate has been introduced for the minimum rate of the Family Payment to replace the 'sudden death' of the payment. On the other hand, people who previously were ineligible for benefits are eligible after the reform, which increases their EMTR.

5.3 Behavioural Simulation Results

Policy reforms, such as those simulated in the previous section, may induce changes to labour supply. Failing to capture these changes can provide misleading results, particularly with regard to the aggregate costs. This section presents the results of the policy simulations using MITTS-B. Labour supply transition matrices showing the probability of changing to particular discrete levels of hours worked per week for married men and women are presented in the first subsection. The extent of changes in work probabilities and predicted hours by gender are discussed in subsection 5.3.2. Subsection 5.3.3 presents the effect of labour supply responses on government revenue and expenditure.

5.3.1 Labour Supply Transition Matrices

Tables 5.5 to 5.8 show the labour supply transition matrices for married men and women respectively. Tables 5.5 and 5.7 show the results of the Policy I reforms while Tables 5.6 and 5.8 show the results of the Policy II reforms. These matrices show the probability of moving between discrete hours levels resulting from a policy reform. The probabilities on the diagonal represent the individuals who were not induced to vary their number of hours worked. The elements in the lower triangular of the matrix (below the diagonal) represent the individuals who are expected to work less whereas the upper triangular elements (above the diagonal) represent those expected to work more. For example, the first row and fifth column of Table 5.5 show that the probability of moving from 0 to 40 hours worked is 0.1 per cent. The '-' denotes an empty cell. Fewer labour supply points are included for men than for women because the number of men working part-time hours is smaller than the number of women. Distinguishing five-hour intervals for men would result in cells with few observations at the lower end of labour supply.

The policy changes have a negligible effect on the supply of labour, with very small proportions of both married men and women located off the diagonals in the matrices. This means few people alter their hours of work.

Policy I, of reducing the withdrawal rate for Family Payment, makes work more attractive for a small proportion of married males and induces them not only to participate in the workforce, but to work full time. The income effect associated with this policy change causes a small proportion of married men to reduce their hours of work.

Table 5.5 Married men's labour supply transitions (rows to columns): Policy I

Hours	0	10	20	30	40	50	Pre-reform
0	99.7	-	0.0	0.0	0.1	0.1	42.0
10	-	100.0	-	-	-	-	1.3
20	-	-	100.0	-	-	-	1.3
30	-	-	-	99.9	0.1	0.0	2.9
40	0.0	-	0.0	0.1	99.8	0.1	32.2
50	0.0	-	0.0	0.1	0.2	99.6	20.3
Post-reform	41.9	1.3	1.3	3.0	32.3	20.3	100.0

Table 5.6 Married men's labour supply transitions (rows to columns): Policy II

Hours	0	10	20	30	40	50	Pre-reform
0	100.0	-	-	-	0.0	0.0	42.0
10	-	100.0	-	-	-	-	1.3
20	-	-	100.0	-	-	-	1.3
30	-	-	-	100.0	0.0	0.0	2.9
40	0.0	-	0.0	0.0	99.9	0.1	32.2
50	-	-	-	0.0	0.1	99.9	20.3
Post-reform	42.0	1.3	1.3	2.9	32.2	20.4	100.0

The reforms associated with Policy II, increasing the income threshold for the minimum rate of Family Payment and replacing the 'sudden death' income test with a gradual withdrawal rate, have virtually no effect on the labour supply choices of married men. Small effects are observed for men working full-time hours. Given the high level of income at which households are affected, it is not surprising that the policy change does not affect men working part time. The increase in net income resulting from the policy change is relatively small.

As is typically the case, married women are more responsive to the policy changes. However, contrary to males, the reduction in labour supply due to their more pronounced response to the income effect tends to outweigh any increase in labour supply due to the substitution effect. From Table 5.7, the higher incomes resulting from the decrease in the withdrawal rate for

Table 5.7 Married women's labour supply transitions (rows to columns): Policy I

Hours	0	5	10	15	20	25	30	35	40	45	50	Pre-reform
0	99.9	0.0	0.0	0.0	0.0	0.0	0.0	0.0	0.0	0.0	0.0	55.1
5	-	100.0	-	-	-	-	-	-	-	-	-	1.5
10	0.0	-	100.0	-	-	0.0	-	-	-	-	-	2.5
15	0.4	0.0	0.0	99.6	-	-	-	-	-	-	-	3.7
20	0.4	0.0	0.0	0.0	99.4	0.0	0.0	0.0	0.0	-	0.0	4.9
25	0.3	0.0	0.0	0.0	0.0	99.7	0.0	-	-	-	0.0	4.1
30	0.6	0.0	0.0	0.0	0.0	0.0	99.3	0.0	0.0	0.0	0.0	4.0
35	0.2	0.0	0.0	-	-	0.0	-	99.8	0.0	-	-	5.2
40	0.2	0.0	0.0	0.0	0.0	0.0	0.0	-	99.8	-	0.0	13.0
45	0.1	-	-	-	-	-	-	0.0	-	99.8	-	2.2
50	0.0	-	-	-	-	0.0	0.0	-	-	-	99.9	3.8
Post-reform	55.2	1.5	2.5	3.7	4.9	4.1	3.9	5.2	13.0	2.2	3.8	100.0

Family Payment (and possibly the increased labour supply of their partners) induce some married women to exit the workforce. Withdrawal from the labour market is less apparent following the Policy II reforms (see Table 5.8). Also associated with the Policy II reforms are some increases in working hours and some decreases. However, these transitions are trivial. The much smaller effect of Policy II is a reflection of the much smaller proportion of the population who are likely to be affected by the change, and the relatively small size of the change for the group who is affected.

The labour supply responses are summarised in Table 5.9. The labour supply effects associated with the reforms, particularly the Policy II reforms, are very small. The higher return to working for certain individuals associated with a reduced withdrawal rate in Policy I induces 0.1 per cent of married men to move into the workforce and 0.03 per cent to work more hours.

However, a higher level of net income results in 0.01 per cent of married men dropping out of the workforce and 0.1 per cent reducing their hours of work, essentially counterbalancing the increase in labour supply and leading to an overall average increase in hours worked of only 0.03 hours.

Table 5.8 Married women's labour supply transitions (rows to columns): Policy II

Hours	0	5	10	15	20	25	30	35	40	45	50	Pre-reform
0	99.9	0.0	0.0	0.0	0.0	0.0	0.0	0.0	0.0	0.0	0.0	55.1
5	-	100.0	-	-	-	-	-	-	-	-	-	1.5
10	0.1	-	99.8	0.0	0.0	0.0	-	-	0.0	-	-	2.5
15	0.1	-	0.0	99.7	0.0	0.0	0.1	0.0	0.0	0.0	0.0	3.7
20	0.2	-	0.0	0.0	99.7	0.0	0.0	0.0	0.0	0.0	0.0	4.9
25	0.1	0.0	-	0.0	0.0	99.7	0.0	0.0	0.0	0.0	0.0	4.1
30	0.1	-	-	-	0.0	0.0	99.8	0.0	0.0	0.0	0.0	4.0
35	0.0	0.0	0.0	0.0	0.0	0.0	0.0	99.9	0.0	0.0	-	5.2
40	0.0	-	0.0	0.0	0.0	0.0	0.0	0.0	99.9	0.0	0.0	13.0
45	-	-	-	0.0	0.0	0.0	-	0.0	0.0	99.9	-	2.2
50	0.0	-	-	0.0	-	0.0	0.0	0.0	0.0	0.0	99.9	3.8
Post-reform	55.1	1.5	2.5	3.7	4.9	4.1	4.0	5.3	13.0	2.2	3.8	100.0

As mentioned above, the net effect of the Policy I reforms on married women's labour supply is negative, with an overall average decrease of 0.02 hours in weekly labour supply. This is mainly due to a negative effect on participation, with a net reduction of 0.06 per cent (0.05 minus 0.11) of married women in the workforce.

Table 5.9 Behavioural responses: change in labour supply for couples

	Policy I		Policy II	
	Men	Women	Men	Women
Per cent workers pre-reform	58.66	45.73	58.66	45.73
Per cent workers post-reform	58.75	45.67	58.66	45.74
Per cent moving from non-work to work	0.10	0.05	0.00	0.03
Per cent moving from work to non-work	0.01	0.11	0.00	0.02
Per cent workers working more hours	0.03	0.01	0.04	0.04
Per cent workers working less hours	0.10	0.02	0.03	0.03
Average hours change	0.03	-0.02	0.00	0.01

Policy II has a negligible effect on labour supply, particularly for married men. Married women show a minimal level of movement both into and out of the workforce with a small net positive effect on participation, and women working more outweighing those working less. Overall, increasing the threshold for the minimum rate of Family Payment and introducing a more gentle withdrawal of the payment can be expected to lead to a marginal increase in the average hours worked by married women of 0.01 hours per week.

5.3.2   Effect on Work Probability and Hours Worked

This section examines the effects of the reforms on the probability of work and predicted hours of work by gender. The effects of the reforms on the probability of working are presented in Table 5.10. The table shows the proportion of individuals that show a change in their probability of working after the policy reform. For example, Table 5.10 shows that 2 per cent of females experience a 2-10 per cent decrease in the probability of working when the Family Payment withdrawal rate is reduced from 50 per cent to 30 per cent. The table shows that the majority of individuals show no change in their work probabilities, with females slightly more affected than males. Reducing the taper rate on more-than-minimum Family Payment has a larger effect on work probabilities than the combination of increasing the threshold for minimum Family Payment and introducing a gradual taper on the minimum rate. Even for those showing a change in work probability, the probability change is small, with only a 2 to 10 percentage point difference from the pre-reform work probability.

Table 5.10 Percentage point change in work probability by gender (row percentages)

Policy I							
	Decrease			Increase		Average	Count
Gender	10-50	2-10	None	2-10	10-50		
Female	0	2	96.0	1	-	-0.1	4217
Male	-	0	98.0	1	0	0.1	4217
Total	0.0	1.3	97.2	1.3	0.1	0.0	8435
Policy II							
Female	-	2	96.0	1	-	-0.1	4217
Male	-	0	98.0	1	-	0.1	4217
Total	-	1.3	97.2	1.3	-	0.0	8435

Table 5.11 shows the changes in the predicted hours of work by gender associated with the Policy I and II reforms respectively. For instance, around 1 per cent of females show a decrease in predicted hours of less than 5 hours a week when the withdrawal rate for more-than-minimum Family Payment is reduced. There is virtually no change in predicted hours, particularly with regard to Policy II. Consistent with the work probabilities, even for those experiencing a change in predicted hours, it is only a small change with an increase/decrease of less than 5 hours a week.

Table 5.11 Change in predicted hours by gender (row percentages)

Policy I						
	Decrease		Increase		Average	Count
Gender	1-5	None	1-5	5-10		
Female	1	99	0	-	0.0	4217
Male	0	98	1	0	0.0	4217
Total	0.8	98.5	0.7	0.1	0.0	8435
Policy II						
Female	-	100.0	0.0	-	0.0	4217
Male	-	100.0	0.0	-	0.0	4217
Total	-	99.9	0.1	-	0.0	8435

5.3.3 Effect of Behavioural Responses on Government Revenue and Expenditure

This section examines the effects of the reforms on government revenue and expenditure incorporating expected labour supply responses. Table 5.12 presents the effects of the reforms on couples with and without taking into account labour supply effects under Policy I. The first column under the heading 'Pre-reform' gives the amount of income taxes and transfer payments under the March 1998 tax system. These values are weighted to reflect the Australian population. The second column provides an estimate of net change in revenue and expenditure as a result of the policy reform by allowing individuals to respond to the policy changes through changing their number of hours worked. The third column expresses the net change in percentages. The last two columns assume fixed labour supply.

Government revenue and expenditure in the pre-reform column of Table 5.12 do not match the amounts presented in Table 5.1 exactly because of the discrete nature of modelling and predicting labour supply. For example, for an individual who is observed to work 19 hours, all the calculations are done as if 20 hours were worked in the MITTS-B module. Consequently, the amounts shown in Table 5.12 are less accurate as income taxes and payments are not evaluated at the actual hours but at the closest quintuple for women and the closest decuple for men. In addition, a few observations are dropped in the MITTS-B simulation due to unrealistic wages. Considering these two differences between MITTS-A and MITTS-B, the calculated pre-reform expenditures and revenues in MITTS-B are close to those calculated in MITTS-A.

Table 5.12 Behavioural responses: change in tax and transfer costs (Policy I)

	Pre-reform ($m)	Allowing for labour supply responses		Keeping labour supply fixed	
		Abs. change ($m)	Rel. change (%)	Abs. change ($m)	Rel. change (%)
Couples					
Government revenue					
Income tax	48005.5	75.6	0.2	82.9	0.2
Medicare	2955.3	-0.4	0	0	0
Total revenue	50960.8	75.2	0.1	82.9	0.2
Government expenditure					
Tax rebates	2472.7	9.0	0.4	0	0
Family Payment	4001.7	218.8	5.5	219.3	5.5
FTP/FTB	394.1	86.2	21.9	82.9	21
Allowances	6717.6	-45.9	-0.7	0	0
Pensions	10850.8	-0.1	0	0	0
Pharmaceutical Allowance	117.5	0.0	0	0	0
Rent Allowance	524.7	63.8	12.2	61.6	11.7
Total expenditure	25079.0	331.7	1.3	363.8	1.5
Net expenditure	-25881.8	256.6	-1.0	280.9	-1.1

Table 5.13 Behavioural responses: change in tax and transfer costs (Policy II)

	Pre-reform ($m)	Allowing for labour supply responses		Keeping labour supply fixed	
		Abs. change ($m)	Rel. change (%)	Abs. change ($m)	Rel. change (%)
Couples					
Government revenue					
Income tax	48005.5	5.2	0	0	0
Medicare	2955.3	0.1	0	0	0
Total revenue	50960.8	5.2	0	0	0
Government expenditure					
Tax rebates	2472.7	-0.3	0	0	0
Family Payment	4001.7	126.9	3.2	125	3.1
FTP/FTB	394.1	-0.2	0	0	0
Allowances	6717.6	-2.5	0	0	0
Pensions	10850.8	0.0	0	0	0
Pharmaceutical Allowance	117.5	0.0	0	0	0
Rent Allowance	524.7	-0.1	0	0	0
Total expenditure	25079.0	123.8	0.5	125	0.5
Net expenditure	-25881.8	118.6	-0.5	125	-0.5

As the labour supply effects associated with the reforms are small, the difference between the amounts of government revenue and expenditure in the arithmetic case compared with the behavioural case is also small. However, there are differences, which highlights the importance of taking into account labour supply effects. From Table 5.12, reducing the withdrawal rate on more-than-minimum Family Payment is costly. The policy reform induces a small positive labour supply response and thus slightly reduces the expenditure required on Family Payment. As more people work after the policy change, expenditure on allowances and even on pensions to a slight extent is reduced. As some people may reduce their hours of work to become eligible for the more-than-minimum Family Payment, expenditure on Rent Assistance and Family Tax Payment increases. Another adverse effect of Policy I is that income tax revenue is reduced due to the distribution of labour supply variations and Australia's progressive tax system. Revenue is lost as a result of the reduction in labour supply (to take advantage of the increase in Family Payment) by those initially working longer hours outweighing the revenue gain associated with the increase in the labour supply of those initially either not working or working a low number of hours. The overall effect of allowing for behavioural responses is however a positive one, with the increase in labour supply leading to a slightly lower increase in net expenditure than would have been the case without behavioural effects.

As Policy II produces virtually no labour supply response, no major differences in the revenue and expenditure estimates with and without labour supply response are expected: see Table 5.13. Family Payment is a little more expensive after labour supply responses are factored into the simulation. Some households adjust their hours of work to take advantage of the increased generosity of minimum Family Payment and thus expenditure on the payment increases. The slight increase in the overall labour supply of couples decreases expenditure on basic allowances and increases income tax revenue, thus reducing the amount of net expenditure required to finance the policy reform.

5.4   Conclusions

This chapter has examined the effects on the labour supply decision of couples with dependent children of reforms to the Family Payment. Couples of all ages are included in the simulations, although behavioural changes are calculated only for those younger than 65. Simulating policy reforms provides information about the changes to the various components of government revenue and expenditure. It also simulates the potential labour supply responses as a result of a change in the tax and transfer system.

The first policy reform, Policy I, involves a reduction of withdrawal rate from 50 to 30 per cent for the maximum rate of Family Payment for household income above the minimum income limit. The second policy reform, Policy II, introduces a gradual withdrawal of the minimum rate of Family Payment of 30 cents in the dollar for household incomes over $73,000 per annum. Policy I is designed to provide more generous support for families earning a low-to-medium income whereas Policy II concerns families with a medium-to-high income.

Both policies have the effect of increasing the net income of couples with dependent children who are earning an income of either above the minimum income limit (Policy I) or above the maximum income limit (Policy II). The simulated policy reforms induce small labour supply responses. The increasing return to work within certain hours and income ranges induces some individuals to increase their labour supply. However, the increase in net income associated with either reform or the higher effective marginal tax rates for some individuals causes other individuals to reduce their labour supply, with some individuals moving out of the labour force completely. This latter effect is most pronounced for married women, possibly because of an increased income level of their partners. Overall, policies provoke a positive labour supply response, albeit very small (particularly in the case of Policy II). This has the effect of reducing the amount of net expenditure required by the government to fund these policy reforms.

Compared with reductions in the taper rate of allowances and pensions, the effect on household net income of a reduction in the Family Payment taper rate is small. In addition, the households affected are those in the medium income range rather than the households on the lowest incomes. Both factors lead to a smaller labour supply effect.

6 Distributional Change and the Safety Net

Behavioural microsimulation models, like MITTS, are based on discrete hours labour supply models, as described briefly in chapter 1. The full budget set is replaced by a finite number of net incomes corresponding to discrete hours points. This type of modelling is essentially probabilistic. It does not identify a particular level of hours worked for each individual after a policy reform, but generates for each individual a probability distribution over the discrete hours levels used. Hence the standard approach to poverty and inequality measurement cannot be applied.

This has meant that earlier microsimulation modellers have either not examined summary measures of distributions, concentrating on results for particular cases, or have simply used an expected income measure for each individual, obtained using the incomes at all hours points along with their probabilities. This measure understates the true variability in income in the population.

This chapter compares alternative methods of obtaining summary measures of inequality and poverty in the context of discrete hours behavioural microsimulation modelling of tax policy changes. Section 6.1 introduces the outcomes available after simulating policy reforms using a discrete hours labour supply model, and discusses three alternative approaches to poverty and inequality measurement. In view of the limitations of the use of average income for each individual, it is important to devise an alternative method that provides both a good approximation to the true measure (which requires a prohibitive computational burden) and is relatively quick to use in the context of large cross-sectional datasets with a realistic number of hours levels.

In addition, section 6.2 examines a substantial policy change involving the elimination of the safety net for sole parents provided by the Australian tax and transfer system. This has the advantage of allowing empirical comparisons of the results of applying the alternative distributional approaches, and contrasts the results from behavioural with non-behavioural simulations in the context of a large policy reform where the assumption of fixed labour supply would be quite unrealistic. Although it is clear that the abolition of benefits for sole parents in Australia would have a negative effect on sole parents' welfare, the simulation gives an indication of the potential magnitude of the overall effect of social transfers on labour supply, government expenditure, poverty and inequality.

6.1   Some Analytical Results

When simulating labour supply effects of policy reforms using microsimulation models, the result is a set of probabilities of being at different income levels for each individual. This section derives analytical results to compare the performance of three alternative approaches to estimating summary measures of the income distribution after simulating changes in labour supply resulting from a policy reform. The three measures are described in subsection 6.1.1. In subsections 6.1.2 to 6.1.4, some properties of the methods are discussed and compared. These analytical results are for the variance; other inequality measures are too intractable to examine in this way.

6.1.1   Alternative Approaches

For convenience the following discussion is in terms of individuals, but it can easily be extended to couple households. Suppose there are n individuals and k possible outcomes of labour supply (hours levels) for each individual. This would result in k^n possible combinations of labour supply, and thus income distributions. Each outcome results in a different value for poverty and inequality measures.

Under the reasonable assumption that individuals' distributions of hours are independent, the probability of each income distribution or outcome (P_q) is given by the product of the relevant probabilities. Hence if $p_{i,j}$ is the probability that individual j is at hours level i the joint probability P_q is equal to $p_{i,1}p_{j,2}\cdots p_{r,n}$, where q runs from 1 to k^n, and i, j, r can attain values between 1 and k (indicating the labour supply points chosen in combination q for each individual). In principle, each inequality or poverty measure can be calculated as the weighted sum of the measures over all possible outcomes with weights equal to the probabilities P_q, where the sum over all P_q is equal to one. However, for any realistic sample size, even for few discrete labour supply points, the large number of possible combinations makes it computationally impractical to calculate all k^n distributions and associated probabilities P_q. It would be impossible to store all the information needed, although this would not be necessary as the appropriate weighted average could be obtained cumulatively using an algorithm for systematically working through all the k^n combinations. However, the computing time needed would be extremely long.

Instead of examining all combinations of income levels, it would be possible to adopt a sampling approach. A large number of possible income distributions could be obtained by taking random draws from each individual's hours distribution. This can be achieved by using a random number generator which produces random uniform variates between 0 and 1 which are then compared with the cumulative distribution at the hours points for each individual in order to select the relevant hours and income levels for each sample drawn. Each choice of discrete hours is drawn with the probability of it occurring for the relevant individual, so no weighting is required in averaging inequality measures over the samples. With a sufficiently large number of randomly selected samples, the proportion of each hours combination would replicate the precise probabilities discussed above. This approach still requires a large computational effort, depending on the number of draws needed to obtain a good approximation. However, it provides a valuable way of examining the performance of alternative, less computer-intensive, approaches against this benchmark in a Monte Carlo experiment.

In considering alternatives which offer more practical solutions, the most obvious is perhaps a simple approach where the expected income is calculated for each individual and is used as if it were a single 'representative' level of income for that individual. See for example, Gerfin and Leu (2003). In addition, we explore an approach where all possible outcomes for every individual are used as if they were separate observations. The outcomes are weighted by the individual probabilities of labour supply to produce a pseudo distribution.

To illustrate the alternative approaches by a simple example, imagine a two-person population with two hours choices available. Person 1 has a wage of 2 and a probability 0.8 of working 10 hours and 0.2 of working 20 hours, and person 2 has a wage of 3 and a probability 0.3 of working 10 hours and 0.7 of working 20 hours. The exact approach has four possible outcomes {(20,30),(40,30),(20,60),(40,60)} with probabilities 0.24, 0.06, 0.56 and 0.14 of occurring. The Lorenz curve would have an income proportion of 0.4, 0.43, 0.25 and 0.4 at the 0.5 fraction of the population for the respective outcomes. The average Lorenz curve (using the above probabilities) would have an income proportion of 0.3178 at 0.5.

Using the expected income approach, person 1 is expected to earn 24 $(2 \times 10 \times 0.8 + 2 \times 20 \times 0.2)$ and person 2 is expected to earn 51 $(3 \times 10 \times 0.3 + 3 \times 20 \times 0.7)$. At a fraction 0.5 of the population, we would have an income proportion of 0.32. Using the pseudo approach described here and constructing a pseudo income distribution, we have outcomes 20, 30, 40 and 60 with probabilities 0.4, 0.15, 0.1 and 0.35. Thus at fraction 0.4 we have an income proportion of 0.13, at fraction 0.55 we have an income proportion of 0.33, and at fraction 0.65 we have an income proportion of 0.6.

6.1.2 The Mean and Variance of the Income Distribution

Suppose there are n individuals and k discrete hours levels, $h_1,...,h_k$. Let $y_{j,i}$ and $p_{j,i}$ denote respectively the ith person's income at hours level j and the probability of hours level j. On the assumption that the probability distributions for different individuals are independent, the joint probabilities of the k^n possible alternative combinations are as shown in Table 6.1. An arbitrary combination m from the set of all possible combinations consists of the set of hours points $h_{1m},h_{2m},...,h_{nm}$ for persons 1 to n respectively, where h_{im} has a value between 1 and k, indicating one of the k possible hours points for each person.

Consider the arithmetic means of each possible combination, denoted $\bar{Y}_i$. The arithmetic mean of all these means, $\bar{Y}$, is given by:

$$\bar{Y} = p_{1,1}p_{1,2}...p_{1,n}\bar{Y}_1 + ... + p_{h_{1m},1}p_{h_{2m},2}...p_{h_{nm},n}\bar{Y}_m + ... + p_{k,1}p_{k,2}...p_{k,n}\bar{Y}_{k^n} \qquad (6.1)$$

Table 6.1 Alternative possible income distributions

q	Incomes of persons:			g_q Distributional	P_q
Combination	1	2	n	measure	Probability
1	$y_{1,1}$	$y_{1,2}$	$y_{1,n}$	g_1	$P_{1,1}P_{1,2}\cdots P_{1,n}$
m	$y_{h_{1m},1}$	$y_{h_{2m},1}$	$y_{h_{nm},n}$	g_m	$P_{h_{1m},1}P_{h_{2m},2}\cdots P_{h_{nm},n}$
k^n	$y_{k,1}$	$y_{k,2}$	$y_{k,n}$	g_{k^n}	$P_{k,1}P_{k,2}\cdots P_{k,n}$
Exact expected distributional measure:				$\sum_{q=1}^{k^n} P_q g_q$	

Substituting for $\overline{Y}_m = \frac{1}{n}\sum_{l=1}^{n} y_{h_{lm},l}$, gives:

$$\overline{Y} = \frac{1}{n}\sum_{l=1}^{n}\sum_{h=1}^{k} P_{h,l} y_{h,l} \tag{6.2}$$

The arithmetic mean, $\overline{S}^2$, of the variances for each possible combination, S_l^2, is:

$$\overline{S}^2 = P_{1,1}P_{1,2}\cdots P_{1,n}S_1^2 + \ldots + P_{h_{1m},1}P_{h_{2m},2}\cdots P_{h_{nm},n}S_m^2 + \ldots + P_{k,1}P_{k,2}\cdots P_{k,n}S_{k^n}^2 \tag{6.3}$$

Where $S_m^2 = \frac{1}{n}\sum_{l=1}^{n} y_{h_{lm},l}^2 - \overline{Y}_m^2$.
Hence:

$$\overline{S}^2 = \sum_{m=1}^{k^n} P_{h_{1m},1}P_{h_{2m},2}\cdots P_{h_{nm},n}\frac{1}{n}\sum_{l=1}^{n} y_{h_{lm},l}^2$$

$$- \sum_{m=1}^{k^n} P_{h_{1m},1}P_{h_{2m},2}\cdots P_{h_{nm},n}\left(\frac{1}{n}\sum_{l=1}^{n} y_{h_{lm},l}\right)^2$$

$$= \frac{1}{n}\sum_{h=1}^{k}\sum_{l=1}^{n} P_{h,l} y_{h,l}^2 - \frac{1}{n^2}\sum_{h=1}^{k}\sum_{l=1}^{n} P_{h,l} y_{h,l}^2$$

$$- \frac{1}{n^2}\sum_{m=1}^{k^n} P_{h_{1m},1}P_{h_{2m},2}\cdots P_{h_{nm},n}\left(2\sum_{l=1}^{n}\sum_{j=1}^{l-1} y_{h_{lm},l} y_{h_{jm},j}\right)$$

$$= \frac{1}{n}\sum_{h=1}^{k}\sum_{i=1}^{n} p_{h,i} y_{h,i}^2 - \frac{1}{n^2}\sum_{h=1}^{k}\sum_{i=1}^{n} p_{h,i} y_{h,i}^2$$

$$-\frac{1}{n^2}\left[2\sum_{i=1}^{n}\sum_{j=1}^{i-1}\sum_{h=1}^{k}\sum_{l=1}^{k} p_{h,i} y_{h,i} p_{l,j} y_{l,j}\right] \tag{6.4}$$

6.1.3 The Mean and Variance Using the Expected Income Method

Consider the use of the arithmetic mean income for each individual as a representative income. Other possible candidates are the median and the mode of the hours distribution for each individual. These are rejected here on the grounds that they ignore potentially important information, as they are based on just one value in the distribution, and the arithmetic means of resulting income distributions do not correspond to $\overline{Y}$. Using expected incomes, $\overline{y}_1 = \sum_{h=1}^{k} p_{h,1} y_{h,1}$ to $\overline{y}_n = \sum_{h=1}^{k} p_{h,n} y_{h,n}$, the overall mean of the n individual means, $\overline{Y}_m$, is identical to (6.2). The variance of the individual mean incomes, S_m^2, is:

$$\overline{S}_m^2 = \frac{1}{n}\sum_{i=1}^{n}\overline{y}_i^2 - \overline{Y}_m^2$$

$$= \frac{1}{n}\sum_{i=1}^{n}\left(\sum_{h=1}^{k} p_{h,i} y_{h,i}\right)^2 - \left(\frac{1}{n}\sum_{i=1}^{n}\sum_{h=1}^{k} p_{h,i} y_{h,i}\right)^2$$

$$= \frac{1}{n}\sum_{i=1}^{n}\left(\sum_{h=1}^{k} p_{h,i}^2 y_{h,i}^2 + 2\sum_{h=1}^{k}\sum_{l=1}^{h-1} p_{h,i} y_{h,i} p_{l,i} y_{l,i}\right)$$

$$-\frac{1}{n^2}\sum_{i=1}^{n}\sum_{h=1}^{k} p_{h,i}^2 y_{h,i}^2 - \frac{2}{n^2}\sum_{i=1}^{n}\sum_{h=1}^{k}\sum_{l=1}^{h-1} p_{h,i} y_{h,i} p_{l,i} y_{l,i}$$

$$-\frac{2}{n^2}\left(\sum_{i=1}^{n}\sum_{j=1}^{i-1}\sum_{h=1}^{k}\sum_{l=1}^{k} p_{h,i} y_{h,i} p_{l,j} y_{l,j}\right) \tag{6.5}$$

The terms in this expression contain powers of the various probabilities. Hence $S_m^2 \neq \overline{S}^2$. The arithmetic means, as linear functions, are identical but the variances, involving nonlinear functions of the various terms, are unequal. A similar feature is expected for any inequality measure that is expressed as a nonlinear function of incomes. The difference between the method using all combinations and the method using the expected income is:

$$\overline{S}_m^2 - \overline{S}^2 = \left(\frac{1}{n} - \frac{1}{n^2}\right)\left[\sum_{i=1}^{n}\left(\sum_{h=1}^{k} p_{h,i} y_{h,i}\right)^2 - \sum_{i=1}^{n}\sum_{h=1}^{k} p_{h,i} y_{h,i}^2\right]$$

$$= \left(\frac{n-1}{n^2} \right) \sum_{i=1}^{n} \left[\left(\overline{y_i} \right)^2 - \overline{y_i^2} \right] \leq 0 \tag{6.6}$$

This confirms the trivial case where the two approaches give identical results for the variance if either the hours distributions are concentrated on a single hours level for each individual or the incomes are the same irrespective of the hours worked. The method using the expected income always underestimates the true expected variance. The square of the expected value is always smaller than or equal to the expectation of the squared values. This is as expected given that the use of the expected income understates the variety in incomes in the population.

6.1.4 The Mean and Variance Using the Pseudo Income Distribution Method

Consider the pseudo income distribution with nk income levels, each associated with a corresponding probability. The incomes are $y_{h,i}$, where h ranges from 1 to k, i ranges from 1 to n and associated probabilities are $p_{h,i}/n$. The division by n ensures that the sum of the probabilities adds to 1. The $y_{h,i}$ values are placed in a single vector, $z = \{y_{h,i}\}$ with nk elements, with the associated probabilities given by $p' = \{p_{h,i}/n\}$. Hence:

$$\sum_{j=1}^{nk} p'_j = \sum_{i=1}^{n} \sum_{h=1}^{k} p_{h,i}/n = 1 \tag{6.7}$$

The arithmetic mean of this pseudo distribution, $\overline{Y}_p$, is equal to $\overline{Y}$ in (6.2) above. The variance of this pseudo distribution, S_p^2, is given by:

$$\overline{S}_p^2 = \frac{1}{n} \sum_{i=1}^{n} \sum_{h=1}^{k} p_{h,i} y_{h,i}^2 - \left[\frac{1}{n} \sum_{i=1}^{n} \sum_{h=1}^{k} p_{h,i} y_{h,i} \right]^2$$

$$= \frac{1}{n} \sum_{h=1}^{k} \sum_{i=1}^{n} p_{h,i} y_{h,i}^2 - \frac{1}{n^2} \sum_{h=1}^{k} \sum_{i=1}^{n} p_{h,i}^2 y_{h,i}^2$$

$$- \frac{2}{n^2} \sum_{i=1}^{n} \sum_{h=1}^{k} \sum_{l=1}^{h-1} p_{h,i} y_{h,i} p_{l,i} y_{l,i}$$

$$- \frac{2}{n^2} \left(\sum_{i=1}^{n} \sum_{j=1}^{i-1} \sum_{h=1}^{k} \sum_{l=1}^{k} p_{h,i} y_{h,i} p_{l,j} y_{l,j} \right) \tag{6.8}$$

Again, this expression depends on the powers of the various probabilities, which appear in the term in square brackets, so it cannot be expected to equal the arithmetic mean of the individual sample variances. The difference between the method using all combinations and that using the pseudo method is:

$$
\begin{aligned}
\overline{S}_p^2 - \overline{S}^2 &= -\frac{1}{n^2}\left(\sum_{h=1}^{k}\sum_{i=1}^{n}\left(p_{h,i}^2 y_{h,i}^2 - p_{h,i} y_{h,i}^2 \right) + 2\sum_{i=1}^{n}\sum_{h=1}^{k}\sum_{l=1}^{h-1} p_{h,i} y_{h,i} p_{l,i} y_{l,i} \right) \\
&= -\frac{1}{n^2}\left(\sum_{h=1}^{k}\sum_{i=1}^{n}\left[p_{h,i}^2 y_{h,i}^2 + 2\sum_{l=1}^{h-1} p_{h,i} y_{h,i} p_{l,i} y_{l,i} \right] - \sum_{h=1}^{k}\sum_{i=1}^{n} p_{h,i} y_{h,i}^2 \right) \\
&= -\frac{1}{n^2}\left(\sum_{i=1}^{n}\left(\sum_{h=1}^{k} p_{h,i} y_{h,i} \right)^2 - \sum_{h=1}^{k}\sum_{i=1}^{n} p_{h,i} y_{h,i}^2 \right) \\
&= -\frac{1}{n^2}\sum_{i=1}^{n}\left[\left(\overline{y}_i \right)^2 - \overline{y_i^2} \right] \geq 0
\end{aligned}
\tag{6.9}
$$

The pseudo method always overestimates the true expected variance, which is as expected because the method exaggerates the true variety of incomes by treating all individual hours points as separate observations with weights relative to the probability of occurring. Comparing this difference with the difference for the method using expected income demonstrates that, for samples of more than two persons, estimates of the variance using the pseudo method are closer to the variance calculated in the method using all combinations, compared with estimates using the expected income method. Furthermore, the true outcome lies in between the pseudo method and the expected income method. The difference is expected to become smaller for the pseudo method as the sample size increases, indicating that the exaggeration of the income variability becomes less important when the number of individuals in the sample increases.

6.2 Eliminating the Safety Net

In this section the performances of the three methods are illustrated by examining the results of a hypothetical policy simulation. To keep the present exercise manageable, the comparisons are based on a particular demographic group, rather than the complete database. The three alternative approaches can just as easily be applied to other larger demographic groups, including couple families. However, given that we want to benchmark the results of the three alternative approaches against 100,000 draws from all possible combinations, the use of a larger sample would be computationally burdensome.

The results relate to sole parents, of which there are 560 in the survey. In the behavioural simulation, 70 sole parents had their labour supply fixed. These included 14 disabled persons, 27 students, 27 self-employed individuals, 1 person over 65 years of age, and 1 person with an imputed wage that was considered too low to be reliable. This leaves 490 individuals where labour supply can vary over 11 discrete hours points. Therefore, for this small example there are 11^{490} possible combinations that should be considered, if measures were to be calculated exactly. This is an extremely large number.

The policy reform involves completely eliminating the safety net that the social security system provides. All basic benefits and family-related payments are thus removed without changing the income tax system, including rebates. Such a drastic policy change is examined partly because it is expected to have substantial effects on predicted labour supply, so that a comparison of behavioural and non-behavioural results is likely to reveal large differences, both in terms of government tax revenue and expenditure, and the distribution of income. Furthermore, it is useful to compare the present results with those obtained from a similar exercise using US data.

The question at issue is that, while the elimination of benefits is undoubtedly likely to lead to an increase in labour supply among sole parents, it is far from clear that (even if it were to lead to actual employment - depending on demand considerations) the resulting income levels would enable them to rise above a pre-determined poverty line. However, it is not expected that the effects of such a drastic change could be accurately predicted by a partial equilibrium model - any discussion of the results must be qualified by the point that in practice it would be desirable to allow for general equilibrium changes in wage rates that are likely to result from such large labour supply changes.

The revenue and labour supply effects are summarised in subsection 6.2.1. To obtain results at the population level, the base dataset is weighted by the weights provided by the Australian Bureau of Statistics (ABS). Subsection 6.2.2 compares the outcomes for a range of distributional measures, using the alternative methods discussed above. The individual is the unit of measurement in all distributional measures calculated in this chapter. Subsection 6.2.3 discusses the distributional implications of the policy change and compares the results with some US results.

6.2.1 Revenue and Labour Supply Changes

When examining average hours, the labour supply after the change for each individual is based on the average value over the successful draws, for which the error term leads to the correct predicted hours before the change. This is equivalent to calculating the expected hours of labour supply after the change, conditional on starting from the observed hours before the change. In computing government revenue from income tax and government expenditure on social security payments, an expected value is also obtained after the policy change. That is, the revenue and expenditure for each of the accepted draws are computed for each individual and an average over these is taken.

A summary of the implications for revenue and expenditure is provided in Table 6.2. The fixed labour supply case applies to a non-behavioural simulation in which all individuals have their discretised labour supplies held constant. In this case, income taxes fall because some of the eliminated benefits are taxable. With an increase in labour supply, income tax revenue increases. It would be possible, using a search procedure, to investigate a revenue-neutral package in which one or more income tax rates (or thresholds) are reduced so that expected net revenue is unchanged.

Table 6.2 Tax and expenditure changes

	Pre-reform ($m)	Changes assuming:			
		Variable labour supply		Fixed labour supply	
		($m)	(%)	($m)	(%)
Government revenue					
Income tax revenue	1796.9	754.7	42	-313.7	-17.5
Government expenditure					
Tax rebates	278.3	-257.5	-92.5	-267.4	-96.1
Basic benefits	4008.5	-4008.5	-100.0	-4008.5	-100.0
Family-related benefits	3099.6	-3093.3	-99.8	-3093.3	-99.8
Total expenditure	7386.4	-7359.3	-99.6	-7369.3	-99.8
Net expenditure	5589.5	-8114	-145.2	-7055.5	-126.2

For both fixed and variable labour supply cases, all basic benefits are obviously reduced to zero, regardless of other income received by the household.

A summary of the behavioural responses is given in Table 6.3, which is based on expected hours for each person. This shows a doubling in the preference of sole parents for participation in the labour force. This shift from the no-work corner solution dominates the responses, with only about 12 per cent working longer hours. The very small proportion moving from work to non-work is caused by one person in the dataset. This person (a 50-year-old woman with one child aged between 5 and 12 years) reported working 11 hours a week, at a low gross wage of just over $5 per hour. Only five sole parents are found to have such a low wage rate. After the change, she has a probability of 0.36 of not working, 0.44 of working 10 hours and 0.11 of working 45 hours, while the other discrete hours levels attract lower probabilities. At this low wage level and without any social transfers, it is difficult to earn more than the estimated fixed cost of working, which is around 200 dollars for sole mothers. In total, 423 sole parents would have zero income at zero hours if no benefits were available. Of these sole parents, 172 have a non-zero probability of being at zero hours.

Table 6.3 Summary of behavioural responses

Labour market state	Percentage
Participation (pre-reform)	42.44
Participation (post-reform)	85.14

Behavioural responses	Percentage point change
Move from non-work to work	42.83
Move from work to non-work	0.14
Workers with higher average hours	11.98
Workers with lower average hours	0.00
Average hours change	21.23

Further details of the transitions are in Table 6.4, which shows the transition probabilities (expressed in percentage form) for movements from rows to columns between the discrete hours levels used. For example, of those working 10 hours before the reform, there is a probability of 17.6 per cent of working the same number of hours after the change. The proportions are calculated by starting each individual from the observed pre-reform discretised hours level and using all 100 successful draws for each individual in obtaining post-reform hours levels; hence, each person is represented 100 times in constructing Table 6.4. The 'total' row and column refer to the overall proportions in each category. It can be seen that the proportions of workers before and after the reform match those in Table 6.3, and the majority of movements is to full-time work of 35 hours or more. The probability of moving into full-time from part-time work is also high for those working 10 and 15 hours.

Table 6.4 Movements between hours (percentages)

Hours	0	5	10	15	20	25	30	35	40	45	50	Total
0	25.6	0.0	0.0	0.2	0.9	2.0	5.1	10.4	14.1	18.4	23.3	57.6
5	-	36.5	0.1	0.1	2.0	6.4	2.0	5.8	13.7	18.9	14.6	3.6
10	4.3	-	17.6	-	0.5	1.4	5.2	7.3	12.9	23.0	27.9	3.2
15	-	-	-	25.4	1.6	8.9	2.7	6.8	11.1	15.5	28.0	2.8
20	-	-	-	-	54.9	0.1	0.6	2.5	10.0	11.3	20.5	3.9
25	-	-	-	-	-	73.5	0.8	2.3	2.7	7.8	12.9	3.7
30	-	-	-	-	-	-	74.4	2.1	3.4	8.8	11.3	3.3
35	-	-	-	-	-	-	-	89.4	1.6	2.2	6.8	3.2
40	-	-	-	-	-	-	-	-	90.6	1.7	7.7	12.2
45	-	-	-	-	-	-	-	-	-	98.3	1.7	1.0
50	-	-	-	-	-	-	-	-	-	-	100	5.5
Total	14.9	1.3	0.6	0.8	2.7	4.4	5.8	9.7	21.1	14.7	23.9	100

6.2.2 Comparison of the Alternative Approaches

To examine the effects of this policy change on the distribution of income before and after labour supply changes, several summary measures are presented. Two measures of inequality, the Gini coefficient, G, and the Atkinson measure of inequality, $A(\varepsilon)$, using an inequality aversion parameter of $\varepsilon = 0.5$, are examined. Some sole parents have zero net incomes in the post-reform situation; these are set equal to 1 for the purpose of computing the Atkinson measure.

For the measurement of poverty, three special cases of the Foster, Greer and Thorbecke (1984) family of measures, P_α, are used, where

$$P_\alpha = \frac{1}{N} \sum_{y_i < y_p} \left(\frac{y_p - y_i}{y_p} \right)^\alpha$$

(6.10)

and y_p is the poverty line, with α a parameter to be set by the user. Substitution of the appropriate value for α shows that P_0 is equal to the headcount measure; P_1 is equal to the headcount measure multiplied by a term that depends on the arithmetic mean income of those in poverty; and P_2 depends on the headcount measure, the average poverty gap and the coefficient of variation of those in poverty.

The poverty measures were obtained for a fixed poverty line set at $y_p = 176$ per week. This value is half the median income over the entire population before the reform, with income defined as income unit total income per equivalent adult. The income unit used was the individual and the survey weights from the Survey of Income and Housing Costs (SIHC) were used to generate population estimates. The equivalence scales used are those proposed by Whiteford (1985), which use a scaling of 1 for the adult and 0.32 for each child. The Whiteford scales also have weights for second and subsequent adults in the unit but these are irrelevant here as we are only dealing with single adult income units.

The poverty line used, and resulting poverty estimates, may differ quite substantially from other published results. This is due to a number of reasons emanating from the fact that net incomes are calculated for individuals in the population based on reported income from earnings and non-benefit sources. Other studies generally rely fully on income details provided by the survey data. Published studies tend to omit observations with zero or negative incomes, as such levels of income are thought to be unsustainable. Here the simulation process entitles these cases to a positive level of benefit income, given that complete take-up of benefits is assumed. As a result, more people are on low incomes and there is a risk of overestimating net incomes for this group. In addition, no allowance is made for the presence of assets and other unobservable factors which determine eligibility for benefits. This may also lead to an overestimation of net incomes at the lower end of the income distribution. Finally, the choice of a poverty line y_p is always a difficult issue and the absolute poverty measures are sensitive to y_p (along with the equivalence scales used). However, the emphasis in this chapter is on differences in poverty, produced by different methods of generating the income distribution when discrete hours labour supply models are used in simulation, rather than on the absolute values of poverty.

As indicated previously, evaluation of the distributional implications of reforms using a complete enumeration of all possible income distributions is not feasible. Instead, comparisons are based on the use of a benchmark case involving 100,000 samples, which is sufficiently large for the measures to have converged.[1]

Table 6.5 shows alternative values of the summary measures. The first row of the table shows the pre-reform values, obtained using discretised hours levels, while the second row is the benchmark case. The last three rows of the table show the differences between the benchmark values and the measures obtained using the alternative strategies, of calculating expected incomes, calculating the pseudo distribution or just taking 10 random draws from all conceivable distributions. The use of 10 random

Table 6.5 Alternative summary measures resulting from behavioural simulation

	Inequality		Poverty Foster *et al.* family			Mean	Variance
	Gini	Atkinson	P_0	P_1	P_2	X	of income
Pre-reform	0.2185	0.0411	0.0432	0.0103	0.0029	311.71	22216.35
Post-reform using different methods							
10^5 draws	0.3508	0.1644	0.2400	0.1620	0.1439	264.37	32762.20
Expected	0.3201	0.1253	0.2445	0.1156	0.0948	264.37	29107.10
Pseudo	0.3508	0.1644	0.2400	0.1620	0.1439	264.37	32768.90
10 draws	0.3512	0.1639	0.2470	0.1624	0.1431	264.10	32639.10
Difference from the method using 100,000 draws							
Δexpected	-0.0307	-0.0392	0.0045	-0.0464	-0.0491	0.0001	-3655.06
Δpseudo	0	0	0	0	0	0.0001	6.70
Δ10 draws	0.0004	-0.0006	0.007	0.0004	-0.0008	-0.2752	-123.06

[1] Creedy, Kalb and Scutella (2004) show that convergence of the mean of the distribution takes place at roughly 50,000 draws, so at 100,000 draws the calculated measures should be stable.

draws was chosen as this produces a similar computational burden and ease of application as that of the pseudo distribution. The results in Table 6.5 show that the performance of the pseudo distribution method is superior to the other two methods for all measures.

6.2.3 Implications of the Reform

The non-behavioural results are summarised in Table 6.6. These results are based on the actual observed hours, rather than the discretised hours levels used in the behavioural model. For this reason, the pre-reform values differ slightly from those shown above, which are based on discretised hours. As anticipated, all the inequality and poverty measures show substantial increases after the reform, particularly the poverty measures.

Table 6.6 Summary of non-behavioural results

	Pre-reform	Post-reform	Change inequality
Gini	0.2245	0.6871	0.4626
Atkinson (0.5)	0.0438	0.4859	0.4421
Poverty (with poverty line of $176 per week)			
P_0	0.047	0.6688	0.6218
P_1	0.0117	0.572	0.5603
P_2	0.0033	0.5337	0.5304

The increase in inequality and poverty when allowing for labour supply changes is substantially lower than is indicated by this non-behavioural simulation exercise. However, it is clear from Table 6.5 that, despite the large positive impact on labour supply behaviour, there are large increases in poverty and inequality. Thus, even if sole parents were able to move freely into employment at their desired hours, they would remain much worse off by the abolition of the safety net, due to their demographic structure and low wage levels.

In practice, many sole parents may be expected to experience difficulty in finding employment even if they were willing to work. This would imply that more sole parents may find themselves in poverty as a result of the change than are predicted by the model. Furthermore, the measures used here are based on net incomes only and do not account for disutility arising from the expected increase in labour supply, which is substantial at an average of more than 21 hours per week. The distributional changes based on the behavioural outcomes in Table 6.5 are therefore probably the least negative possible. The actual outcome is likely to lie somewhere in between the static and the behavioural simulation result.

Hoynes (1996) carried out a comparable exercise for the US and found similar results for couples participating in welfare, although the predicted increase in hours worked is lower than here. She found that 'if the AFDC-UP program was [sic] eliminated, the increase in labor force participation and hours of work is not sufficient to make up for the loss of welfare benefits' (1996, p. 325).[2]

A similar observation was made in the review paper by Moffitt (1992) for sole parents. He reported an average hours of work increase of 1 to 9.8 hours per week, and concluded, 'the labor supply effects, while statistically significant are not large enough to explain the high rates of poverty among female heads; most AFDC women would, apparently, be poor even in the absence of the AFDC program' (1992, p. 56). In other words, the predicted increase in labour supply after abolishing AFDC is not enough to compensate for the loss in welfare income. A probable explanation for the larger simulated effect in Australia compared with the U.S. is Australia's more generous welfare system.

6.3   Conclusions

This chapter has compared alternative approaches to the measurement of inequality and poverty indices in the context of behavioural microsimulation with discrete hours labour supply models. Special consideration is needed because microsimulation modelling using a discrete hours approach does not identify a particular level of hours worked for each individual after a policy change. Instead it generates a probability distribution over the discrete hours levels used. This makes analysis of the distribution of income difficult because, even for a small sample with a modest range of hours points, the range of possible labour supply combinations becomes too large

---

[2] AFDC-UP stands for Aid to Families with Dependent Children - Unemployed Parent Program, which is a welfare programme in the U.S.

to handle. However, in comparing alternative approaches, a benchmark value for the measures was created by taking 100,000 draws from the hours distributions, which is sufficient for convergence to be reached.

The approaches examined include the use of an expected income level for each individual. Alternatively, a simulated approach could be used in which labour supply values are drawn from each individual's hours distribution and summary statistics of the distribution of income are calculated by taking the average over each set of draws. Finally, the construction of a pseudo income distribution was proposed. This uses the probability of a particular labour supply value and associated income, occurring for each individual (standardised by the population size) to refer to a separate value in an artificial, or pseudo, income distribution. The total number of values in this pseudo income distribution consists of the product of the number of individuals and the number of discrete hours levels used.

By examining an extreme reform of the Australian social security system it was shown that the pseudo method clearly performs better than the expected income method or the sampling approach with just 10 draws. The latter has a similar computational burden and ease of use as the pseudo approach. The pseudo method takes much less time to run than the approach using 100,000 draws. Nevertheless, the measures calculated with these two methods are very close. For larger samples, the gain in computation time will be larger than for the example given here, which consisted of just 560 individuals.

Another major finding resulting from the application studied in this chapter is that even if sole parents were able to move into the labour force to help compensate for a loss of all social security benefits, they would remain much worse off financially than under the system before the change, where a safety net is in place. The calculations reported here do not allow for a potential lack of demand for sole parents' skills or for the disutility from working. Therefore they are likely to provide a picture of the situation for sole parents after abolishing the safety net which is overly optimistic.

7 Survey Reweighting for Population Ageing

This chapter investigates the use of sample reweighting, in a behavioural tax microsimulation model, to examine the implications for government taxes and expenditure of population ageing in Australia. Tax microsimulation models are based on large-scale cross-sectional surveys containing substantial information about the characteristics of individuals and households. Each household has a sample weight provided by the statistical agency responsible for collecting the data, and these weights are used to 'gross up' from the sample in order to obtain estimates of population values. This applies to aggregates such as income taxation, the number of recipients of a particular social transfer or the number of people in a particular demographic group. In addition, the weights are used in the estimation of measures of population inequality and poverty.

The possibility therefore arises of adjusting the sample weights to reflect anticipated changes in the population age structure. Such a change in population structure could have important policy implications. Consider, for example, an increase in the proportion of individuals over 65, who in principle are eligible for the Age Pension and traditionally have low labour force participation rates, relative to the proportion of individuals between 25 and 64. If age-specific participation rates do not change, an increase in the proportion of individuals over 65 gives rise to higher government expenditure and lower government revenue. Revised weights, based on the changed population structure, can be used to estimate implications for labour force participation and government expenditures, on the assumption that other characteristics remain unchanged. That is, at the individual level, the outcomes remain unchanged. What changes is the weight assigned to each of the individuals' outcomes when calculating the aggregate effects. Any population age structure could be assessed, allowing the effects of alternative future scenarios to be evaluated. Other possibilities of adapting individual characteristics could also be considered at the same time, including for example the potential effects of real wage growth or of changes to the tax and benefit regime. Such changes are of course likely to arise partly as a response to the pressures of population ageing, so it is useful to be able to examine the precise nature of those pressures.

The microsimulation approach combined with reweighting contrasts with a popular method of examining population ageing, which combines population projections with age-specific per capita expenditures on a range of benefits in order to obtain projected social expenditures. These are typically combined with GDP projections based on age-specific labour force participation and unemployment ratios, along with productivity growth assumptions. While accounting frameworks of this type have proved useful, they necessarily lack the kind of policy modelling, detail and heterogeneity available in microsimulation models.[1]

This chapter begins by describing a calibration approach to sample reweighting which achieves specified population totals for selected variables, subject to the constraint that there are minimal adjustments to the weights. A formal statement of the problem of obtaining 'minimum distance' weights and a general approach to the solution are described in section 7.1. Section 7.2 applies the approach to the Survey of Income and Housing Costs (SIHC), and considers whether – before examining population ageing – the SIHC needs to be reweighted for tax simulation purposes.[2] Reweighting to allow for population ageing is examined in section 7.3, which makes use of Australian Bureau of Statistics (ABS) population projections. The analysis abstracts from changes in population size and concentrates purely on changes in the age structure. Section 7.4 reports simulation results of a tax policy change with the revised weights, reflecting the aged population structure.

---

[1] On this type of modelling, see Alvarado and Creedy (1998).

[2] The ABS weights are calibrated to provide correct aggregates at the population level with regard to, for example, age and household composition, but not necessarily to provide a good representation of benefit recipient groups, such as for example sole parents on Parenting Payments Single or families receiving NewStart Allowance. Given the importance of these groups in tax microsimulation, reweighting might be necessary if the ABS weights are not adequate to represent these groups correctly.

7.1 The Calibration Approach

This section discusses methods of calibration. Subsection 7.1.1 provides a general statement of the problem of minimising the overall distance between two sets of weights, subject to a set of calibration conditions. The following subsections examine a class of distance functions giving rise to a convenient structure and present an iterative solution procedure.

7.1.1 Statement of the Problem

For each of K individuals in a sample survey, information is available about J variables; these are placed in the vector:

$$x_k = \begin{bmatrix} x_{k,1} \\ . \\ . \\ . \\ x_{k,J} \end{bmatrix}$$

(7.1)

For present purposes these vectors contain only the variables of interest for the calibration exercise. Most elements of x_k are likely to be 0/1 variables. For example, $x_{k,j} = 1$ if the kth individual is in a particular age group, and zero otherwise. The sum $\sum_{k=1}^{K} x_{k,j}$ therefore gives the number of individuals in the sample who are in the age group.

The sample design weights, provided by the statistical agency responsible for data collection, are s_k for $k = 1,...,K$. These weights can be used to produce estimated population totals, $\hat{t}_{x|s}$, based on the sample, given by the J-element vector:

$$\hat{t}_{x|s} = \sum_{k=1}^{K} s_k x_k$$

(7.2)

The calibration approach can be stated as follows. Suppose that other data sources, for example census or social security administrative data, provide information about 'true' population totals, t_x. The problem is to compute new weights, w_k, for $k = 1,...,K$ which are as close as possible to the design weights, s_k, while satisfying the set of J calibration equations:

$$t_x = \sum_{k=1}^{K} w_k x_k$$

(7.3)

It is thus necessary to specify a criterion by which to judge the closeness of the two sets of weights. In general, denote the distance between w_k and s_k as $G(w_k, s_k)$. The aggregate distance between the design and calibrated weights is thus:

$$D = \sum_{k=1}^{K} G(w_k, s_k) \tag{7.4}$$

The problem is therefore to minimise (7.4) subject to (7.3), for which the Lagrangean is:

$$L = \sum_{k=1}^{K} G(w_k, s_k) + \sum_{j=1}^{J} \lambda_j \left(t_{x,j} - \sum_{k=1}^{K} w_k x_{k,j} \right) \tag{7.5}$$

where λ_j for $j = 1, ..., J$ are the Lagrange multipliers.

7.1.2 A Class of Distance Functions

Suppose that $G(w_k, s_k)$ is such that the differential with respect to w_k can be expressed as a function of w_k / s_k, so that:

$$\frac{\partial G(w_k, s_k)}{\partial w_k} = g\left(\frac{w_k}{s_k} \right) \tag{7.6}$$

The K first-order conditions for minimisation can therefore be written as:

$$g\left(\frac{w_k}{s_k} \right) = x_k' \lambda \tag{7.7}$$

Write the inverse function of g as g^{-1}, so that if $g(w_k/s_k) = u$, say, then $w_k/s_k = g^{-1}(u)$. From (7.7) the k values of w_k are expressed as:

$$w_k = s_k g^{-1}(x_k' \lambda) \tag{7.8}$$

If the inverse function, g^{-1}, can be obtained explicitly, equation (7.8) can be used to compute the calibrated weights, given a solution for the vector, λ.

The Lagrange multipliers can be obtained by post-multiplying (7.8) by x_k, summing over all $k = 1, ..., K$ and using the calibration equations, so that:

$$t_x = \sum_{k=1}^{K} w_k x_k = \sum_{k=1}^{K} s_k g^{-1}(x_k' \lambda) x_k \tag{7.9}$$

Finally, subtracting $\hat{t}_{x|s} = \sum_{k=1}^{K} s_k x_k$ from both sides of (7.9) gives the nonlinear equations:

$$t_x - \hat{t}_{x|s} = \sum_{k=1}^{K} s_k \left\{ g^{-1}\left(x_k'\lambda\right) - 1 \right\} x_k \tag{7.10}$$

where $s_k \left\{ g^{-1}\left(x_k'\lambda\right) - 1 \right\}$ is a scalar and the left hand side is a known vector. An iterative procedure to solve these equations is given in the following subsection.

7.1.3 An Iterative Procedure

Writing $t_x - \hat{t}_{x|s} = a$, the equations in (7.10) can be written as:

$$f_i(\lambda) = a_i - \sum_{k=1}^{K} s_k x_{k,i} \left\{ g^{-1}\left(x_k'\lambda\right) - 1 \right\} = 0 \tag{7.11}$$

for $i = 1, \ldots, J$. The roots can be obtained using Newton's method. This involves the following iterative sequence, where $\lambda^{[I]}$ denotes the value of λ in the Ith iteration:

$$\lambda^{[I+1]} = \lambda^{[I]} - \left[\frac{\partial f_i(\lambda)}{\partial \lambda_\ell} \right]_{\lambda^{[I]}}^{-1} \left[f(\lambda) \right]_{\lambda^{[I]}} \tag{7.12}$$

The Hessian matrix $\left[\partial f_i(\lambda)/\partial \lambda_\ell \right]$ and the vector $f(\lambda)$ on the right hand side of (7.12) are evaluated using $\lambda^{[I]}$. The elements $\partial f_i(\lambda)/\partial \lambda_\ell$ are given by:

$$\frac{\partial f_i(\lambda)}{\partial \lambda_\ell} = -\sum_{k=1}^{K} s_k x_{k,i} \frac{\partial g^{-1}\left(x_k'\lambda\right)}{\partial \lambda_\ell} \tag{7.13}$$

which can be written as:

$$\frac{\partial f_i(\lambda)}{\partial \lambda_\ell} = -\sum_{k=1}^{K} s_k x_{k,i} x_{k,\ell} \frac{dg^{-1}\left(x_k'\lambda\right)}{d\left(x_k'\lambda\right)} \tag{7.14}$$

Starting from arbitrary initial values, the matrix equation in (7.12) is used repeatedly to adjust the values until convergence is reached, where possible.

As mentioned earlier, the application of the approach requires that it is limited to distance functions for which the form of the inverse function, $g^{-1}(u)$, can be obtained explicitly, given the specification for $G(w,s)$. Hence the Hessian can easily be evaluated at each step using an explicit expression for $dg^{-1}(x_k'\lambda)/d(x_k'\lambda)$. As these expressions avoid the need for the numerical evaluation of $g^{-1}(x'_k\lambda)$ and $dg^{-1}(x'_k\lambda)/d(x'_k\lambda)$ for each individual at each step, the calculation of the new weights can be expected to be relatively quick, even for large samples. Using numerical methods to solve for each $g^{-1}(u)$ and $dg^{-1}(u)/du$, for $u = x'_k\lambda$, for every individual in each iteration, would increase the computational burden substantially. However, a solution does not necessarily exist, depending on the distance function used and the adjustment required to the vector $t_x - \hat{t}_{x|s}$.

7.1.4 A Distance Function

The solution procedure requires only an explicit form for the inverse function $g^{-1}(u)$, from which its derivative can be obtained. Hence it is not necessary to start from a specification of $G(w,s)$. Deville and Särndal (1992) suggested the use of an inverse function $g^{-1}(u)$ of the form:[3]

$$g^{-1}(u) = \frac{r_L(r_U - 1) + r_U(1 - r_L)\exp\alpha u}{(r_U - 1) + (1 - r_L)\exp\alpha u} \tag{7.15}$$

where r_L and r_U are the lower and upper limit of the allowed proportionate change in weight with $r_L < 1 < r_U$ and:

$$\alpha = \frac{r_U - r_L}{(1 - r_L)(r_U - 1)} \tag{7.16}$$

Thus $g^{-1}(-\infty) = r_L$ and $g^{-1}(\infty) = r_U$, so that the limits of w/s are r_L and r_U. Hence the new weights are kept within the range, $r_L s_k < w_k < r_U s_k$, without the need to make checks during computation.

The derivative required in the computation of the Hessian is:

$$\frac{dg^{-1}(u)}{du} = g^{-1}(u)\{r_U - g^{-1}(u)\}\frac{(1 - r_L)\alpha\exp\alpha u}{(r_U - 1) + (1 - r_L)\exp\alpha u} \tag{7.17}$$

Since $g^{-1}(u)$ solves for w/s, (7.15) can be rearranged, by collecting terms in $\exp\alpha u$, to give:

---

[3] Singh and Mohl (1996), in reviewing alternative calibration estimators, refer to this 'inverse logit-type transformation' as a Generalised Modified Discrimination Information method. Folsom and Singh (2000) propose a variation on this, which they call a 'generalised exponential model', in which the limits are allowed to be unit-specific. In practice, they suggest the use of three sets of bounds for low, medium and high initial weights.

$$\frac{\frac{w}{s}-r_L}{1-r_L}=\frac{r_U-\frac{w}{s}}{r_U-1}\exp\alpha u \qquad (7.18)$$

so that the gradient of the distance function is:

$$g\left(\frac{w}{s}\right)=u=\frac{1}{\alpha}\left[\log\left(\frac{\frac{w}{s}-r_L}{1-r_L}\right)-\log\left(\frac{r_U-\frac{w}{s}}{r_U-1}\right)\right] \qquad (7.19)$$

7.2 The Survey of Income and Housing Costs

This section checks the performance of the ABS weights provided with the SIHC against an extensive set of calibration conditions, and reports revised weights and MITTS totals. The most recent dataset available at the time of analysis was for 2001. The calibration conditions include demographic variables, such as age, family composition, unemployment by age and income support recipiency. For the first three variables, population information is taken from Census data (ABS, 2002), while information on the last variable is obtained from administrative data on income support payments.

Details of the calibration conditions are given in tables presented in Appendix 7-A. A comparison between SIHC and census numbers on the age distribution of males and females reveals that the SIHC appears to have too many people in the lower age groups and too few in the higher age groups, particularly in the highest age group for women.[4]

With regard to family composition, except for the group of sole parents with dependent and non-dependent children, all groups appear to be over-represented in the SIHC.[5] Furthermore, the ABS weights understate the number of unemployed men in all but the 15-19 and 35-44 age groups. In contrast, the ABS overstates the number of unemployed women in all but the 20-34 age group. The numbers of income support recipients are taken directly from the observed values in the SIHC, according to self-reported responses. There are both under- and overestimates of particular subgroups.

---

[4] This is probably caused by the fact that the SIHC excludes people in institutions or people living in remote areas, whereas these groups are included in the Census. An alternative reweighting could be based on total numbers from the Census excluding these groups if possible.

[5] The number of families in the group 'other types of family' is omitted from the calibration conditions to avoid singularities.

The iterative approach described in section 7.1 was applied using the calibration conditions listed in Appendix 7-A. Lower and upper bounds of 0.68 and 1.87 were obtained after experimentation to find the smallest possible range. Figure 7.1 presents the distribution of the ratio of the new weight to the ABS weight. Relatively few people have a new weight that is more than 1.4 times as large as the ABS weight. Around 50 per cent of all observations are reweighted by a factor between 0.85 and 1.20.

Figure 7.1 Ratio of new weight to ABS weight

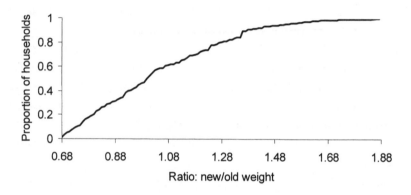

Before considering the performance of MITTS with these new weights, it is useful to compare a few summary measures resulting from calculations using the old and the new weights. First, consider the simulated number of income support recipients based on the two sets of weights, shown in Table 7.1. The reweighting has had little effect on most types of income support recipients. The two main exceptions are Disability Support pensioners, which show an improvement, and Age Pensioners, where the difference between actual and simulated numbers becomes bigger. The latter is caused by the reweighting on age, putting additional weight on the older age groups. The MITTS model overestimates the proportion of older persons eligible for the Age Pension as a result of the lack of information on assets held by households. People over 60 are among those most likely to have built up assets in the form of superannuation or other investments[6].

---

[6] Some alternative approaches are reported in Cai, Creedy and Kalb (2004). For example, observed benefit receipt was used as a requirement for taking up of Age Pension, and people with

Table 7.1 Actual and simulated numbers (×1000) of income support recipients

	Actual from FaCS[1] (1)	Simulated using ABS weights (2)	Simulated using new weights (3)	Difference between (1) and (2)	Difference between (1) and (3)
Parenting Payment					
(Single and Couple)	639	674	602	-35	37
Sickness Allowance	11	21	22	-10	-11
Widow's Allowance	36	1	0	35	36
AUSTUDY/ABSTUDY	42	135	150	-93	-108
NewStart Allowance	541	660	690	-119	-149
Mature Age Allowance	39	47	47	-8	-8
Youth Allowance	393	674	671	-281	-278
Special Benefit	12	232	246	-220	-234
Partner Allowance	90	215	212	-125	-122
Age Pension	1786	1935	2094	-149	-308
Disability Support Pension	624	575	615	49	9
Wife's Pension	78	101	93	-23	-15
Widow B Pension	9	41	38	-32	-29
Carer's Payment	57	33	33	24	24
Total	4357	5344	5513	-987	-1156

(1) Source: Department of Family and Community Services (FaCS) (2003).

The aggregate expenditures for a range of benefits produced directly by the SIHC for the old and new weights may be compared; that is, the actual benefits reported as being received by individuals in the SIHC are used. Comparisons are shown in Table 7.2, which reports estimated expenditure obtained directly from the SIHC when aggregated using the ABS weights and when aggregated using the revised weights. There seems to be a slight overall improvement resulting from using the new weights. However, when examining particular payment types separately, for some types the amount is much further from the actual amount than before the reweighting, whereas for other types an improvement is evident.

Finally, the performance of MITTS with regard to expenditures using the different sets of weights is illustrated in Table 7.3, which is similar to Table 7.2 but compares the simulated expenditure based on the reweighted SIHC data with the simulated expenditure based on the original SIHC data.

---

eligibility for benefits under $10 per week were assumed not to take-up these benefits. Using observed eligibility for the Age Pension instead of assets (which are not observed) improves the simulation of the number of recipients but does not improve the estimated expenditure.

Hypothetical Policy Reforms

Table 7.2 Actual and estimated expenditure on income support

	Actual from FaCS[1] ($m) (1)	SIHC using ABS weights ($m) (2)	SIHC using new weights ($m) (3)	Difference between (1) and (2)	Difference between (1) and (3)
Parenting Payment (Single and Couple)	5327.0	4911.3	4303.7	415.7	1023.2
Sickness Allowance	95.9	212.7	223.0	-116.8	-127.1
Widow's Allowance	330.2	402.5	369.1	-72.3	-39.0
AUSTUDY/ABSTUDY	255.6	n/a[2]	n/a		
NewStart Allowance	4918.3	3466.2	3858.9	1452.1	1059.5
Mature Age Allowance	353.1	329.1	304.9	24.1	48.2
Youth Allowance	2121.6	1446.2	1521.1	675.4	600.5
Special Benefit	113.8	150.5	164.9	-36.6	-51.1
Partner Allowance	717.1	605.2	668.2	111.9	48.9
Age Pension	15571.8	14233.9	15681.1	1337.9	-109.4
Disability Support Pension	5837.4	5182.7	5656.3	654.7	181.1
Wife's Pension	680.0	491.7	445.0	188.3	235.0
Widow B Pension	75.3	n/a[2]	n/a		
Carer's Payment	478.3	605.2	582.3	-127.0	-104.0
Total	36875.4	32037.2	33778.5	4507.4	2765.8

(1) Source: FaCS (2001).
(2) AUSTUDY and Widow B Pension cannot be identified from the SIHC data.

Table 7.3 Actual and simulated expenditure on income support

		Simulated using			
	Actual from FaCS[1] ($m) (1)	ABS weights ($m) (2)	New weights ($m) (3)	Difference between (1) and (2)	Difference between (1) and (3)
Parenting Payment (Single and Couple)	5327.0	5037.5	4454.7	289.5	872.3
Sickness Allowance	95.9	181.7	193.6	-85.8	-97.7
Widow's Allowance	330.2	4.9	3.5	325.3	326.7
AUSTUDY/ABSTUDY	255.6	947.1	1000.6	-691.5	-745.0
NewStart Allowance	4918.3	4268.1	4562.9	650.2	355.4
Mature Age Allowance	353.1	221.2	244.3	131.9	108.8
Youth Allowance	2121.6	2475.7	2463.7	-354.1	-342.1
Special Benefit	113.8	1910.2	2036.1	-1796.4	-1922.3
Partner Allowance	717.1	1493.2	1492.4	-776.1	-775.3
Age Pension	15571.8	15865.0	17401.7	-293.2	-1829.9
Disability Support Pension	5837.4	5133.8	5610.6	703.6	226.8
Wife's Pension	680.0	792.9	729.9	-112.9	-49.9
Widow B Pension	75.3	398.2	360.5	-322.9	-285.2
Carer's Payment	478.3	274.1	272.4	204.2	205.9
Total	36875.4	39003.6	40826.9	-2128.2	-3951.5

(1) Source: FaCS (2001).

Comparing Tables 7.2 and 7.3, it can be seen that the difference between the actual expenditure and the simulated expenditure is smaller than the difference between the actual expenditure and the expenditure observed from the SIHC. However, the reweighting does not improve the simulated expenditure. The difference between actual and simulated expenditure for 2001 is small with the initial weights, although there are a few exceptions. Regarding the Widow's Allowance and the Widow B Pension it seems that the two payments cannot be separated as they should, but in aggregate, the simulated amount paid on these is quite close to the actual amount. Similarly, adding the NewStart Allowance and the Partner Allowance seems to smooth out differences between actual and simulated amounts.

There remain AUSTUDY and Special Benefit, both of which are overestimated in MITTS because not all necessary information is available in the SIHC for an accurate calculation of the payments. From the lack of improvement - indeed deterioration - in simulated expenditures after reweighting, the conclusion is drawn that reweighting the base data for simulations of policy in the current time period cannot be recommended. [7]

7.3   Population Ageing

The previous section showed that reweighting the base sample for the current time period is unlikely to improve the outcome of simulations. This section explores the use of MITTS in combination with reweighting to examine the implications of population ageing. Projected population distributions by age and gender for 2050 from ABS (2003b) are used to reweight the population in the 2000/01 SIHC. However, to avoid the effects of changes in population size, it is assumed that the total population size does not change: only the proportion in each subgroup is used. The calibration conditions in the reweighting exercise then consist of the reallocated population totals by age and gender.

Three series of projections for 2050 are presented in ABS (2003b). Series B results in a medium-sized stable population, based on a fertility rate of 1.6 babies per woman, a net overseas migration of 100,000 persons and a life

---

[7] A wide range of alternatives, including the imposition of take-up conditions and basing the calibration on numbers calculated by MITTS, based on entitlement according to reported characteristics, are discussed in Cai, Creedy and Kalb (2004).

expectancy at birth of 84.2 for men and 87.7 for women. Series A presents a larger population based on a fertility rate of 1.8 babies per woman, a net overseas migration of 125,000 persons and a life expectancy at birth of 92.2 for men and 95.0 for women. Series C presents a declining population size based on a fertility rate of 1.4 babies per woman, a net overseas migration of 70,000 persons and a life expectancy at birth of 84.2 for men and 87.7 for women.

The distributions across age-gender groups are also different for the three scenarios. Figure 7.2 presents the age-gender distribution in the three population projection series. It shows that the proportion of young individuals is lowest in series C and highest in series A. The proportion of older individuals is highest for series C and lowest for series B.[8] Finally, series B has the largest proportion of the population in the working age category.[9] Therefore, series A, B and C are referred to in this chapter respectively as the young, medium and old population projections.

Figure 7.2 shows that the relative proportion of older persons versus younger persons is expected to change between 2001 and 2050. Due to different assumptions, there are some differences between the three projections provided by the ABS, but generally the three alternatives are relatively close to each other, especially when compared with the 2001 situation. All three alternatives are based on plausible assumptions about the fertility and mortality rates. To provide an insight into the effect of this changed population composition, the SIHC can be reweighted to reflect the composition of the 2050 Australian population before running a simulation. By using the three alternatives, the sensitivity of changes in government expenditure and revenue to the alternative population scenarios can be analysed. Given the current fertility and mortality rates, it is clear that the 2001 population composition must change. Therefore, a simulation based on the 2001 population structure to inform us about the future is not satisfactory.

In all three projections, the proportion of older persons has increased relative to the younger age groups. Assuming that people's behaviour

---

[8] The proportion of the population aged 65 and over for series A, B and C is 28.03, 26.94 and 29.45 per cent respectively.

[9] The proportion of the working age population for series A, B and C is 56.71, 59.00 and 58.49 per cent respectively.

remains similar to current behaviour of comparable individuals, the effect
on expenditure and revenue can be simulated. Under the same assumption,
behavioural responses to policy changes can be simulated as well. The
reweighting procedure is discussed in subsection 7.3.1, followed by the
microsimulation results using the alternative weights in subsection 7.3.2.

**Figure 7.2 Gender and age distributions for 2001 and for projected
populations**

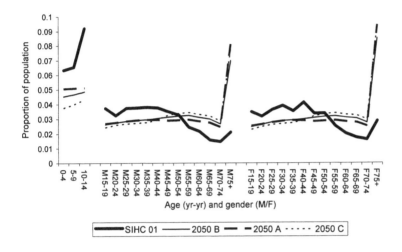

7.3.1 The Reweighting Procedure

As mentioned above, the calibration conditions are constructed from the
population projections for 2050 by ABS (2003b). Figure 7.2 also presents
the age-gender distribution of the 2000-2001 SIHC sample.[10] From the
graph, it is clear that there is a decrease in the younger age groups (up to
about 54 years) and an increase in the proportion of older Australians. The
patterns are similar for men and women. Only the proportion of older
women is slightly higher than the proportion of older men for the 2001
population and for all projected populations. This is no surprise, given the
longer life expectancy of women.

---

[10] Up to age 14, only age can be observed in the SIHC; gender is not available for this group.

The proportions presented in Figure 7.2 are used to calculate revised
weights based on the original ABS weights. Given the low impact of the
reweighting discussed in the previous section, the reweighting here is based
only on the updated age and gender distribution. Figure 7.3 presents the
distribution of the ratio of the new weights resulting from this procedure
relative to the ABS weights.

**Figure 7.3 Ratio of new weight for 2050 population structures and ABS
weight**

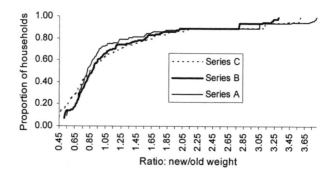

As anticipated, the weights in this section deviate more from the ABS
weights than the earlier revised weights (which had a range for the ratio of
new to old weights of 0.68 to 1.87). The substantial changes in the age
structure of the population require some age groups to be weighted up and
others to be weighted down. The minimum range that could be imposed in
the Deville and Särndal approach increased to [0.51, 3.25] for the 2050
reweighting using the medium population projection (series B). The upper
boundary seems relatively more affected by the difference in age structure,
which can be explained by the relatively sharp increase needed for the older
age group compared with the smaller decrease of the other groups, which
are spread across a wider age range. Comparing the restrictions on the
bounds that can be achieved in the different scenarios shows that the range
is narrowest for the medium population scenario. This may be explained by
the fact that although series B has a higher proportion of people over 50
than the young population, the proportion of people over 75 is lower. This

means that this relatively small group of people over 75 needs to have a larger increase in their weights in series A and C.

The effects on wage and salary income distributions of reweighting are shown in Figure 7.4 for the three population series. This figure shows for each income level the reweighted frequency minus the initial frequency. In each case, there is little change in the proportion of persons on very high wages, but the proportion on medium wage and salary incomes, in particular, has decreased. This has mostly gone to an increase in the proportion of people who have no wage and salary income. This is not shown in Figure 7.4, but the differences at zero income for series A to C respectively are 13.17, 12.08 and 13.55. The income from wage and salary distribution is further from the 2001 distribution in series A and C compared with B. A possible explanation for this is that the younger population has a larger proportion of children whereas the older population has a larger proportion of potentially retired people. The medium-aged population, B, on the other hand, has the highest proportion in the working-age category, resulting in a larger proportion of the population on non-zero wage and salary income.

7.3.2 Population Ageing, Taxes and Expenditure

This section examines the effect of population ageing on government expenditure and revenue, if the changed demographic structure of the population were realised in 2001. Table 7.4 presents the results for the medium population projection (series B). As expected, a larger proportion of people pay income tax, as there are fewer children and dependent adolescents, but at a lower level given the lower income of retirees. This results in a decrease in the revenue from taxation. Similarly, the Medicare levy decreases and rebates increase.

On the expenditure side, the number of people on pensions increases substantially, while the number of people on allowances and Family Payments decreases. The Age Pension sees the largest increase, in line with the ageing population, and a smaller increase is observed for the Disability Support Pension, which also tends to be received by older individuals.

Figure 7.4 Difference of frequency distribution of weekly wage and salary income using ABS weights versus new weights for projected population structure of 2050

ABS: series A

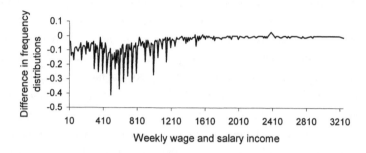

ABS: series B

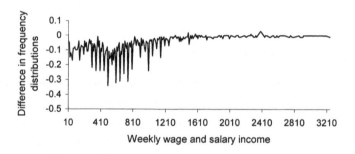

ABS: series C

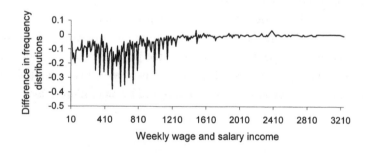

When eligibility for the Age Pension is based on observed receipt in the SIHC (to account for the lack of information on assets), the expenditure on the Age Pension becomes smaller, as shown in the last two columns in Table 7.4. However, the relative increase in the expenditure due to population ageing, when compared with the expenditure in 2001 based on observed eligibility for Age Pension (not presented in Table 7.4[11]), is similar to the relative increase in the middle two columns compared with the first two columns in Table 7.4. Of the allowances, only the Mature Age Allowance and the Partner Allowance increase.

Table 7.5 presents the results for the two alternative population projection scenarios A and C. Comparing the change in net expenditure, series B is the least costly. In 2050, revenue is somewhat higher and expenditure is somewhat lower for B than for A and C, which is caused by the larger proportion of population B in the working age groups. Assuming similar employment rates as there were in 2000/01, a larger proportion of population B is therefore going to be self-sufficient without the need for government support.

7.4 Policy Simulation with Aged Population Structure

Population ageing is of course likely to lead to a different response to policy changes. Hence this section examines a policy change using the reweighted sample, which accounts for population ageing, rather than the sample weighted with the original 2000-2001 ABS weights. The policy change involves a reduction to 30 per cent in all benefit taper rates over 30 per cent. Results are reported for population series B. Table 7.6 compares the labour supply response to this policy change for the 2001 population and for the updated population. The first row in each of the two panels in Table 7.6 presents the percentage of workers in the pre-reform situation.

Comparing the two sets of results, lower participation rates for all groups except sole parents are evident in the series B age structure. The labour supply responses are similar for both sets of results.

For sole parents the change is minimal. This group may have become smaller, but the age composition of this group is unlikely to have shifted

---

[11] See Cai, Creedy and Kalb (2004) for these numbers in 2001.

Table 7.4 Simulated impact of population ageing

| | Simulation using ABS weight | | Simulation using weights derived from projected medium population (B) in 2050 | | | |
| | | | Using calculated Age Pension eligibility | | Using observed Age Pension eligibility | |
	Rev/exp ($m)	Persons (1000)	Rev/exp ($m)	Persons (1000)	Rev/exp ($m)	Persons (1000)
Government revenue						
Income tax	79707.8	12103	71294.3	13411	71143.5	13286
Medicare levy	5727.8	7762	5102.2	7271	5087.4	7223
Total revenue	85435.6		76396.5		76230.9	
Government expenditure						
Tax rebates	2889.1	6294	4515.7	8410	4463.7	8287
FTP/FTB	9548.4	1935	6198.6	1277	6198.6	1277
Allowances	16539.6	2657	14222.8	2239	14222.8	2239
Pensions	26437.0	3102	52076.8	6127	50410.0	5868
Pharmaceutical Allowance	383.8	3556	665.9	6472	640.7	6211
Rent Allowance	2033.5	1454	1971.1	1597	1925.8	1558
Total expenditure	57831.5		79651.0		77861.5	
Net expenditure	-27604.1		3254.5		1630.6	
Allowance						
Parenting Payment (Single)	3253.6	389	2259.3	267	2259.3	267
Parenting Payment (Couple)	1783.9	285	1196.7	192	1196.7	192
Sickness Allowance	181.7	21	176.3	20	176.3	20
Widow's Allowance	4.9	1	2.5	0	2.5	0
AUSTUDY/ABSTUDY	947.1	135	722.7	103	722.7	103
NewStart Allowance	4268.1	660	3811.2	584	3811.2	584
Mature Age Allowance	221.2	47	303.0	60	303.0	60
Youth Allowance	2475.7	674	1820.4	491	1820.4	491
Special Benefit	1910.2	232	1992.5	246	1992.5	246
Partner Allowance	1493.2	215	1938.3	275	1938.3	275
Total allowance cost	16539.6		14222.8		14222.8	
Pension						
Age Pension	15865.0	1935	34148.3	4171	32733.9	3947
Disability Support Pension	5133.8	575	6144.3	682	6144.3	682
Wife's Pension	792.9	101	1099.2	139	1082.4	136
Widow B Pension	398.2	41	311.7	32	311.7	32
Carer's Payment	274.1	33	371.9	44	371.9	44
Veteran Pension	1812.7	233	5327.5	672	5125.2	644
Veteran Disability Pension	1063.5	101	2357.4	213	2324.0	208
War Widow Pension	1096.9	83	2316.6	174	2316.6	174
Total pension cost	26437.0		52076.8		50410.0	
Rebate						
Beneficiary Rebate	457.9	1193	433.5	1119	433.5	1119
Pension Rebate	2388.3	2213	5137.6	4781	5168.8	4771
Sole Parent Pension Rebate	256.1	349	177.7	243	177.7	243
Low-Income Rebate	1250.6	8715	1531.9	10608	1533.7	10620
Dependent Spouse Rebate	423.3	416	481.5	512	576.8	569
Total rebate cost	4776.3		7762.2		7890.5	

Table 7.5 Simulated government revenue and costs for 2050 projections

| | Simulation using ABS weight | | Simulation using weights derived from projected population structures A and C | | | |
| | | | Young population | | Old population | |
	Rev/exp ($m)	Persons (1000)	Rev/exp ($m)	Persons (1000)	Rev/exp ($m)	Persons (1000)
Government revenue						
Income tax	79707.8	12103	68629.0	13230	71222.3	13774
Medicare levy	5727.8	7762	4889.2	7005	5106.1	7331
Total revenue	85435.6		73518.2		76328.4	
Government expenditure						
Tax rebates	2889.1	6294	4560.2	8416	4814.7	8811
FTP/FTB	9548.4	1935	6765.0	1365	5309.0	1111
Allowances	16539.6	2657	14004.8	2206	13869.2	2176
Pensions	26437.0	3102	53206.0	6233	56644.3	6658
Pharmaceutical Allowance	383.8	3556	683.0	6592	715.4	6972
Rent Allowance	2033.5	1454	2029.2	1622	1940.6	1620
Total expenditure	57831.5		81248.2		83293.2	
Net expenditure	-27604.1		7730.0		6964.9	
Allowance						
Parenting Payment (Single)	3253.6	389	2466.9	290	1961.3	233
Parenting Payment (Couple)	1783.9	285	1274.7	204	1054.2	168
Sickness Allowance	181.7	21	158.9	18	185.5	21
Widow's Allowance	4.9	1	2.6	0	2.2	0
AUSTUDY/ABSTUDY	947.1	135	710.3	101	689.9	100
NewStart Allowance	4268.1	660	3631.0	554	3831.1	586
Mature Age Allowance	221.2	47	271.8	54	320.0	63
Youth Allowance	2475.7	674	1878.2	507	1697.2	458
Special Benefit	1910.2	232	1879.2	233	2053.0	254
Partner Allowance	1493.2	215	1731.0	246	2074.8	293
Total allowance cost	16539.6		14004.8		13869.2	
Pension						
Age Pension	15865.0	1935	34762.7	4224	37243.1	4545
Disability Support Pension	5133.8	575	5743.9	636	6510.2	722
Wife's Pension	792.9	101	1032.2	130	1182.1	149
Widow B Pension	398.2	41	288.3	30	310.0	32
Carer's Payment	274.1	33	359.3	43	399.8	47
Veteran Pension	1812.7	233	6037.6	759	5867.4	739
Veteran Disability Pension	1063.5	101	2565.7	230	2560.0	231
War Widow Pension	1096.9	83	2416.2	181	2571.8	193
Total pension cost	26437.0		53206.0		56644.3	
Rebate						
Beneficiary Rebate	457.9	1193	413.5	1066	437.0	1125
Pension Rebate	2388.3	2213	5310.4	4913	5605.0	5211
Sole Parent Pension Rebate	256.1	349	193.5	264	154.6	211
Low-Income Rebate	1250.6	8715	1533.0	10610	1586.9	10983
Dependent Spouse Rebate	423.3	416	430.7	465	518.3	552
Total rebate cost	4776.3		7881.1		8301.8	

Table 7.6 Simulated impacts on labour supply of population ageing

	Married men	Married women	Single men	Single women	Single parents
		ABS weights			
All workers (% base) [1]	71.67	55.42	62.04	50.06	49.62
Worker, hrs known (% base)	58.08	48.61	54.94	47.09	42.64
Worker, hrs known (% post)	58.02	47.67	55.12	47.38	44.81
Non-work to work (%)	0.59	0.41	0.23	0.35	2.31
Work to non-work (%)	0.65	1.36	0.05	0.06	0.14
Workers working more	0.23	0.24	0.01	0.05	1.03
Workers working less	1.30	0.77	0.78	1.69	1.27
Average hours change	-0.20	-0.45	-0.06	-0.18	0.73
	Projected population structure of 2050 series B				
All workers (% base) [1]	54.35	42.20	53.77	38.15	48.93
Worker, hrs known (% base)	42.60	36.15	46.31	35.73	41.81
Worker, hrs known (% post)	42.63	35.48	46.47	35.94	44.00
Non-work to work (%)	0.53	0.34	0.21	0.26	2.33
Work to non-work (%)	0.50	1.01	0.05	0.05	0.14
Workers working more	0.17	0.18	0.01	0.03	1.01
Workers working less	0.94	0.59	0.66	1.33	1.32
Average hours change	-0.12	-0.34	-0.04	-0.15	0.73

Note (1): The group in this first row includes the self-employed for whom no hours of work are observed. Only the effect for wage and salary earners (for whom hours are known) is simulated in MITTS.

towards the 60-and-over group to a large extent. Similarly, there is little change in the effect for single persons. The negative effects for singles and married men and women are slightly smaller in the aged population. For married men and women, the proportion moving to non-work or working fewer hours after the policy change has decreased in the aged population, possibly because they are already at a lower level of participation in the updated population. This causes the slightly less negative labour supply response for men and women.

Finally, the effects of the policy change on government expenditure and revenue are shown in Table 7.7, which compares results with those obtained using the original ABS weights. Although total expenditure on couples is projected to increase as a result of population ageing, it is mostly through pensions. People on age and disability pensions are assumed to be non-responsive to financial incentives and most of them are not working, so they do not benefit from the taper rate reduction. Therefore, a smaller proportion of the 2050 population is expected to benefit from the policy change. As a result, the cost of the policy change is lower for couples in the 2050 projection compared with 2000-2001. For single men and women the cost is similar to before, although the total expenditure increases just as for couples. For sole parents both the total expenditure and the cost of the policy change are lower with the projected 2050 population structure. This is the result of a reduced number of sole parents as a proportion of the total population when the revised weights are used.[12]

7.5 Conclusions

This chapter has investigated the use of sample reweighting in MITTS to examine the implications of population ageing for government revenue and expenditure in Australia. First, a calibration approach to sample reweighting was described. This produces new weights which achieve specified population totals for selected variables, subject to the constraint that there are minimal adjustments to the weights. Second, the performance of the ABS weights provided with the 2001 SIHC, for obtaining aggregate government expenditure and revenue estimates and numbers of people receiving various benefits, was examined. This was needed because population aggregates for variables not used in official calibrations may deviate from population values obtained from other data sources, such as official administrative data on tax revenue and expenditures. It was found that reweighting does not improve the simulation outcomes, so the original ABS weights were retained for 2001.

Third, the implications of changes in the age distribution of the population were examined, based on ABS population projections to 2050. A 'pure' change in the age distribution was examined by keeping the aggregate population size fixed and changing only the relative frequencies in different age groups. Using the reweighted sample as the base dataset in microsimulation allows an analysis of the potential changes in government revenue and expenditure, conditional on a population with a different age structure but otherwise similar characteristics as the 2001 population. This example of an ageing population shows that the cost of social security is

---

[12] The weighted number of sole parents is 589,287 using ABS weights and 411,727 using weights derived from the projected 2050 population structure.

Table 7.7 Simulated tax and transfer costs allowing for labour supply responses

	ABS weights		2050 series B	
	Pre-reform value ($m)	Change after reform value ($m)	Pre-reform value ($m)	Change after reform value ($m)
Couples				
Government revenue				
Income tax	57474.3	112.1	48841.7	302.9
Medicare	4023.6	75.6	3403.8	73.5
Total revenue	61497.9	187.7	52245.5	376.4
Government expenditure				
Tax rebates	1537.6	-135.0	2540.2	-197.0
FTP/FTB	6006.6	886.2	3838.7	549.8
Allowances	6065.6	5030.3	5627.7	4481.4
Pensions	13641.1	476.9	28705.7	968.4
Pharmaceutical Allowance	134.0	8.1	276.7	13.5
Rent Allowance	647.3	234.3	570.7	194.7
Total expenditure	28032.1	6500.9	41559.7	6010.7
Net expenditure	-33465.9	6313.2	-10685.8	5634.4
Single men				
Government revenue				
Income tax	12839.4	251.9	12882.7	272.4
Medicare	1019.2	22.9	1008.3	23.9
Total revenue	13858.6	274.8	13891.0	296.2
Government expenditure				
Tax rebates	414.7	-12.9	702.5	-23.0
Allowances	4298.9	1132.3	3993.8	1053.6
Pensions	4085.4	107.7	8230.0	226.4
Pharmaceutical Allowance	65.8	1.8	131.0	2.9
Rent Allowance	465.0	395.5	578.8	369.4
Total expenditure	9329.8	1624.3	13636.1	1629.3
Net expenditure	-4528.8	1349.5	-254.9	1333.1
Single women				
Government revenue				
Income tax	7510.5	130.9	8279.0	145.7
Medicare	592.9	13.6	629.3	14.2
Total Revenue	8103.4	144.5	8908.4	159.9
Government expenditure				
Tax rebates	650.1	-14.9	1071.0	-22.6
Allowances	2633.9	964.1	2120.2	874.7
Pensions	8529.4	116.2	15030.6	223.0
Pharmaceutical Allowance	124.8	1.8	217.4	2.6
Rent Allowance	344.1	279.7	424.3	235.3
Total expenditure	12282.3	1347.0	18863.4	1313.0
Net expenditure	4178.9	1202.5	9955.0	1153.1

expected to increase and the revenue from income tax is expected to decrease. It is suggested that this type of exercise provides an insight into the implications for government income tax revenue and social security expenditure of changes in the population. The likely pressures for policy changes are thereby indicated.

Finally, the effects of a reduction in benefit taper rates in Australia were compared using 2001 and 2050 population weights. Assuming that labour force participation rates have not changed between 2001 and 2050, this shows that the cost of such a policy is expected to be slightly less in absolute terms and considerably less in relative terms (as a proportion of the expenditure before the policy change) for the 2050 population. The larger proportion of the population out of the labour force means that fewer people benefit from the taper rate reduction. As a result, a taper rate reduction is expected to be less costly in the older population.

Sample reweighting could be used to examine other types of change, including for example changes in unemployment rates. It is suggested that the kind of reweighting approach discussed here provides much scope for providing insights into the implications of changes to the population composition.

Appendix 7-A. Calibration Conditions for 2001

Table 7.8 Population age distribution

	Required total from Census 2001[1]	Estimated total from the SIHC using ABS weights	Difference
Population aged under 15[2]			
0-4	1243969	1214517	29452
5-9	1331926	1253801	78125
10-14	1336580	1765168	-428588
Males			
15-19	677513	713250	-35737
20-24	629319	617182	12137
25-29	654456	715695	-61239
30-34	688049	719950	-31901
35-39	703544	729525	-25981
40-44	705817	720095	-14278
45-49	651987	673475	-21488
50-54	624315	628445	-4130
55-59	490155	468993	21162
60-64	394631	414462	-19831
65-69	322901	302613	20288
70-74	292636	280859	11777
75 and over	427221	404355	22866
Females			
15-19	647751	668439	-20688
20-24	611763	607638	4125
25-29	664501	696427	-31926
30-34	716182	748909	-32727
35-39	728089	676943	51146
40-44	730838	789864	-59026
45-49	667860	646603	21257
50-54	624170	647963	-23793
55-59	480580	485004	-4424
60-64	394376	385841	8535
65-69	337686	333367	4319
70-74	326947	306560	20387
75 and over	663487	546531	116956
Total	18769249	19162474	-393225

(1) Source: ABS (2002).
(2) The number of children variables in the SIHC for the different age categories are mostly censored at two. Therefore, the exact number of children in the different age categories cannot be calculated using information from the SIHC. In this table, we treated the censored number as the actual number, which is unlikely to be far from the actual value given the available age categories in the SIHC (that is, 0-2, 3-4, 5-9 and 10-14 years of age).

Table 7.9 Family composition

	Required total from Census 2001[1]	Estimated total from the SIHC using ABS weights	Difference
Couples without children	1764167	1886483	-122316
Couples with dependent children only	1661963	1767752	-105789
Couples with dependent and non-dependent children	242159	285577	-43418
Couples with non-dependent children only	417043	459372	-42329
Sole parents with dependent children only	465932	530460	-64528
Sole parents with dependent and non-dependent children	64037	58827	5210
Sole parents with non-dependent children only	232663	250421	-17758

(1) Source: ABS (2002).

Table 7.10 Number of unemployed people

	Required total from Census 2001[1]	Estimated total from the SIHC using ABS weights	Difference
Males			
15-19 years	59493	66202	-6709
20-24 years	67585	53863	13722
25-34 years	93416	84334	9082
35-44 years	74300	80405	-6105
45-54 years	59110	48071	11039
55-64 years	37011	19851	17160
Females			
15-19 years	50921	55461	-4540
20-24 years	45704	36408	9296
25-34 years	61263	54502	6761
35-44 years	56553	60112	-3559
45-54 years	38463	43212	-4749
55-64 years	12319	16831	-4512
Total	656138	619252	36886

(1) Source: ABS (2002).

Table 7.11 Number of income support recipients

	Required total from FaCS[1]	Estimated total from the SIHC using ABS weights	Difference
A. Disability Support Pension			
Couples			
Males with dependants	172666	183435	-10769
Females with dependants	68295	96924	-28629
Singles			
Males with dependants	219688	175091	44597
Females with dependants	163277	129364	33913
B. Parenting Payments (Single + Couple)			
Males			
Under 39	29634	28824	810
40–49	18641	14647	3994
50 and over	5349	4700	649
Females			
Under 29	180100	196069	-15969
30–39	250438	298710	-48272
40–49	137478	182098	-44620
50 and over	17695	16195	1500
C. Wife Pension, Carers' Payment and Widow Allowance			
Under 39	16667	13291	3376
40–49	30806	31408	-602
50–59	91354	107956	-16602
60 and over	32480	31083	1397

(1) Source: FaCS (2003).

PART III. ACTUAL AND PROPOSED REFORMS

8 The Australian New Tax System

In July 2000, several reforms were made to the Australian Income Tax and Social Security System. These changes were introduced simultaneously with the new 10 per cent Goods and Services Tax (GST), the abolition of wholesales tax and some of the States' expenditure taxes, and were at least partly meant to offset the increase in net taxes paid through expenditures.[1] It raises the question of whether they did more than that. Important changes in this reform were the decrease in personal income taxes, increases in benefit levels of pensions, allowances and additional benefits such as Rent Assistance and assistance available to families with children, which also underwent a substantial amount of restructuring.

An evaluation of this reform is difficult to perform. First, no suitable data covering the period just before and after the reform are available. Second, even if such data were available, disentangling the effects of the separate components of the reform and other events taking place at the same time would be complicated.

This chapter takes an alternative approach and investigates, through simulation, the effects of the social security and income tax reform on government expenditure and on labour supply of Australian households taking into account price changes resulting from the net increase in expenditure taxes. The before reform date is set at January 2000 and the after reform date is set at July 2000. This chapter focuses on behavioural responses from the supply side of the labour market.

Warren *et al.* (1999a, 1999b), Harding *et al.* (2000) and Johnson *et al.* (1998) analysed distributional effects of this reform while plans were still in a developmental stage. They indicate the difficulties of assessing the effect of the reform while not knowing the impact of the net increase in expenditure taxes on price levels. This chapter uses the level of inflation, calculated by comparing the Consumer Price Index (CPI) of the first and

---

[1] About 8 of the 10 percentage points of GST replaced the former wholesales tax and some of the States' expenditure taxes.

third quarter of 2000 (the before and after reform dates), to take out the effect of the GST and other price effects.[2] The Commonwealth Treasury of Australia (2003b) takes a similar approach to deal with the GST and provides a brief overview of the distributional impacts. However, it does not account for behavioural responses or examine individual components of the reform.

The effects that the changes to the tax and transfer system have had on the effective marginal tax rates (EMTRs) and net incomes of Australian households and on the overall budget cost are described here. This chapter also explores the changes in costs of the different payments and rebates. First, the effects are simulated without taking into account any potential labour supply responses, resulting from the changed EMTRs at the different hours of labour supply. Later, labour supply responses are taken into account as well. It examines the effects on couples with and without children, single men, single women and sole parents separately.

After analysing the overall effect of the reforms, some of the more relevant individual changes are studied separately to reveal their effect on labour supply, net income and costs. Individual changes examined here include the personal income tax changes, introduction of the new Family Tax Benefits (parts A and B), and the change in the pension taper rate.[3] The combined effect of changes is not necessarily equal to the sum of all separate changes.

Section 8.1 discusses the approach taken for the simulations and the data used. It also outlines the qualifications needed in interpreting the results. First, the complete package is evaluated in section 8.2. Section 8.3 discusses the results from simulating individual components of the reform. Details of the tax and transfer system are given in Appendix 8-A.

---

[2] The CPI is an average measure and the impact of the GST is likely to be different for the different households. However, it is not possible to allow for this here. Creedy (1998) analysed the introduction of the GST in New Zealand and concludes that it did not have a substantially larger effect on low-income groups than on high-income groups. This supports the idea of using an average price increase, especially since the focus of this chapter is on the reforms to the social security and income tax system.

[3] The change in the second threshold for recipients of the partnered Parenting Payment had little effect on net income, costs or labour supply, so the results are not reported here. The small effect is not surprising given that the reform only had a minor effect on the net incomes of a small proportion of the population.

8.1 The Simulation Procedure

The basic simulation procedure within MITTS has been described in chapter 1. This involves, for example, the use of estimated wages for non-workers in the sample, the assumptions regarding eligibility and take-up of benefits, the use of labour supply modelling to estimate behavioural responses, and the calibration procedure. This section discusses the need to combine information from different years and the need to simulate changes starting from a year for which no data are yet available. Furthermore, it is necessary to account for the net increase in expenditure taxes and price changes more generally.

8.1.1 Combining Different Years of Data

The simulation procedure involves data from several years of the Survey of Income and Housing Cost (SIHC) and information on the taxation and social security regimes of several years. A few transformation steps are needed to combine these years in the analysis.

First, the behavioural part of the simulation procedure is based on labour supply models. These models are estimated using the Survey of Income and Housing Cost from 1994/95, 1995/96, 1996/97 and 1997/98 with the corresponding taxation and social security rules. Combining several years of data actually helps to identify the model, since slightly different tax regimes were operational in the four years. This provides more variation in net incomes at different hours of labour supply than would otherwise be the case. To estimate one model combining the four years, the net incomes calculated over a range of different possible hours have to be made comparable over the four years. This can be achieved by expressing the calculated net incomes in each of the years in the dollar value of one year. That is, we have to account for the change in the real value of the dollar. All net incomes are in 1997/1998 dollars and the CPI is used to inflate the other years' net incomes to the corresponding 1997/98 level before using them in the labour supply model.

Second, we need to use data from 1997/98 (which was the most recent dataset available at the time of this analysis) for simulations of the effect of a change in taxation and social security rules from January 2000 to July 2000. Therefore, the wage rates of the respondents and the level of their other income (excluding social security payments) were updated to the wage rates and other income that similar households would have experienced in January 2000 and July 2000 respectively. The average wage rate increase measured over this time and the CPI are used to update the wages and the value of other income respectively, to the values expected in January and July 2000. Additionally, we update the observed labour supply of 1997/98 to the predicted modal level given the change to the January 2000 taxation regime and social security system. In this way, an artificial dataset is created for January and July 2000 based on the 1997/98 data with updated values for labour supply, income and wages.

The availability of more recent data would have made this last step unnecessary, or at least bridging fewer years between the year of data collection and the year of interest would have made the uncertainty associated with creating an artificial dataset smaller. Obviously, better and more up-to-date data would improve the quality of simulations.[4]

Finally, when calculating the expected labour supply under a particular regime, the net incomes need to be translated from their January 2000 or July 2000 value to the 1997/98 values needed as input in the labour supply model. For this, the CPI is used again. The costs are expressed in July 2000 dollars.

8.1.2 Accounting for the Net Increase in Expenditure Taxes

The effect of the reform on prices was measured by comparing the CPI of the first and the third quarter of 2000, the before and after reform dates, to take out the effect of the GST and other price effects. The CPI uses average budget shares whereas the real income effects are likely to differ across groups of individuals. Hence the exact changes in real incomes at the individual level are not measured. The level of inflation between the two quarters was 4.6 per cent, which includes the effect of the net increase in expenditure taxes and the usual inflation. Although the approach accounts for the increased price resulting from the net increase in expenditure taxes, the increased revenue from the GST is not included in the comparison of the costs to the government before and after the reform.

---

[4] At the time of analysis, these data were not available.

Whenever real tax and transfer systems at different moments in time are compared in MITTS, the results are corrected for the different price levels (here during the first and the third quarter of 2000). This prevents nominal changes in benefits from having an effect whenever the nominal change is equal to the general increase in prices. The assumption in the labour supply model underlying the behavioural results is that households are aware of the actual price changes after introduction of the GST and other indirect tax changes, and the effect this has on their real incomes. This may not have been true immediately after 1 July 2000, but in the longer term the real implications of the new system should become clear to most households and they are expected to behave accordingly.

8.1.3 Labour Supply Responses

Labour supply is held constant for some groups who are expected to differ in their responses (that is, be less responsive) compared with the average working-age individual. These groups are the self-employed (864 cases), those on disability payments (508 cases), full-time students (256 cases) and people over 65 years of age (1601 cases). This leaves 8022 households for whom MITTS is used to simulate the effect of the policy reform on labour supply.

8.2 The Effect of All Changes in the New Tax System

The first simulation examines the full effect of all changes for the total population. Subsection 8.2.1 describes the non-behavioural results and EMTR changes briefly, and subsections 8.2.2 to 8.2.6 discuss behavioural and non-behavioural results by demographic group.

8.2.1 Non-behavioural Simulation Results

The reduction in marginal tax rates and the increase in income thresholds have reduced tax revenue for the government by over 10 billion dollars as can be seen in the next section, when adding revenues for all demographic groups. With the reform of Family Assistance, several rebates have been abolished (-1.3 billion dollars) and the old Family Payments (-6.6 billion dollars) have been transferred to the FTP/FTB (Family Tax Payment/Family Tax Benefit) category (+9.5 billion dollars). The number and amount of allowances declined (-0.6 billion dollars) because the basic Parenting Allowance has been integrated into the Family Assistance system. The combined change in these three categories indicates that the overall support for families increased by about 1 billion dollars. Combining the decrease in tax revenue with the increase in support for families, it is clear that families with children gain most. Warren *et al.* (1999a) and the Commonwealth Treasury of Australia (2003b) observe a similar effect.

Table 8.1 presents the income gainers and losers by income decile. It shows that the higher income deciles have on average the highest increase in income. This is mainly driven by the income tax reform, which reduced taxation rates and increased income tax thresholds, thus reducing the amount of tax paid, particularly by those on higher incomes. More than 90 per cent of individuals in the top three deciles gain more than 10 dollars per week in average income-unit income per person in the income unit. For the top decile, the average increase in average income-unit income per person is 51.70 dollars. Selected components of the reform are analysed separately in section 8.3.1. The largest percentage of households losing income is observed in the sixth and seventh deciles, just above median income.

Table 8.1 Income gain/losses ($ per week) by net income-unit income deciles (row percentages, individual level per capita non-equivalised net income-unit income[a])

Decile	Decrease				Increase			Average
	> 10	5-10	1-5	None	1-5	5-10	> 10	
1	-	0.1	4.1	24.5	71.4	-	-	1.2
2	0.4	0.1	5.3	7.4	55.2	15.0	16.7	5.7
3	0.5	-	1.1	7.7	70.7	7.6	12.4	5.4
4	1.3	0.1	0.4	2.6	36.1	34.8	24.8	8.3
5	3.2	1.5	0.5	1.6	5.6	36.2	51.4	13.4
6	5.6	1.8	1.7	0.9	3.1	19.1	67.8	18.4
7	3.9	2.0	3.3	1.5	6.1	15.2	68.0	22.0
8	2.2	0.2	0.2	-	1.1	3.0	93.4	23.3
9	1.4	-	-	-	0.3	1.5	96.7	37.3
10	2.0	0.6	0.3	0.3	1.1	1.9	93.7	51.7
Total	1.9	0.6	1.6	4.7	24.7	14.2	52.3	18.6

Note a: This is the average income per person in the income unit, without accounting for economies of scale or the difference between an additional child and adult.

The various taper rate changes combined with the tax regime reform have decreased the effective marginal tax rate for the majority of the population. However, the decreased taper rate has also drawn some previously ineligible households into the social security system, increasing their effective marginal tax rate. The shifts in EMTRs can be seen in Table 8.2. These results imply that the policy reform of July 2000 is likely to have had labour supply effects. There are substitution effects through the changes in EMTRs and income effects through the increase (or decrease in a few instances) in net income-unit income. The changed incentives could affect individuals' hours worked and the decision to enter or leave the labour force. The resulting effect is ambiguous in theory, because the two effects may be in opposite directions. The following subsection discusses the predicted labour supply effects, based on the SIHC 1997/1998 sample.

Table 8.2 Distribution of EMTRs (row percentages): pre-ANTS[a] to post-ANTS (from rows to columns)

EMTR Lower bound	0	0	10	20	30	40	50	60	70	80	90	100	
EMTR Upper bound	0	10	20	30	40	50	60	70	80	90	100	∞	Total
0	99.6	0.0	0.1	0.2	-	-	0.0	-	-	-	-	-	28.6
0-10	100.0	-	-	-	-	-	-	-	-	-	-	-	0.1
10-20	6.7	0.7	89.9	-	0.5	0.8	1.4	-	-	-	-	-	2.1
20-30	8.0	-	53.8	6.3	23.8	3.5	0.5	2.2	0.3	1.1	-	0.4	4.5
30-40	0.1	-	-	0.2	90.6	0.3	1.2	6.3	0.0	0.5	0.4	0.3	24.3
40-50	-	0.1	0.0	0.3	41.4	50.9	1.4	3.8	2.0	0.2	-	0.1	26.4
50-60	-	-	-	2.1	8.6	41.0	31.7	12.8	3.9	-	-	-	0.5
60-70	-	-	0.2	0.3	14.1	2.5	52.2	26.9	2.9	0.5	-	0.4	3.8
70-80	0.1	-	0.2	0.3	0.7	3.8	6.6	27.8	54.3	6.1	-	-	4.0
80-90	-	-	-	8.7	0.9	0.4	9.4	25.4	11.1	41.4	2.7	-	3.1
90-100	-	-	-	-	-	-	0.5	3.4	1.7	20.8	73.6	-	2.0
>100	-	-	-	-	0.7	18.6	1.5	8.1	42.4	11.4	6.7	10.5	0.6
Total	29.1	0.0	4.4	0.8	34.7	14.3	3.4	5.7	3.5	2.2	1.7	0.2	100.0

Note a: ANTS = Australian New Tax System.

8.2.2 Behavioural and Non-behavioural Simulation Results for the Subgroups

The effect of all changes taken together is also simulated for the four subgroups separately. Using the weights provided by the Australian Bureau of Statistics (ABS), the results are weighted to represent 2,067,719 couples with children, 2,216,424 couples without children, 2,203,166 single men, 2,048,685 single women and 504,015 sole parents. These weights have not been updated to represent the Australian population size in 2000 and thus the expenditure and revenue are likely to be somewhat underestimated as a result. ABS estimated the Australian population to be 18,711,271 persons in June 1998 and 19,153,380 persons in June 2000 (ABS, 2003a), so the underestimation is likely to be between 2 and 3 per cent.

For each subgroup, the behavioural labour supply responses are presented in Table 8.3 and the effects on government expenditure by payment type and revenue with and without accounting for behavioural responses are presented in Table 8.4. Expenditure and revenue calculated in the discretised framework, before the reform and when assuming fixed labour supply after the reform, are slightly different from the expenditure and revenue calculated using the observed hours of labour supply, due to the rounding of observed hours to multiples of ten hours (for married men) or five hours (for everyone else). The results are discussed by subgroup in the following subsections.

Table 8.3 Behavioural responses: change in labour supply after reform (percentages)

| | Couples | | | | Singles | | |
| | W/out children | | With children | | | | |
Workforce participation	Men	Women	Men	Women	Men	Women	Parents
Pre-ANTS	45.43	40.08	72.82	51.67	59.94	45.15	42.44
Post-ANTS	46.50	41.17	74.27	54.03	61.54	46.35	43.89
Non-work to work	1.07	1.09	1.45	2.38	1.60	1.20	1.52
Work to non-work	0.00	0.01	0.00	0.02	0.00	0.00	0.06
Workers working more	0.22	0.29	0.53	0.44	0.13	0.03	1.07
Workers working less	0.29	0.11	0.99	0.20	0.32	0.82	0.53
Average hours change	0.41	0.35	0.53	0.67	0.59	0.26	0.40

Table 8.4 Behavioural responses: changes in income tax revenue and transfer costs ($m per year) for couples with and without children

| | Couples w/out children | | | Couples with children | | |
| | Abs. Change | | | Abs. Change | | |
	Pre-ANTS	Allowing for labour supply response	Keeping labour fixed	Pre-ANTS	Allowing for labour supply response	Keeping labour fixed
Government revenue from income tax						
Income tax	23264.3	-3097.4	-3310.6	30876.8	-3469.7	-3742.8
Medicare	1471.1	9.9	-8.8	1856.9	-1.7	-28.4
Total	24735.4	-3087.5	-3319.4	32733.7	-3471.4	-3771.2
Government expenditure on social security						
Tax Rebates	1434.5	-187.2	-172.7	1221.2	-1000.8	-988.5
Family Payment	0.0	0.0	0.0	4292.3	-4292.3	-4292.3
FTP/FTB	0.0	0.0	0.0	409.9	6493.6	6609.3
Allowances	2859.6	-156.9	62.9	4329.6	-1129.2	-744.9
Pensions	10600.5	481.4	500.5	793.8	26.7	35.9
Pharmaceutical Allowance	110.1	3.6	3.9	9.3	-0.2	0.0
Rent Allowance	176.3	2.7	7.2	363.8	98.2	105.8
Total	15180.9	143.6	401.8	11419.8	196.1	725.4
Net expenditure		3231.2	3721.2		3667.5	4496.6

8.2.3   Couples without Dependent Children

Similar to the results for other groups, tax payments of couples without dependent children decrease and hence tax rebates also decrease. Table 8.4 shows a slight increase in the expected labour supply. Both men and women in this group are more likely to move into work and women are more likely to increase their working hours whereas men are more likely to decrease their working hours. However, all changes are small. Notwithstanding the small effects, the increased labour supply reduces the additional expenditure associated with the reform and reduces the decrease in revenue. In other words, the labour supply effects help to reduce the cost of the policy changes to the government by about 0.5 billion dollars (from 3.7 billion dollars).

8.2.4 Couples with Children

The simulation shows that government expenditure on benefit payments has increased more for couples with children than for couples without children. This is due to a large component of the change involving Family Payments, which are payable only to households with children. To see this most clearly we need to look at the combined effect of tax rebates, Family Payments, FTP/FTB and allowances in both groups. Pension payments are excluded because the payments to couples without children mostly consist of Age Pensions, which means that the recipients are an older age group than most couples with children. Couples with children receive an additional 620.7 million dollars in these categories, whereas there is a reduction for couples without children as a result of the lower rebates. The reduction in allowances is caused by the abolition of the Basic Parenting Payment for couples. However, this payment is replaced by increased FTP/FTB payments for one-earner families. Similarly, the reduction in rebates is mainly caused by the abolition of the rebate for a dependent spouse with children, and families have been compensated for this through FTP/FTB payments.

The labour supply effects for couples with children are larger than for couples without children. There were more changes in social security payments and income tax as a result of the introduction of the new system for households with children than for those without. Therefore, the larger effect does not necessarily indicate that couples with children are more responsive to changes. From Table 8.4, the labour supply responses in all directions are somewhat larger for the group with children. The reforms are estimated to induce an additional 2.4 per cent of married women with children into the labour market, which is the largest participation effect observed for any of the demographic groups. This may be due to several changes that have been made to Family Assistance, including reducing the number of different taper rates, which may be more important for women than for men.

8.2.5 Single Men and Women without Children

Table 8.5 shows that the largest difference in the tax and social security changes for singles compared with couples is on the expenditure side. The decrease in rebates is relatively large whereas the increase in allowance payments and pensions is relatively small, making the overall increase smaller than for couples. The relative increases in nearly all payment rates are smaller than for couples, with a decrease evident for Youth Allowance, AUSTUDY/ABSTUDY, the Veterans' Disability Pension and War Widows' Pension. The latter does not mean that the payment rates for these four groups have actually gone down, but only that the rates have not increased by enough to keep up with price changes. From January 2000 to July 2000 prices increased by 4.6 per cent, due in part to the effect of the net increase in indirect taxes.

Table 8.5 Behavioural responses: changes in income tax revenue and transfer costs ($m per year) for single men and women without children

	Single men			Single women		
		Abs. change			Abs. change	
	Pre-ANTS	Allowing for labour supply response	Keeping labour fixed	Pre-ANTS	Allowing for labour supply response	Keeping labour fixed
Government revenue from income tax						
Income tax	13742.7	-1806.0	-1960.8	7965.9	-1050.3	-1078.3
Medicare	939.1	-4.5	-18.5	525.9	7.5	3.6
Total	14681.8	-1810.5	-1979.3	8491.8	-1042.7	-1074.7
Government expenditure on social security						
Tax rebates	427.1	-88.3	-77.0	741.1	-131.5	-127.5
Family Payment	0.0	0.0	0.0	0.0	0.0	0.0
FTP/FTB	0.0	0.0	0.0	0.0	0.0	0.0
Allowances	3095.1	-201.6	34.5	1949.9	-80.4	14.7
Pensions	3320.2	99.2	104.3	7746.9	135.6	174.0
Pharmaceutical Allowance	56.0	0.5	0.8	117.3	1.3	1.5
Rent Allowance	379.2	-3.2	12.5	310.5	4.5	7.7
Total	7277.7	-193.3	75.1	10865.7	-70.5	70.4
Net expenditure		1617.2	2054.4		972.3	1145.1

There are also differences between single men and women, with a large proportion of single women receiving a pension whereas single men are nearly equally divided between allowances and pensions. Women are also more likely to receive a rebate given the pension-linked rebate. A larger proportion of single women than single men receive the Age Pension. This can be explained by the slightly lower pension age for women at the time of the reform and women being more likely to live to an older age. In addition, women are less likely to have participated in superannuation schemes during their working lives or to have worked at all. As a result, they are more likely to depend on the Age Pension than are men.

The average change in labour supply of married men with children is similar to that of single men. However, smaller proportions of single men, already working before the reform, change the amount of labour supply than married men, whereas a slightly larger proportion of nonparticipating single men move into work. The reduction in government revenue after taking into account labour supply responses is similar to that for couples. The increase in expenditure with fixed labour supply becomes a decrease when taking labour supply changes into account, largely as a result of the decreased allowance payments. The increase in net expenditure decreases by about 20 per cent after accounting for potential labour supply changes.

The behavioural changes for single women are generally smaller than for single men, which can be explained by the large proportion of Age Pensioners among single women. Behavioural changes are not simulated for people over 65 years of age. The effects in this older age group are likely to be small anyway. Fewer single women move into work or increase their working hours, and a larger proportion decreases their working hours, resulting in a smaller expected increase in the average hours worked. Therefore, the difference between expenditure while taking into account behavioural changes and expenditure while keeping labour supply at the pre-reform hours is not as large as for single men. However, expenditure on single women still turns from an increase to a decrease after accounting for the labour supply changes.

8.2.6 Sole Parents

The largest expenditures for sole parents are on Parenting Payment single allowances (that is, the Sole Parent Pension) and on family allowances. Table 8.6 shows that the relative change in revenue for sole parents is similar to that in the other groups. However, the relative change in total expenditure is higher for sole parents than for other groups except couples with children. More was spent on allowances (mainly the Parenting Payment single) and Family Payments for sole parents after the reform.

Table 8.6 Behavioural responses: changes in income tax revenue and transfer costs ($m per year) for sole parents

| | Sole parents | | |
| | | Absolute change | |
	Pre-ANTS	Allowing for labour supply response	Keeping labour fixed
Government revenue from income tax			
Income tax	1963.9	-235.9	-253.2
Medicare	84.8	1.3	0.1
Total	2048.7	-234.5	-253.1
Government expenditure on social security			
Tax rebates	584.6	-307.4	-307.5
Family Payment	2289.8	-2289.8	-2289.8
FTP/FTB	234.9	2845.5	2850.8
Allowances	3190.2	102.7	136.0
Pensions	167.3	0.8	2.3
Pharmaceutical Allowance	51.2	1.8	2.2
Rent Allowance	423.5	21.4	20.9
Total	6941.5	375.0	414.8
Net expenditure		609.6	667.9

The labour supply effect of sole parents is smaller than the labour supply effect of married women with children but larger than the effect observed for single women or married women without children. The expected increase in expenditure is lower after accounting for labour supply changes than it was before. However, the reduction in the increase is not as pronounced as for some other groups, such as couples with children or single men. This is as expected given the smaller behavioural response. Similarly, the reduction in the expected increase in net expenditure is lower than for these other groups. The changes in the payments relevant to sole parents may have had lower work incentive effects than the changes for other demographic groups. This is further explored in the following sections, where the effects of individual components of the reform are analysed separately.

Comparing results from the above subsections, the largest increases in expenditure are on households with children. Warren *et al.* (1999a) and the Commonwealth Treasury of Australia (2003b) come to a similar conclusion in their distributional analysis. This can be explained by the major focus of the reform on the restructuring of Family Assistance.

8.3   Selected Components of the Reform

This section examines the effect of individual components of the reforms. The effect of each change is simulated by examining the difference between the New Tax System and the New Tax System where one of the new components is taken out and replaced by the January 2000 values. Tables 8.7 to 8.10 present a summary of the predicted effect of these separate components on labour supply and on government expenditure and revenue.

Table 8.7 Labour supply response in average hours per week changes

| | Couples | | | | Single | | |
| | No children | | With children | | | | |
	Men	Women	Men	Women	Men	Women	Parents
Income tax reform	0.17	0.21	0.22	0.24	0.24	0.20	0.96
Introduction of FTB-A	-	-	0.06	-0.18	-	-	0.93
Introduction of FTB-B	-	-	0.10	0.27	-	-	-3.30
Decreasing the pension taper rate	-0.01	0.00	0.00	0.00	0.00	0.00	0.36

Table 8.8 Behavioural responses: change in total income tax revenue and transfer costs (in million dollars per year) for couples

	Couples w/out children		Couples with children	
Allowing for labour supply response	Yes	No	Yes	No
Income tax reform				
Govt revenue	-3279.9	-3524.1	-3879.7	-4182.2
Govt expenditure	-403.8	-312.9	-231.9	-69.0
Net expenditure	2876.1	3211.1	3647.8	4113.1
Introduction of FTB-A				
Govt revenue	-	-	225.6	235.3
Govt expenditure	-	-	1605.5	1643.5
Net expenditure	-	-	1379.9	1408.2
Introduction of FTB-B				
Govt revenue	-	-	314.0	178.1
Govt expenditure	-	-	-937.2	-791.5
Net expenditure	-	-	-1251.2	-969.6
Decreasing the pension taper rate				
Govt revenue	60.1	64.7	0.8	1.6
Govt expenditure	322.6	323.1	22.3	22.2
Net expenditure	262.5	258.3	21.5	20.6

8.3.1 Marginal Tax Rates and Tax Thresholds

One of the major reforms of the July 2000 tax and transfer system was the increase in income thresholds and the decrease in taxation rates. The effect of this component of the overall reform is a large part of the overall effect. The reduction in taxation rates after July 2000 is expected to decrease revenue, but this is partly compensated (a reduction in the decrease of about 34 per cent for sole parents and about 7 per cent for the other groups) by the increased labour supply resulting from the improved work incentives.

Table 8.9 Behavioural responses: change in total income tax revenue and transfer costs (in million dollars per year) for singles

	Single men		Single women	
Allowing for labour supply response	Yes	No	Yes	No
Income tax reform				
Govt revenue	-1797.9	-1932.5	-1198.6	-1288.6
Govt expenditure	-216.8	-114.3	-286.0	-198.6
Net expenditure	1581.0	1818.2	912.6	1090.0
Introduction of FTB-A				
Govt revenue	-	-	-	-
Govt expenditure	-	-	-	-
Net expenditure	-	-	-	-
Introduction of FTB-B				
Govt revenue	-	-	-	-
Govt expenditure	-	-	-	-
Net expenditure	-	-	-	-
Decreasing the pension taper rate				
Govt revenue	14.1	14.1	24.8	24.7
Govt expenditure	59.8	59.8	94.7	95.4
Net expenditure	45.7	45.7	69.9	70.7

8.3.2 Introduction of Family Tax Benefit Part A

Family Tax Benefit Part A (FTB-A) was a payment replacing three former payments: Family Allowance (including Minimum Family Allowance), Family Tax Payment Part A (FTP-A) and Family Tax Assistance Part A (FTA-A). Payment rates and income test thresholds were increased by much more than the inflation rate, with the payments tapered out at a more gradual rate than they were prior to July 2000. From the distribution of EMTRs, it can be seen that the change in the income-free area and the change in the withdrawal rate of the maximum rate of FTB-A are the main causes of any work-incentive changes for families with children. The abolition of the 'sudden death' income test for the minimum payment was less relevant. The July 2000 values result in slightly lower net incomes for parents. Overall, FTB-A contributes significantly to the expenditure of the government. Obviously expenditure on Family Allowance decreases with the inclusion

Table 8.10 Behavioural responses: change in total income tax revenue and transfer costs (in million dollars per year) for sole parents

	Sole parents	
Allowing for labour supply response	Yes	No
Income tax reform		
Govt revenue	-209.8	-319.4
Govt expenditure	-243.8	-97.4
Net expenditure	-34.0	222.0
Introduction of FTB-A		
Govt revenue	89.3	0.0
Govt expenditure	-347.1	-158.1
Net expenditure	-436.4	-158.1
Introduction of FTB-B		
Govt revenue	-65.1	68.4
Govt expenditure	1001.8	761.5
Net expenditure	1066.8	693.1
Decreasing the pension taper rate		
Govt revenue	33.1	27.5
Govt expenditure	45.9	92.6
Net expenditure	12.7	65.2

of FTB-A in the ANTS reform, where the change in expenditure on FTB-A more than outweighs this for couples with children but not for sole parents. The change in income tax revenue is due to the re-arrangement of FTA-A (FTA-A was paid out through the tax system as an increase in the tax-free income range), which is part of FTB-A after the ANTS reform and is paid through the social security system. An increase in income tax revenue is evident as the tax-free threshold is effectively decreased with the amount of FTA-A.

The expenditure changes on Family Payments are the main influences on the overall net effect on government expenditure. As the number of individuals in receipt of FTB-A is greater than the number on Family Allowance, the expenditure on Rent Assistance is also higher in the new Family Payments system since eligible families will receive Rent Assistance over a larger range of income, given that it is associated with the receipt of Family Payments.

The introduction of FTB-A, conditional on all other changes already being implemented, is expected to have a positive labour supply effect on sole parents (which can be explained by the higher amount of Family Payments paid to sole parents in the old system), a negligible positive effect on married men and a slightly adverse effect on married women.

In conclusion, the cost of implementing FTB-A, conditional on all other changes already being implemented, is lower when labour supply responses are taken into account than would be expected under the assumption of a fixed labour supply. The reduction in expenditure on sole parents is even more apparent once the increased hours of work for this group are taken into account. Expenditure on allowances and Family Payments is reduced when allowing for labour supply responses. This is caused by the increase in workforce participation and working hours for married men and sole parents, which reduce the amount of Parenting Payment Single and Partnered claimed. The reduced expenditure on sole parents in the new system is probably mainly due to a decreased overall payment rate, where the different components before the reform added up to a larger amount than the payment after the reform for a substantial number of sole parents. However, sole parents may be compensated for the lower amount received under Part A by a larger amount under Part B. This is explored in the next subsection.

8.3.3   Introduction of Family Tax Benefit Part B

In July 2000, six forms of assistance - three social security payments and three forms of assistance available through the taxation system - which were all available to single income earner families (including sole parent families) were simplified and merged into one Family Tax Benefit Part B (FTB-B). The new FTB-B payments, explicitly designed for single income and sole parent families, were more generous, particularly for sole parents on lower incomes.

Overall, net government expenditure is slightly lower after the inclusion of FTB-B, with increased spending on sole parents but a decrease in spending on couples with children. The decrease in spending on couples mainly comes through the abolition of Basic Parenting Payment and the Dependent Spouse Rebate.

EMTRs for couples with children are generally lower with the introduction of FTB-B. As many payments are merged and the overlapping tapers on Basic Parenting Payment and Dependent Spouse Rebate are replaced by a single payment and a single income test, a reduction in the EMTRs of most families is expected with the introduction of FTB-B. For some sole parents the EMTR is lower after the introduction of FTB-B. However, for the majority of sole parents, FTB-B increases the EMTRs by a substantial amount. For a large proportion of sole parents initially facing EMTRs of between 30 and 40 per cent, EMTRs are increased to between 50 and 60 per cent. The explanation for this is that with the introduction of FTB-B the Sole Parent Rebate was abolished. This rebate, replaced by a lump sum payment in FTB-B (which is not income tested for sole parents), used to decrease the amount of tax paid for some of the sole parents and thus the EMTR.

Sole parents are the most responsive to the FTB-B reform. This is due to an income and a substitution effect. As sole parents receive a net increase in their benefit income and EMTRs increase for a substantial proportion of sole parents, they move out of the workforce and work less hours. Even the prospect of being able to keep the additional benefit regardless of the level of income earned does not induce sole parents to increase their labour supply. Married men and women with children are much less responsive. Introducing FTB-B has a small positive effect, mainly on participation in the workforce, more so for women than for men, possibly due to the overlapping tapers on the second earner's income in the January 2000 system. However, the effect on average hours is small compared with that for sole parents. Introducing FTB-B is expected to result in a net government expenditure saving, which is further increased by the labour supply response. Although the labour supply response for couples with children is small, the size of the group within the population makes the further saving in cost quite large. This more than outweighs the additional cost involved with sole parents.

These results show that FTB-A and FTB-B work in opposite directions for couples and sole parents. The higher expenditure on FTB-B more than compensates for the lower expenditure on FTB-A for sole parents, and the higher expenditure on FTB-A more than compensates for the lower expenditure on FTB-B for couples. This indicates that payments are perhaps

more targeted to low-income couples independent of whether they are one-
or two-earner households after the ANTS reform. The labour supply effects
for couples are quite small, with opposite effects for married women as a
result of introducing FTB-A and FTB-B. The overall labour supply effect
for sole parents is negative, with the negative effect resulting from the
introduction of FTB-B being much larger than the positive effect from the
introduction of FTB-A.

8.3.4 Decreasing the Pension Taper Rate

In July 2000, all pension and Parenting Payment Single withdrawal rates of
50 per cent for income above the free area decreased to 40 per cent. As a
result, the overall net expenditure has increased. This is caused first by the
larger number of households who are eligible after the increase in taper rate
and second by the larger amounts of benefits paid to households with other
income. Couples without children contribute most to the additional cost
because this group contains the highest number of recipients eligible for
pensions. The relative contribution of sole parents is however similar in
size. The contribution of the group of single women is much smaller than
that of the sole parents even though they receive quite a large amount of
pension payments. It is unlikely that many single women on Age Pension
participate in the labour force, which means the change in their taper rate
will not affect them. The effect on the pension payments flows on to the
amount of income tax and Medicare levy paid by households and to the
amount of rebate received. Family Payments, Pharmacy Allowance and
Rent Allowance, which are all dependent on eligibility for pensions or
allowances, increase as well after the taper rate decrease.[5]

In the simulations accounting for labour supply changes, people of Age
Pension age or people with a disability are not allowed to change their
labour supply. Because these are the largest groups receiving a pension, the
estimated labour supply changes are virtually zero in these groups.
However, the change in taper rate also affected the Parenting Payment

---

[5] While eligibility for Family Payments is not per se dependent on the eligibility for a basic
pension or allowance benefit, the income test is waived for families in receipt of a pension or
allowance. Thus with the increase in pension and allowance receipt, more families are entitled to
the maximum rate of Family Payment.

Single and the recipients of this payment are of working age and mostly able to work.

The net income of a sole parent or a pension recipient with zero earnings has not changed because their basic rate remains the same following the decrease in taper rate in the July 2000 system, whereas net incomes at low part-time hours have increased, making employment more attractive. The simulation results confirm that no one, except a very small group in the category of couples with children, moves out of the labour market. In the group of couples, the increased income of one partner, as a result of the decreased taper rate, may induce the other person to leave the labour force.

For sole parents who are already in the workforce, the increased net income can induce some of them to work fewer hours (the income effect). However, because the net wage rate has increased at the same time, the value of one hour of work may have risen above the value of one hour of leisure and recipients may choose to work more hours and have less non-work time (the substitution effect). Therefore, the effect on labour supply is theoretically ambiguous. On average, labour supply is predicted to increase by about 0.36 hours per week.

The anticipated increase in expenditure on benefit payments and rebates as a result of the reduction of the pension withdrawal rate in the July 2000 reform is nearly halved for sole parents when changes in labour supply are included in the predicted change. Including the reduced pension withdrawal rate in the reform for sole parents is not costly. Overall, the change in the pension taper rates has a relatively minor effect and is not a major component in the overall change.

8.4 Conclusions

This chapter has analysed the effects of introducing the income tax and social security components of the Australian New Tax System, concentrating on behavioural responses from the supply side of the labour market. The effects of the different components of the reform package were examined. Changes to marginal tax rates and income tax thresholds were shown to have had the largest effect because they affected the largest proportion of the Australian population. The change also increased labour supply for all groups, in particular for sole parents, making up part of the loss in tax revenue. Compared with the change in revenue resulting from the complete reform, the increase in expenditure on social security payments is small.

For families with children the changed structure and rates of Family Payments were shown to be important. The effects of the new FTB-A and FTB-B appear different for sole parents and couples with children, FTB-B being more generous towards sole parents and FTB-A more generous towards couples. A strong income effect associated with the increased generosity of FTB-B is estimated to have induced sole parents to reduce labour supply. Other components of the reform provided several positive incentives for sole parents but the Family Payment reforms seem to partly counteract this, resulting in a small positive overall effect. For FTB-A, the introduction of the gradual withdrawal of the minimum rate of Family Payment, rather than the previous 'sudden death' cut-out, had the larger effect as the latter reform only involved a small amount of income at a relatively high level of family income.

The chapter has also shown that the reduction in pension taper rates had little effect on expenditure, given that a large proportion of pensioners are not working because of disability or retirement, and will not be affected by a change in the taper rate. The reduction in the taper rate has a small positive labour supply effect for sole parents.

Looking at the combined effect of all changes, families with children experienced the largest increase in net government expenditure, mainly caused by increased Family Payments. This is also reflected in the average increase in income in these households, which is higher than in other households. Given the large effect of the income tax reform, it is also found that families in higher income deciles had larger average income gains.

Although expenditure on benefit payments increases following the reform of July 2000, it is expected that this increase is lower after taking into account labour supply behaviour. For single men and women, the expectation is that the increase in expenditure may even turn into a saving on expenditure. Similarly, the decrease in revenue is lower after taking into account the increased labour supply among all groups. Thus the expected changes in labour supply should help to reduce the cost of the reform. The increase in net expenditure (expenditure on income support minus income tax revenue) is also lower after accounting for labour supply changes.

Appendix 8-A. Details of the Tax and Social Security System

This appendix provides information on personal income taxes, the Family Assistance schemes, allowances and pensions.

Table 8.11 Marginal taxation rates

1999/2000		2000/2001	
Taxable income $ per week	Marginal tax rate	Taxable income $ per week	Marginal tax rate
0 – 103.56	Nil	0 – 115.07	Nil
103.57 – 396.99	0.20	115.08 – 383.56	0.17
397.00 – 728.77	0.34	383.57 – 958.90	0.30
728.78 – 958.90	0.43	958.91 – 1150.68	0.42
958.91 – ∞	0.47	1150.69 – ∞	0.47

Table 8.12 Medicare levy

1999/2000		2000/2001	
If weekly income more than	Levy rate	If weekly income more than	Levy rate
$256.78 (single)	1.5%	$265.18 (single)	1.5%
$433.31+$40.27 × (no of children (family))	1.5%	$447.48+$40.27 × (no of children (family))	1.5%
Shade-in percentage	20%	Shade-in percentage	20%
$958.90 for singles, additional Medicare levy[a]	1.0%	$990.27 for singles, additional Medicare levy[a]	1.0%
$1917.81 + $28.77 × (no of children –1) for families, additional Medicare levy[a] No shade-in	1.0%	$1980.54 + $28.77 × (no of children –1) for families, additional Medicare levy[a] No shade-in	1.0%

Note a: The additional Medicare levy is only payable for those who do not have private health insurance.

Table 8.13 Family Assistance

	January 2000	July 2000
For all families with children		
	Family Allowance	Family Tax Assistance Part A
Minimum rate per week ≤ 3 children	$12.00	
Minimum rate per week		$18.69
Minimum rate per week (18 to 24 yr old)		$25.06
Large family supplement per week for fourth and each subsequent child	$3.95	$4.00
Maximum basic rate per week		
For 0-12 yr old	$50.80	$58.10
For 13-15 yr old	$66.10	$73.64
For 16-17 yr old	$12.00	$18.69
For 18-24 yr old	$25.00	$25.06
Minimum rate payable for annual income below	$67134+$3359 × (number of children − 1)	$73000 + $3000 × (number of children − 1)
Maximum rate payable for annual income below	$23800 + $624 × (number of children − 1)	$28200
Taper rate for minimum rate	'Sudden death'	
Taper rate for more-than-minimum rate	0.5	
Taper rate for both payments		0.3
Family Tax Payment Part A		
Rate per child per week	$3.85	
Payable to families receiving more than	minimum Family Allowance	
Family Tax Initiative Part A		
Tax-free threshold increases by	$1000 × number of dependent children	
For families with income less than	$70000+$3000 × (number of children −1)	

Table 8.13 continued

For single income families with children	Basic Parenting Allowance	Family Tax Assistance Part B
Maximum rate per week if youngest child is		
<16 years old	$33.10	
5-18 years old		$34.79
0-4 years old		$49.91
Maximum rate payable to second earners with weekly income of less than	$30.00	
Maximum rate payable to all sole parents or second earners with annual income of less than		$1616.00 ($31.08 pwk)
Taper rate	0.5 (up to $70) 0.7 (over $70)	0.3

Family Tax Payment Part B (with child under 5 years)	
Maximum rate per week per family with a 0-4 yr old	$9.62
Payable to all sole parents	
Payable to second earners with weekly income below	$87.90

Family Tax Assistance Part B (with child under 5 years)	
Tax-free threshold per year for family with a 0-4 yr old increases by	$2500
Payable when second earner's annual income less than $4573 and household income less than	$65000 + $3000 × (number of children − 1)

Guardian Allowance	
Maximum rate per week per family	$18.35
Payable to sole parents who get more than	minimum Family Allowance

Dependent Spouse Rebate (with children)	
Maximum rate per year	$1452
Maximum rate payable for spouse with children under 16 years and annual income below	$282
Taper rate	0.25

For single income families with children	
Sole Parent Rebate	
Maximum rate	$1243

Table 8.14 Weekly allowance rates

	January 2000 ($)	July 2000 ($)
Maximum rate single	163.35	172.45
Maximum rate sole parent/single 60 years or older	176.70	186.50
Maximum rate couple (per person)	147.35	155.50
Free area for income below	30.00	31.00
Taper rate of *0.5* for income below	70.00	
Taper rate of *0.5* for women on Parenting Allowance Partnered (with children under 16 years) with income below		121.50
Taper rate of *0.5* for all others for income below		72.00
Taper rate of *0.7* for income over	70.00	
Taper rate of *0.7* for women on Parenting Allowance Partnered (with children under 16 years) with income over		121.50
Taper rate of *0.7* for income over		72.00
Youth Allowance per week (for 16-20 yr olds and 16-24 yr old students)		
Maximum rate for		
16-17 yr olds (live at home)	74.00	76.95
18-20 yr olds (live at home)	88.95	92.50
16-20 yr olds (live away/student/couple)	135.15	140.55
16-20 yr old singles with children	177.05	184.15
16-20 yr old couples with children	148.40	154.35
Free area for income below (students)	115.00	118.00
Free area for income below	30.00	31.00
Taper rate of *0.5* for income below (students)	155.00	159.00
Taper rate of *0.5* for income below	70.00	71.00
Taper rate of *0.7* for income over (students)	155.00	159.00
Taper rate of *0.7* for income over	70.00	71.00

Table 8.15 Weekly pension rates and Parenting Payment Single rate

	January 2000	July 2000
Maximum rate single	$183.25	$193.45
Maximum rate couple (per person)	$152.95	$161.45
Free area for income below (singles)	$51.00+$12.00 × (nr of children)	$53.00+$12.30 × (nr of children)
Free area for income below (couples)	$90.00+$12.00 × (nr of children)	$94.00+$12.30 × (nr of children)
Taper rate of *0.5* for income over	Free area	Free area

9 Inflation and Bracket Creep

This chapter examines the extent of bracket creep since the Australian New Tax System (ANTS) package, and the distribution of effective marginal tax rates (EMTRs). In analysing bracket creep, four alternatives are considered. The first case relates to the actual system as it has developed since the ANTS package, and which is projected to continue forward without any further changes to the tax thresholds beyond the changes made in the 2003/04 budget. In the second case, the introduction of ANTS is accompanied by a systematic indexing of the tax thresholds at the start of each budget cycle by the Consumer Price Index (CPI) increase over the previous budget cycle. The third case is identical to the second, except that indexing is based on increases in average weekly earnings (AWE) rather than CPI. Finally, the fourth alternative has no indexing of thresholds, which are fixed at the 2000/01 levels.

After having outlined the various issues and different state of affairs for the four different indexing schemes in section 9.1, section 9.2 describes the average effective marginal tax rates for four hypothetical families in 2004. To explore alternative ways in which the government could hand back some of the bracket creep and increase work incentives, section 9.3 analyses various tax cut proposals that all have upfront costs that are roughly equal to the dollar amount of bracket creep due to increases in CPI. The alternative tax packages assume that the income tax base does not change when the income tax thresholds change.

9.1 Bracket Creep

9.1.1 The Amount of Bracket Creep

If the ANTS tax reform were to include a policy to index tax thresholds annually by the CPI, by 2005-06 the total personal income tax collected is expected to be $3.8 billion lower than if there were no further increases in the tax thresholds. This amount is calculated from the difference in total income tax under the two systems (a cost of roughly $4.3 billion) and is then adjusted for the difference in total rebates (a saving of roughly half a billion dollars). This $3.8 billion is the dollar amount of bracket creep, expressed in first quarter 2004 dollars, resulting from inflation, as measured by the CPI since 2000-01. The indexing of CPI uprates the thresholds at the start of the financial year with the CPI increase from June to June the previous year. The CPI is adjusted for the Goods and Services Tax (GST) effect based on the press release by the Treasurer (2000) on the Consumer Price Index for the September 2000 quarter. It reports that excluding the ANTS effects, the CPI annual increase was around 3.25 per cent (not corrected for oil prices, only for ANTS effects). Using the quarterly increases in CPI from September 1999 to June 2000, the missing September 2000 quarter increase that generates the 3.25 on an annual basis is calculated to be 0.9115 per cent. Based on this September 2000 quarter CPI increase, the uprating factors for the tax thresholds under the CPI indexing scheme are computed. Indexing with AWE involves uprating the thresholds at the start of the financial year using the increase in male average weekly earnings measured from August to August during the previous year.

The uprating is based on the forecasts for CPI and AWE growth, taken from the Commonwealth Treasury of Australia (2003a). Since only annual numbers are provided, forecast increase in CPI/AWE is assumed to be realised gradually during the year. For CPI the forecasts are 2.25; 2; 2.5; 2.5 for budget cycles 2003-04; 2004-05; 2005-06; 2006-07 respectively. For AWE these are 3.75; 3.5; 3.75; 3.75 for budget cycles 2003-04; 2004-05; 2005-06; 2006-07 respectively. Tables 9.1 and 9.2 give the uprating factors for the tax thresholds based on CPI and AWE respectively.

Table 9.1 Uprating factors based on the CPI

CPI increase from	Is used to uprate for budget cycle	The uprate factor is
Jun00 – Jun01	2001/02	1.031462
Jun01 – Jun02	2002/03	1.028273
Jun02 – Jun03	2003/04	1.027232
Jun03 – Jun04	2004/05	1.022585
Jun04 – Jun05	2005/06	1.020000

Table 9.2 Uprating factors based on average weekly earnings

Male AWE increase from	Is used to uprate for budget cycle	The uprating factor is
Aug00 – Aug01	2001/02	1.04132
Aug01 – Aug02	2002/03	1.04118
Aug02 – Aug03	2003/04	1.05525
Aug03 – Aug04	2004/05	1.03687
Aug04 – Aug05	2005/06	1.03562

9.1.2 The Tax Burden of Bracket Creep

The average income tax rate (AITR) for all Australians, computed as income tax net of rebates expressed as a percentage of gross income, is 15.9 per cent in 2005/06 if the 2003/04 income tax thresholds would not be changed and 15.1 per cent under a policy of yearly CPI indexing of the thresholds. This compares with 14.5 per cent when ANTS was introduced in 2000/01. This increase is largest in relative terms for those in the lowest income deciles, as shown in Table 9.3. A policy of CPI indexing will not keep the average income tax rate constant as wages generally grow faster than the CPI. This is not considered to be bracket creep.

Table 9.3 AITR by income decile with and without inflation adjustment

AITR in	1	2	3	4	5	6	7	8	9	10
					Income decile					
1999/2000	3.19	10.22	11.96	16.10	17.28	19.28	21.74	23.05	25.98	32.33
2000/2001	2.28	8.49	11.09	14.60	16.41	18.14	19.62	20.84	23.16	28.98
2003/2004	3.93	8.65	11.73	15.09	17.16	18.94	20.71	22.03	24.25	30.22
Under CPI indexing	3.23	8.20	11.26	14.71	16.86	18.65	20.18	21.49	23.81	29.71
2005/2006	4.81	8.78	12.81	15.84	17.68	19.85	21.81	23.01	25.13	31.16
Under CPI indexing	3.83	8.10	11.67	15.05	17.02	19.07	20.64	21.98	24.11	30.12

To read Table 9.3, consider someone in income decile 3. In 1999-2000, their average tax rate was 11.96 per cent. The ANTS reforms reduced the average income tax rate to 11.09 per cent; but there was also a net increase in indirect taxes paid. The effect of nominal wage increase, and including the tax rate schedule changes for 2003-04, was for the average tax rate to rise to 11.73 per cent. If brackets had been indexed by the CPI, the average tax rate would have risen to 11.26 per cent; with some increase because real wages rose. With no further changes to the tax schedule over the next two years, the average tax rate rises to 12.81 per cent in 2005-06, an increase of 1.72 percentage points or of 15.5 per cent. By contrast, someone in decile 8 experiences a rise in the average tax rate from 20.84 per cent in 2000-01 to 23.01 per cent in 2005-06, an increase of 2.17 percentage points but only a 10.45 per cent increase in real tax paid.

9.1.3 The Distribution of Individuals Across Tax Brackets

The distribution of people over tax brackets is shown in Table 9.4, for those who pay positive net taxes. When looking at the total Australian population paying positive taxes, the proportion of people in the highest tax bracket under the 2004 system is about 1.7 percentage points higher than it would have been under a system of CPI indexing - at 14.6 per cent and 12.9 per cent respectively. By 2005/06, this difference increases to 4.5 percentage points, with no further changes to the tax threshold beyond those in the 2003/04 budget.

Table 9.4 Per cent distribution of taxpayers by highest tax bracket reached

		Marginal income tax rate			
Budget cycle	0	0.2	0.34	0.43	0.47
1999/2000 (pre-ANTS)	-	28.0	40.1	14.6	17.3
(I) Actual	0	0.17	0.3	0.42	0.47
2000-01 (ANTS)	-	22.6	57.1	8.6	11.6
2003-04	-	22.1	54.1	9.2	14.6
2005-06	-	19.9	52.7	9.0	18.5
(III) Under CPI indexing of tax brackets	0	0.17	0.3	0.42	0.47
2000-01 (ANTS)	-	22.6	57.1	8.6	11.6
2003-04	-	21.9	56.1	9.1	12.9
2005-06	-	20.9	56.0	9.1	14.0

To put these numbers in perspective, between 2000/01 and 2003/04, about 336,000 people moved into the top two tax brackets as a result of bracket creep. Another 500,000 are expected to move up between 2003/04 and 2005/06 if tax thresholds remain at the level of the 2003/04 budget.

9.2   Average EMTRs for Realistic Employment Options

EMTRs can be misleading as they measure the rate applying to one extra dollar, which may not be the relevant unit. Therefore, Table 9.5 presents gross and net income at 0, 20 and 40 hours of work for four different types of families (defined in the first three rows), corresponding to non-work, part-time and full-time employment.

9.2.1   Heads of Households

The financial incentives of taking up employment are higher for sole parents than for families who depend on an allowance when out of work. In the case of part-time take-up, sole parents lose 37 per cent of their earned income in taxes and withdrawn benefits, versus an average of 68 per cent for heads of households in couples. Even a move from non-work to full-time work is more rewarding for sole parents, losing 51 per cent of their earnings compared with 69 per cent for low-wage, 67 per cent for average-wage and 61 per cent for high-wage earning heads in couples.

9.2.2   Spouses as Secondary Earners

The highest proportion of additional income is lost by second earners in low-wage families. This is because these families are eligible for various payments even if the head is working full time. As the second earner starts to earn a higher income these payments are withdrawn, causing a higher EMTR than would have been the case had they been partners of high-wage individuals. The difference is quite large, especially for a second earner taking up part-time employment. In the case of a low-wage family the second earner loses 65 per cent of the extra dollars earned in taxes and withdrawn benefits, compared with 39 per cent for an average wage and 32 per cent for a high-wage earning family. A low-wage secondary earner partnered to a low-wage primary earner also faces lower incentives to increase hours from part-time to full-time levels.

Table 9.5 Gross and net income per week for the hypothetical households at alternative hours of work

	Sole parent	Low wage couple	Medium wage couple	High wage couple
Number of children < 13	1	2	2	2
Hourly wage head ($ per hour)	11.8	11.8	24	48
Hourly wage partner ($ per hour)	-	11.8	18	27
Non-work family				
Gross family income ($ per week)	0	0	0	0
Net family income ($ per week)	422.34	548.17	548.17	548.17
Head works 20 hours per week				
Gross family income ($ per week)	236	236	480	960
Net family income ($ per week)	571.49	624.56	694.16	868.85
Share of extra income from work family loses when moving from non-work to a single part-time job (by the head)	37%	68%	70%	67%
Head works 40 hours per week				
Gross family income ($ per week)	472	472	960	1920
Net family income ($ per week)	653.93	692.48	868.85	1298.67
Share of extra income from work family loses when the head moves from a part-time to a full-time job	65%	71%	64%	55%
Share of extra income from work family loses when the head moves from non-work to a full-time job	51%	69%	67%	61%
Head works 40 hours per week and partner takes up a part-time job (20 hrs)				
Gross family income ($ per week)		708	1320	2460
Net family income ($ per week)		775.28	1089.23	1663.85
Share of extra income the family loses when the spouse takes up a part-time job		65%	39%	32%
Both head and spouse work 40 hours per week				
Gross family income ($ per week)		944	1680	3000
Net family income ($ per week)		885.92	1328.48	2016.33
Share of extra income the family loses when the spouse moves from a part-time to a full-time job		53%	34%	35%
Share of extra income the family loses when the spouse moves from non-work to full-time work		59%	36%	34%

9.3   Alternative Tax Reform Proposals

To assess various reform proposals aimed at addressing the low financial incentives to take-up employment or increase hours worked, several possible tax reforms are analysed.

9.3.1   Description of Alternative Tax Packages

To compare the various tax proposals, all tax reforms are compared with the alternative of holding the January 2004 income tax and social security system fixed. Each of the tax proposals is designed to have a cost of approximately \$3.8 billion when introduced in 2005/06; this is the dollar value of bracket creep in 2005/06 as established above.

Three tax reforms are analysed separately and have much smaller costs. Table 9.6 displays the tax thresholds and tax rates for each of the different reforms. Table 9.7 indicates if an earned income tax credit is introduced, if taper rates are reduced and if NewStart eligibility is restricted. Reforms involving a reduction in taper rates lower the rates from 40 to 30 per cent for sole parents and from 70 to 45 per cent for others. Potentially this could lead to a situation in which a person is working full time, yet remains eligible for some NewStart benefits. However, in principle, individuals in full-time work are not eligible for NewStart; therefore, similar reforms are examined where NewStart eligibility is restricted to those working fewer than 30 hours a week.

The Earned Income Tax Credit (EITC) is effectively a payment to low-income families. It is tapered in at around 5 cents to the dollar, starting at the first dollar being earned. The maximum EITC is \$30 per week. Each working partner is thus eligible for this EITC on his or her own merits. However, the EITC is tapered out based on family income using the same withdrawal scheme as for Family Tax Benefit Part A. First all Family Payments are tapered out at 30 per cent until the minimum level is reached, after which the withdrawal of the EITC starts. Under this proposal, the maximum tax credit any individual can obtain is \$30 a week, but a two-earner couple could get more than this.

Table 9.6 Tax thresholds and rates of alternative tax reform proposals

	Tax bracket				
	1	2	3	4	5
Reform I (January 2004 system)					
Upper tax threshold ($)	6000	21500	52000	62500	-
Tax rate (cents per dollar)	0	17c	30c	42c	47c
Reform II (CPI indexing)					
Upper tax threshold ($)	6818	22727	56819	68183	
Tax rate (cents per dollar)	0	17c	30c	42c	47c
Reform III					
Upper tax threshold ($)	6000	21500	52000	77500	-
Tax rate (cents per dollar)	0	17c	30c	40c	47c
Reform IV					
Upper tax threshold ($)	6000	21500	57000	68000	-
Tax rate (cents per dollar)	0	17c	30c	42c	47c
Reform V					
Upper tax threshold ($)	6000	21500	52000	77500	-
Tax rate (cents per dollar)	0	17c	30c	40c	47c
Reform VI					
Upper tax threshold ($)	6000	21500	57000	68000	-
Tax rate (cents per dollar)	0	17c	30c	42c	47c
Reform VII					
Upper tax threshold ($)	6000	21500	52000	77500	-
Tax rate (cents per dollar)	0	17c	30c	40c	47c
Reform VIII					
Upper tax threshold ($)	6000	21500	57000	68000	-
Tax rate (cents per dollar)	0	17c	30c	42c	47c
Reform IX					
Upper tax threshold	6000	21500	52000	62500	-
Tax rate (cents per dollar)	0	17c	30c	42c	47c
Reform X					
Upper tax threshold	6000	21500	52000	62500	-
Tax rate (cents per dollar)	0	17c	30c	42c	47c
Reform XI					
Upper tax threshold	6000	21500	52000	62500	-
Tax rate (cents per dollar)	0	17c	30c	42c	47c

Table 9.7 Details of the alternative tax reform proposals: tapers and eligibility

	EITC	Reduce tapers	Eligible for NewStart only if hours< 30
Reform I (January 2004 system)	No	No	No
Reform II (CPI indexing)	No	No	No
Reform III	Yes	No	No
Reform IV	Yes	No	No
Reform V	No	Yes	No
Reform VI	No	Yes	No
Reform VII	No	Yes	Yes
Reform VIII	No	Yes	Yes
Reform IX	Yes	No	No
Reform X	No	Yes	No
Reform XI	No	Yes	Yes

Table 9.8 displays the costs of each reform, with and without labour supply responses. The last column of Table 9.8 shows the number of extra workers for each of the tax reforms versus the January 2004 system.

Table 9.8 Costs of the alternative tax reform proposals

	Upfront costs ($b)	Costs after labour supply effects ($b)	Extra labour supply versus reform I (persons)
Reform I (January 2004 system)	base	base	base
Reform II (CPI indexing)	3.85	3.28	23979
Reform III	3.95	3.47	31224
Reform IV	4.01	3.53	33216
Reform V	3.66	3.75	1246
Reform VI	3.71	3.82	2975
Reform VII	3.35	3.48	924
Reform VIII	3.40	3.55	2214
Reform IX	2.33	2.14	28501
Reform X	1.38	1.54	3921
Reform XI	1.18	1.36	4039

9.3.2   Winners and Non-winners under the Tax Reforms

As every reform is in principle a tax cut, there are no losers under any of the reforms. The different tax reform proposals imply different distributions of winners and non-winners, which are presented in Table 9.9. Table 9.10 presents the average win, conditional on being a winner, which also varies greatly under the different tax reform proposals. The proposal with the most winners (78 per cent) is the straightforward indexing of the thresholds. However, the average gain is only $2.50 a week for those in the lowest family income decile, which increases to about $5 for those in the 5th family income decile, and is largest for the highest decile at $28 a week. The tax reforms involving the EITC have 55 per cent of families gaining, versus 44 per cent for reforms involving a reduction in taper rates. Compared with the indexing of all thresholds, some middle- to high-income families do not gain. What the EITC and reduction in taper rates have in common is that, compared with indexation of the thresholds, they take some of the gains for high-income families, in particular the top two family income deciles, and redistribute these to lower-income groups. The EITC tax reforms maintain a relatively even absolute average gain across income deciles, whereas the reforms involving a reduction of taper rates seem to favour the 2nd, 4th and 5th deciles.

Table 9.9 Percentage of winners under the various tax reforms

| | Tax reform | | | | | | |
Decile	II	III	IV	V	VI	VII	VIII
1	16	17	17	12	12	12	12
2	40	35	35	31	31	26	26
3	51	42	42	18	18	12	12
4	78	71	71	20	20	19	19
5	91	38	38	37	37	35	35
6	98	48	48	45	45	45	45
7	100	76	76	59	59	58	58
8	100	58	58	51	51	51	51
9	100	67	67	66	66	66	66
10	100	99	99	99	99	99	99
Total	78	55	55	44	44	43	43

Table 9.10 Average positive gain in after-tax family income in $ per week

Decile	\multicolumn{7}{c}{Tax reform}						
	II	III	IV	V	VI	VII	VIII
1	2.43	6.62	6.62	7.37	7.37	8.78	8.78
2	2.54	13.18	13.18	30.65	30.65	29.16	29.16
3	4.98	20.96	20.96	18.25	18.25	19.62	19.62
4	5.09	20.41	20.41	42.72	42.72	41.01	41.01
5	5.02	14.97	14.97	35.69	35.69	34.79	34.79
6	5.99	17.11	18.03	24.75	25.74	24.05	25.05
7	12.15	12.83	17.18	9.26	14.86	8.96	14.64
8	15.05	17.17	16.85	14.69	14.34	14.69	14.34
9	17.73	13.21	13.25	12.86	12.89	12.86	12.89
10	28.58	21.23	19.36	20.89	19.01	20.89	19.01

9.3.3 Labour Supply Effects of Alternative Reforms

The labour supply effects induced by the tax reforms imply different ex-post costs of the various tax reforms, although each reform proposal has approximately equal upfront costs (except for IX, X and XI). The most expensive tax reform package (IV), with an upfront cost of $4.01 billion, is one of the least expensive reforms after accounting for labour supply responses, with an expected ex-post cost of $3.53 billion. The reason is that this package, which combines indexing the top two thresholds by the CPI with the introduction of the EITC, triggers the largest labour supply response. The labour supply responses, expressed as an increase/decrease in the number of workers compared with the benchmark of tax reform I, show that almost 33,200 extra workers are expected to enter the market under this tax reform.

The tax reforms that include a reduction in the taper rates (reforms V-VIII), although generating extra labour supply, perform less well than a straightforward indexing of tax thresholds (tax reform II). Table 9.11 provides a breakdown of the labour supply effects by partnered men, partnered women, single men, single women and sole parents. It reveals for which group each tax reform has the largest impact. The EITC (reform IX) has relatively large positive aggregate effects for all groups except partnered women. In contrast, the tax reforms involving a reduction in taper rates have

large negative aggregate effects on partnered men and women, but unlike
the case of the EITC, these are only just offset by gains in labour supply for
singles and sole parents. The only tax reform that in aggregate increases the
labour supply of partnered women is the straightforward indexing of the tax
thresholds (tax reform II). This makes sense intuitively, as it is the only tax
reform under consideration that is purely based on individual income.

Table 9.11 Decomposition of the labour supply effects by group

Tax reform	Partnered men	Partnered women	Single men	Single women	Sole parents	Total net employment effect
I	Base	Base	Base	Base	Base	Base
II	5719	7919	3503	2360	4479	23979
III	4399	-7479	5838	7605	20861	31224
IV	4839	-6599	6130	7867	20979	33216
V	-8358	-10998	584	1573	18445	1246
VI	-7919	-10118	876	1573	18563	2975
VII	-7039	-12318	584	1311	18386	924
VIII	-7039	-11438	876	1311	18504	2214
IX	3079	-7919	5254	7343	20743	28501
X	-7479	-7479	0	787	18091	3921
XI	-6599	-7919	0	524	18032	4039

9.4   Conclusions

This chapter has identified the extent to which bracket creep, the extra
amount of tax collected as a result of inflation, has led to an increase in tax
revenue to the Commonwealth Government. According to the calculations,
by the end of 2005-06, bracket creep would have reached $3.8 billion. In
examining alternative policies, this chapter has explored ways to improve
the work incentives of low-income families. The tax credit proposal was the
most effective strategy for making employment, especially full-time
employment, a more attractive proposition for jobless households or
households with only a few hours of work. It is more cost effective than
increasing the tax-free threshold or reducing the taper rate on NewStart
payments. To compensate for bracket creep higher up the income
distribution, the top two tax thresholds were raised. This combination of a

tax credit for low income tax payers and increased tax thresholds for high income tax payers is expected to increase the net number of Australians moving into paid work by about 33,200. The increased tax revenue and reduced welfare benefits paid would reduce the cost to the government of about $4 billion by about $500 million, resulting in a net cost of about $3.5 billion.

In contrast, indexing the tax thresholds by the CPI would increase the movement into paid work by about 24,000. Under indexing, most of the tax revenue is returned to the top four deciles in the distribution of income. Introducing a tax credit and lifting the top two tax thresholds spreads the benefit more evenly across the income distribution so that the bottom half of the distribution gains more in proportion to their income.

10 The 2004 Federal Budget

This chapter examines the labour supply and distributional effects of the tax cuts and changes to family tax benefits announced in the 2004 Federal Budget. The government has emphasised the importance of policies to raise labour force participation and the work effort of Australians. This emphasis arises from the fact that about one in seven households of working age is jobless and one in seven children live in jobless households.

A first priority of the budget was to increase the top two thresholds of the income tax system, to reduce the marginal tax rates of an increasing number of middle to high income earners. The second priority was to lower the taper rates of family tax benefits, to reduce the effective marginal tax rates of low-wage earners in low-income families. Maximum and base rates of family benefits were also increased. The latter component of the reform is first analysed in section 10.1, before examining the effect of the total reform package and alternative packages in section 10.2.

The dataset used in this chapter is the 2000/01 Survey of Income and Housing Costs (SIHC). All amounts are expressed in 2004 dollars. Labour supply effects and costs are compared with the labour supply and costs associated with the tax and social security system that would have been in place without the announced changes.

10.1 Effects of Changes to Family Tax Benefits

In the 2004 budget, the maximum and the base rate of Family Tax Benefit Part A were increased by $600 per year per dependent child under 18 years of age. In addition, instead of being withdrawn at 30 per cent after the income threshold, families face a 20 per cent withdrawal rate between the maximum and the base rate. Family Tax Benefit Part B, which is targeted at sole parents and single-earner families, has an increased income threshold for the secondary earner in a family of $4000 per year instead of $1825. The withdrawal rate for income above this level was changed to 20 per cent

179

instead of 30 per cent. Sole parents' incomes remain untested for Family Tax Benefit Part B.

10.1.1 Distributional Effects

Table 10.1 provides details of the distributional effects of the Family Tax Benefit changes. The benefits go to about 21 per cent of Australian income units, loosely referred to as families. There are about 9.5 million income units.

Table 10.1 Percentage of winners and average amount gained in net weekly income-unit income from the Family Tax Benefit (Part A and B) changes only

Decile	% non-winners	% winners	average gain (if winner)
1	99.47	0.53	11.54
2	99.37	0.63	26.70
3	87.98	12.02	13.89
4	80.21	19.79	21.97
5	79.17	20.83	28.51
6	69.29	30.71	27.39
7	64.12	35.88	34.27
8	60.12	39.88	37.31
9	55.71	44.29	27.92
10	92.26	7.74	22.73
All	78.77	21.23	

The income deciles that are disproportionate winners from changes to the Family Tax Benefits are in the top half of the income distribution. This is because most families with children are in the fourth to the ninth highest deciles in the income distribution. There are few families with children in the bottom two deciles. These deciles tend to be dominated by singles without children, who do not receive Family Tax Benefits. However, significant winners start appearing from the third decile onwards. In the top 10 per cent, there are very few winners because most families' incomes in this decile would be too high to benefit from the increased Family Tax Benefit. The average value of the gain obtained from the increase in Family

Tax Benefits ranges from $11.54 per week for decile 1 to $37.31 per week for those in decile 8.

10.1.2 Labour Supply Responses

The net effect on labour supply of the changes to the Family Tax Benefits is negative, with around 19,000 people expected to move from work to non-work. The overall average effect on working hours is negative and small. Table 10.2 presents estimates of the effect of the changes to family benefits on labour force participation. First, the payment per child for Family Tax Benefit Part A was increased by $600. Second, the withdrawal rate of Family Tax Benefit Part A was reduced from 30 per cent to 20 per cent after the income threshold is reached. Third, Family Tax Benefit Part B has an increased income threshold before it is withdrawn and then it is to be withdrawn at 20 per cent instead of 30 per cent.

Table 10.2 The employment effects of the different packages (in persons)

| | Couples | | Singles | | | |
	Men	Women	Men	Women	Parents	Total
July 2004 absent any changes	Base	Base	Base	Base	Base	Base
FTB Part A $600+ only	-2200	-6159	0	0	-4066	-12425
FTB Part A reduced taper only	1760	-3519	0	0	2770	1010
FTB Part A change only	-440	-9678	0	0	-884	-11002
FTB Part B change only	-7479	-1320	0	0	0	-8798
FTB changes only	-7919	-10558	0	0	-884	-19360
Weighted sample (millions)	4.4	4.4	2.9	2.6	0.6	14.9

The effect of the increase in Family Tax Benefit Part A by $600 per child is estimated to reduce labour supply by about 12,400, with the largest reduction being expected for partnered women. For sole parents, this is largely offset by a positive labour supply effect from reducing the withdrawal rate of Family Tax Benefit Part A. The overall negative labour supply effect is caused to a large extent by the changes to Family Tax Benefit Part B and a large part of the negative effect is for married men.

The negative effect on married men's labour supply, resulting from the changes to Family Tax Benefit Part B, is explained by the extended eligibility for this payment by their partners while receiving Parenting

Payment. Before the change, a family receiving the full amount of Parenting Payment would not receive any Family Tax Benefit Part B if their youngest child was over 4 years old, because the Parenting Payment would be more than the threshold for Family Tax Benefit Part B. After the change, however, these families become partly eligible and will still receive around $1011 in Family Tax Benefit Part B. Similar families with children under 4 received around $729 before the change and will receive about $1894 after the change. This change is illustrated in Figure 10.1 for families with a youngest child between 5 and 18 years old.[1]

This means that across the range of incomes where the primary earner's income is not yet reducing the partner's Parenting Payment, net incomes will become more than $1000 higher after the change. This difference is larger for families with children (aged over 5 years) at the start of the income range where Parenting Payment is withdrawn. This has a negative income effect on labour supply. In addition, the lower taper rate has a negative effect on the primary earner's labour supply as well, through the indirect effect via Parenting Payments for at least part of the income range where Parenting Payments are withdrawn. Once their own benefit payment is completely withdrawn, additional income by the primary earner will impact on the Parenting Payment, reducing it by 70 cents for every dollar they earn (point A in Figures 10.1 and 10.2). This reduction in Parenting Payment in turn increases the Family Tax Benefit Part B, but only by 20 cents for every dollar in Parenting Payment lost instead of by 30 cents for every dollar as was the case before the change. As a result, the effective marginal tax rate of the primary earner increases after the change for part of the range of income that affects their partner's Parenting Payment. These changes are illustrated in Figure 10.2 for a family with a youngest child aged between 5 and 18.

Thus the effect of changes to Family Tax Benefit Part B is to reduce work incentives for some men. This is undoubtedly a case of 'unintended consequences', caused by the fact that the means test for Family Tax Benefit Part B includes income from the secondary worker's Parenting Payment, which in turn is affected by the income of the primary earner.

---

[1] This figure only shows the lower end of the primary earner's income range because that is where the change to the Family Tax Benefit Part B is relevant.

Under the new regime for example, for a couple with a child over 5, it will be possible to receive the full value of NewStart, Parenting Payment and Family Tax Benefit Part A, and a part payment of Family Tax Benefit Part B. Before the budget, such a family would not receive any Family Tax Benefit Part B because Parenting Payment was included in the means test for Family Tax Benefit Part B. The budget relaxed the means test, resulting in eligibility for a part payment. Thus, the family's income becomes higher out of work than it was before the changes, reducing the incentive for the male to work. However, this is not a large effect; of all partnered male workers only a tiny proportion is expected to move out of the labour force.

For secondary earners, there are two counteracting effects of the lower taper rate. First there is an income effect because more of the secondary earner's income can be retained, resulting in a negative effect on the secondary earner's labour supply. Second, there is a substitution effect which makes additional labour supply more attractive, especially at low part-time hours, due to the lower marginal tax rate on earnings. The income effect, which reduces labour supply, is found to outweigh the substitution effect, so there is also a small negative effect on female labour supply.

Figure 10.1 Family with a non-working secondary earner (youngest child aged 5-18)

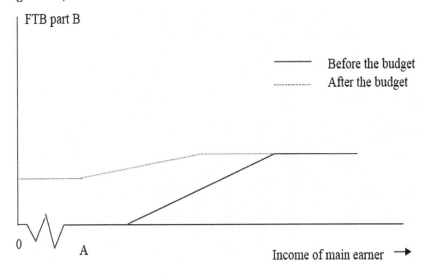

Figure 10.2 Family with a non-working secondary earner (youngest child aged 5-18)

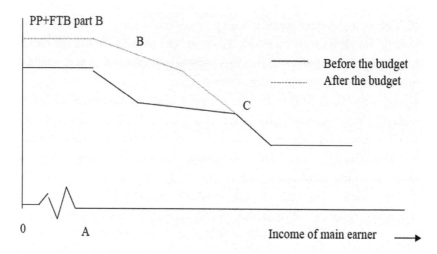

10.2 Effects of All Changes and Some Alternatives

In addition to the more generous Family Payments, the budget contained an increase in the two top tax thresholds in two stages. In 2004-05, the 42 per cent threshold was to be raised to $58,000 and the top threshold was to be raised to $70,000. In 2005-06, these two thresholds were to be raised to $63,000 and $80,000 respectively. The calculations in this section are based on the thresholds for the later year.

10.2.1 Distributional Effects

Tables 10.3 and 10.4 provide details of the distribution of the benefits resulting from raising the top two tax thresholds and the combination of the Family Tax Benefit and income tax changes. For the increase in the tax thresholds, the benefits occur at the top of the income distribution. The first six deciles do not benefit from the changes, as their income is not high enough to be affected.

When combining the gains from the income tax changes with the gains from the changes to the Family Tax Benefits, the majority of income units in the bottom half of the distribution do not receive any additional income, while most of those in the top half of the distribution benefit from the changes. The mean positive gain for the 95 per cent of income units in the top decile is $40 a week. The mean positive gain for the 21 per cent in the fifth decile is $28.50 a week. The mean gain for the 12 per cent of winners in the third decile is $14 a week. Barely anyone in the bottom two deciles, dominated by low-income singles without children or Age Pensioner couples, gains anything from the budget.

Table 10.3 Percentage of winners and average amount gained in net income unit weekly income from the income tax threshold changes alone

Decile	% Non-winners	% Winners	Average gain (if winner)
1 to 6	100.00	0.00	-
7	82.72	17.28	7.61
8	49.29	50.71	23.98
9	48.69	51.31	30.33
10	7.38	92.62	39.54
Total	78.80	21.20	

Table 10.4 Percentage of winners and average amount gained in net income unit weekly income from the Family Tax Benefit and income tax threshold changes

Decile	% Non-winners	% Winners	Average gain (if winner)
1	99.47	0.53	11.54
2	99.37	0.63	26.90
3	87.98	12.02	13.89
4	80.21	19.79	21.97
5	79.17	20.83	28.51
6	69.29	30.71	27.39
7	47.08	52.92	25.72
8	23.81	76.19	35.49
9	27.74	72.26	38.64
10	5.24	94.76	40.50
All	61.93	38.07	

10.2.2 Labour Supply Responses

The tax cuts established by raising the top two thresholds raise the work incentives slightly. However, the negative effect of the changes to the Family Tax Benefit scheme cancels the positive labour supply effect from the tax cuts, because of the income effect resulting from the increase in the family's net income due to the higher Family Tax Benefit payments. In aggregate, the resulting effect on labour supply is simulated to be a net loss of about 10,000 workers (see the first two rows of Table 10.6).

The work incentives could have been increased for all groups; in particular, the work incentives for all low-income families could have been addressed. Apart from work incentives being one of the policy directives, singles and couples without children missed out on benefits from the government's $6 billion outlay on the 2004 budget.

Table 10.5 shows the distribution of winners and the average amount of net gain over the 10 income deciles for the alternative policy of providing working tax credits of $30 per week. The type of working tax credits modelled here has been outlined in Buddelmeyer *et al.* (2004b) and is briefly described in section 9.3.1. It is clear that for this alternative policy the additional expenditure benefits a larger proportion of families than the policy in the budget.

Table 10.5 Percentage of winners and average amount gained in net income unit weekly income from the Working Tax Credit, Family Tax Benefit Part B and full tax changes

Decile	% Non-winners	% Winners	Average gain (if winner)
1	82.92	17.08	6.70
2	85.23	14.77	11.63
3	74.76	25.24	17.67
4	59.24	40.76	22.66
5	30.00	70.00	19.13
6	65.71	34.29	23.01
7	49.11	50.89	21.05
8	30.83	69.17	25.77
9	45.83	54.17	32.29
10	7.02	92.98	40.17
All	53.14	46.86	

In Table 10.6 the labour supply effects of this alternative are compared with the full policy and with components of the policy set out in the budget. Table 10.7 compares the costs of the different components of the budget initiatives with the costs of the alternatives. The cost of the alternative policy is similar to the cost of the policy presented in the 2004 budget. However, since the expected labour supply effects are positive at around 31,000 additional persons in the labour force, the expected cost after taking the effect of labour supply responses into account is lower for this alternative policy. Excluding the Family Tax Benefit Part B changes from the working tax credit package is expected to increase the labour supply effect of the working tax credit to about 36,500 additional labour force participants.

Table 10.6 The employment effects of the different packages (actual numbers)

	Couple		Single			
	Men	Women	Men	Women	Parents	Total
July 2004 absent any changes	Base	Base	Base	Base	Base	Base
Increase tax thresholds ONLY	3519	2200	1168	787	413	8086
FTB changes + maximum tax cut	-3519	-7919	1168	787	-471	-9955
Tax credit + FTB Part B change	-3519	-9238	6130	7867	20566	21805
Tax credit + FTB Part B change + maximum tax cut	880	-6599	7005	8654	20861	30801
Tax credit + maximum tax cut	6599	-6599	7005	8654	20861	36520
All budget changes + tax credit	1760	-14077	7881	8916	18916	23396
All budget changes + reduced tax credit	-880	-10998	4086	4458	10725	7392
Weighted sample (million)	4.4	4.4	2.9	2.6	0.6	14.9

Finally, both the $30 a week working tax credit and a reduced working tax credit of $15 a week were introduced as an addition to the budget. The labour supply effects remain positive for these two packages, with an additional 23400 and 7400 jobless persons expected to enter the labour market for the $30 and $15 tax credit respectively. In addition to the $6 billion for the 2004 budget proposal, the addition of a tax credit would cost an extra $3 billion or $1.3 billion before labour supply effects for the $30 and $15 tax credit respectively. The cost of the smaller working tax credit, measured after taking account of the positive labour supply effects, would be about $1.1 billion.

Table 10.7 Costs of the different packages ($ million)

	Before labour supply responses	After labour supply responses	Difference in cost
July 2004 absent any changes	Base	Base	Base
FTB Part A + $600 ONLY	1998	2331	333
FTB Part A reduced taper ONLY	436	370	-66
FTB Part A change ONLY	2434	2695	261
FTB Part B change ONLY	371	673	302
FTB changes only	2806	3363	557
Increase the tax thresholds ONLY	3198	2726	-472
FTB changes + maximum tax cut	6003	6034	30
Tax credit + FTB Part B change	2855	2934	79
Tax credit + FTB Part B change + maximum tax cut	6053	5618	-435
Tax credit + maximum tax cut	5681	5019	-662
All budget changes + tax credit	8987	8780	-206
All budget changes + reduced tax Credit	7326	7193	-133

10.3 Conclusions

The estimates presented in this chapter suggest that the Family Tax Benefit changes in the 2004 Federal Budget are expected to cause about 19,000 workers to withdraw from the labour market. In turn, this adds an extra $560 million to the cost of the package due to lower tax receipts and higher welfare payments. This effect is mitigated by a positive behavioural effect on tax revenues from raising the top two tax thresholds over the following two financial years.

At no extra cost, part of the Family Tax Benefit changes (only keeping the budget changes to Family Tax Benefit Part B) could have been replaced by a tax credit payment available to all households, structured to increase work incentives. Under this alternative policy, about 31,000 jobless people would have been expected to enter the labour market. If this group could move into jobs then that would reduce the net cost of the changes by $435 million due to higher tax receipts and lower welfare payments. Excluding the changes to Family Tax Benefits Part B as well, an additional 5500 persons are expected to enter the labour force, increasing the total number of jobless people to enter the labour market to 36500. This includes the positive labour supply effect of the tax cut. As a result of the lifting of the income tax thresholds alone, about 8000 people would be expected to move into jobs.

11 The Australian Labor Party's Tax and Family Benefits Package

This chapter analyses a package of policy changes proposed in 2004 by the Australian Labor Party. The Labor Party did not win the following election, so none of the plans were introduced.

The package is described in section 11.1 and the cost to government without allowing for any labour supply responses is presented in section 11.2. Section 11.3 provides estimates of the predicted effect of Labor's package on labour force participation and preferred hours of work. Using Australian and international evidence on a reasonable time path for the increased labour supply to be converted into realised employment, the effect of these behavioural changes on the government's budget over a four-year period is estimated in section 11.4. Section 11.5 concludes.

11.1 The Components of the Policy Package

There are four elements of the tax and Family Payments package analysed here. Details of the four components are outlined in the Labor Party's policy document *Labor's Tax and Better Family Payment Plan Rewarding Hard Work*; Australian Labor Party (2004).

First, Family Tax Benefit Part A and Family Tax Benefit Part B are to be consolidated into one Family Tax Benefit Payment. The new Family Payment no longer has a separate extra payment for single income families and single parents. Single parent and couple families are treated the same in the reform system. In the process, there are some changes to rates of payment and tapers, as outlined in the Australian Labor Party's report (2004). For example, the 'free area' for the consolidated payment (before it is withdrawn according to a family income means test), is to be increased to $50,000. This part of the package is referred to as *Family Tax Benefit Consolidation* (also known as 'Better Family Payment'). This component would have been introduced in financial year 2005-06.

191

Second, a single income family with one or more dependent children will be able to transfer the tax-free area of the partner to the income earner. This is a similar idea to the Dependent Spouse Rebate, as it applied in 2004 to couples without children. This part of the package is referred to as the *Single Income Tax Offset* (also known as the 'Tax Free Guarantee for Families'). The Single Income Tax Offset is also available to single parents, paid out through the tax system for single parent families with an income of over $50,000 or as an add-on to the new Family Payment for single parent families with an income of less than $50,000. This can be viewed as a form of compensation to single income families who no longer receive Family Tax Benefit Part B as the result of Family Tax Benefit Consolidation. This part of the package would also be introduced in financial year 2005-06.

Third, individual taxpayers with an income of less than $56,160[1] per year are to receive a tax cut which does not go to taxpayers with higher incomes. This is achieved by an extension of the low-income tax offset, so that a taxpayer with an income of between $7382 and $56160 receives a tax cut of the value of up to $8 per week. Taxpayers with an annual income below $8453 (this increased from $7382) no longer pay tax. This part of the package is called the *Low and Middle Income Tax Offset* (also known as the 'Working Tax Bonus'). It would also have been introduced in financial year 2005-06.

Fourth, the top income tax threshold is to be increased by $5000 to $85,000. This part of the package would have been introduced in financial year 2006-07.

11.2   Costs Before Behavioural Effects

On its own, the consolidation of Family Tax Benefit Part A and Part B represents a saving compared with the budget in 2005-06 of about $288 million. Thus, bearing in mind that the combined value of Family Tax Benefit Part A and Family Tax Benefit Part B is over $15 billion, this is close to a revenue-neutral change.

---

[1] Taxpayers on an income of over $52,000 will receive a reduced offset as they are still in the tapering-out range.

When the Single Income Tax Offset is added to the consolidation of Family Tax Benefits, the estimated cost in 2005-06, assuming no behavioural effects, is about $797 million. Thus, the net effect on the budget of the Single Income Tax Offset by itself is estimated to be about $1.1 billion.

When the Low and Middle Income Tax Offset is added to the package, this raises the estimated cost, without behavioural effects, to $3.093 billion. The addition of the increase in the top income tax threshold in 2006-07 raises the costs (in 2005-06 prices) to an estimated $3.254 billion.

Table 11.1 Estimated cost of policies before behavioural effects (negative numbers indicate a saving)

Policy	Estimate of annual cost of policies without behavioural response ($b) in 2005-06 prices
Family Package:	
FTB Consolidation	−0.288
Tax Package:	
FTB Consolidation plus Single Income Tax Offset	+0.797
FTB Consolidation plus Single Income Tax Offset plus Low and Middle Income Tax Offset	+3.093
FTB Consolidation plus Single Income Tax Offset plus Low and Middle Income Tax Offset, plus an increase in the top income tax threshold (to be implemented in 2006-07)	+3.254

11.3 Labour Supply Effects

This section discusses anticipated and simulated labour supply effects by the separate components of the policy package. In addition, it presents the effect on the government's budget of the package allowing for the expected labour supply changes.

11.3.1 Anticipated Labour Supply Effects by Each Component

Family Tax Benefit Consolidation

The main effect of Family Tax Benefit Consolidation is expected to be an increase in the labour supply of partnered women and single parents. This is because the policy involves the removal of that part of Family Tax Benefits that is designed for single income families. The removal of Family Tax Benefit Part B is expected to reduce the incentive to be a single earner family and thus increase the incentive to be a dual earner family. This mostly affects the labour supply of partnered women who do not already participate in the labour market, and a small number of partnered men who do not already participate but whose spouses do. This change also affects single parents, as they no longer have access to the non-means-tested Family Tax Benefit Part B. However, changes to payment and withdrawal rates, which occur at the same time, also affect the incentive to work for some 'primary earner' males and females.

Single Income Tax Offset

The Single Income Tax Offset would increase the rewards to single earner couples relative to dual earner couples and to non-earner single parents relative to single parents in employment. Therefore, the increase in partnered women's labour supply from Family Tax Benefit Consolidation is likely to be at least partially reversed by the Single Income Tax Offset.

Low and Middle Income Tax Offset

The Low and Middle Income Tax Offset has the effect of increasing the reward to work for those individuals who receive the tax rebate involved. This has income and substitution effects. The substitution effect causes people to be more inclined to participate in the labour market and to work more hours (due to the relative increase in the price of non-working time versus the price of other consumption goods). The income effect causes some people to take advantage of the higher income at a lower level of labour supply by reducing their labour supply. Empirical evidence suggests that especially for those with relatively low earnings, the group targeted by the offset, the substitution effect tends to outweigh the income effect. Thus, an increase in labour supply is likely.

Increasing the Top Tax Threshold

The increase in the top tax threshold has both income and substitution effects, which could raise or lower labour force participation and hours of work. The analysis, in chapter 10, of the 2004 Federal Budget, which raised the top two income tax thresholds, suggests that the positive substitution effect on labour supply dominates. Given the usually lower wage elasticity of high-income earners, the labour supply responses to the increase in the top tax threshold are likely to be relatively modest.

11.3.2 Simulated Effects on Labour Supply

Table 11.2 presents the expected effects of the package on labour supply behaviour, at unchanged real wages.[2] The labour supply effect of the Family Tax Benefit Consolidation is primarily to increase the labour supply of partnered females, involving about 29000 additional participants. A substantial positive effect is also found for single parents (about 7000 additional labour force participants, increasing their participation rate from about 61.6 per cent to about 62.7 per cent) and a smaller effect for partnered males. The overall estimated effect of the Family Tax Benefit Consolidation is an increase of about 37000 labour force participants, raising the participation rate of all those aged 15 and over from 63.5 per cent to just over 63.7 per cent.

The Single Income Tax Offset partially reverses the positive effect, on the labour supply of partnered women, of the Family Tax Benefit Consolidation, while having a small positive effect on partnered males' labour supply. There is also a small negative effect on single parents' labour supply. Adding the Single Income Tax Offset is found to reduce labour supply by about 19000 persons. However, this negative effect is not as large as the negative effect Family Tax Benefit Part B has on labour supply. As a result, the overall increase in labour force participation, combining the Single Income Tax Offset and the Family Tax Benefit consolidation, is from

---

[2] The individual weights used in MITTS are uprated to reflect the total population in 2005/06. This is achieved by multiplying the person weights in the underlying data from the 2000/01 Survey of Income and Housing Costs (SIHC) with a growth rate that is gender and age specific. The resulting weights should reflect the population in 2005/06. The growth rates are based on the population projections provided by the Australian Bureau of Statistics (ABS) (2003a) by gender and age.

about 63.5 per cent to just under 63.6 per cent, an increase of about 17500 persons.

Table 11.2 Estimated effect of policies on labour force participation (persons, % point changes in parentheses)

	Partnered males	Partnered females	Single males	Single females	Single parents
Participation rate for everyone over 15 before Labor's policy changes(%)[a]	72.83	56.61	69.17	53.56	61.56
New policy					
Family Benefits package:					
FTB Consolidation (A)	+958	+28739	0	0	+7036
	(+0.02)	(+0.60)			(+1.14)
Adding tax package:					
A plus Single Income Tax Offset (B)	+1437	+12454	0	0	+3641
	(+0.03)	(+0.26)			(+0.59)
B plus Low and Middle Income Tax Offset (C)	+5748	+21554	+3423	+2829	+10060
	(+0.12)	(+0.45)	(+0.11)	(+0.10)	(+1.63)
C plus increase in top income tax threshold	+6227	+21554	+3423	+2829	+10183
	(+0.13)	(+0.45)	(+0.11)	(+0.10)	(+1.65)

Note a) It is assumed unemployment and employment rates remain as they were in 2001, when the data were observed, before adding the predicted changes in labour supply.

Consistent with expectations, adding the Low and Middle Income Tax Offset has a positive labour supply effect for every category. The largest percentage changes are for single parents, but small positive effects are found for the other groups. Thus the overall estimated effect on labour force participation, of those elements of the package to be introduced in the first year, is to raise it from about 63.5 per cent to just under 63.8 per cent, an increase of about 43500 persons.

Finally, the increase in the top income tax threshold has a small positive labour supply effect for partnered males, increasing the estimated total labour force participation effect by a few hundred persons.

The final two columns of Table 11.3 show, respectively, the potential change in the number of jobless families if all the increased labour supply were converted into employment and the estimated effect on average desired hours of work.

Table 11.3 Estimated effect of policies on the number of jobless families and hours of work

	Total participation effect (in persons)	Potential change in the number of jobless families/income units [a]	Change in average desired hours of work (hours) [b]
	Rate of all	Jobless families:	Average
Totals before Labor's	over 15	1671948	hours:
policy changes [c]	63.48%	(20.82%)	28.8
New policy			
Family Benefits package:			
	+36733	-10426	
FTB Consolidation (A)	(+0.23)	(-0.13)	+0.14
Adding tax package:			
A plus Single Income	+17532	-9347	
Tax Offset (B)	(+0.11)	(-0.12)	+0.05
B plus Low and Middle	+43614	-25364	
Income Tax Offset (C)	(+0.27)	(-0.32)	+0.15
C plus increase in top	+44216	-25787	
income tax threshold	(+0.27)	(-0.32)	+0.16

Notes a) The number of jobless income units is calculated for the working-age population alone excluding full-time students.

b) Average hours are calculated only for those who are allowed to change their labour supply in MITTS (this excludes the self-employed for whom no hours of work are recorded in the data, full-time students, disabled individuals and people over 65).

c) It is assumed unemployment and employment rates remain as they were in 2001, when the data were observed, before adding the predicted changes in labour supply.

Regarding jobless families, if all the labour supply increase were converted into employment, the number of jobless families would be reduced by about 26,000, a one third of a percentage point decrease in the incidence of jobless families. The term 'family' includes singles or couples with or without children. This decrease is mainly caused by the increased incentive to move from welfare to work arising from the Low and Middle Income Tax Offset, which is found to increase single parents' labour supply in particular. However, in addition to single parents' increased labour supply, a significant number of jobless singles and partnered males and females in jobless families are expected to want to move into work after the policy changes are introduced. Finally, the desired average hours of work increase from 28.8 to 29.0 (also included in this calculation are those who desire zero hours of work).

11.3.3 Effects on the Government Budget

Table 11.4 presents estimates of the potential impact on the annual cost of
the policy changes caused by these behavioural changes, if all the estimated
increase in labour supply were converted into employment. The budget
savings due to the Family Tax Benefit Consolidation have the potential to
be increased by an estimated additional $335 million due to the behavioural
response. However, adding the Single Income Tax Offset, the total cost of
these two parts of the package is only reduced from about $797 million to
about $694 million, if all the modelled labour supply effects were converted
into employment, thus reducing the overall behavioural savings to an
estimated $103 million only.

Table 11.4 Estimates of full potential feedback effects on the budget

	Estimate of annual cost of policies ($b) in 2005-06 prices		
Policy	Without behavioural response	If full labour supply response were realised	Potential saving (in $b)
Family Benefits package:			
FTB Consolidation	−0.288	−0.623	+0.335
Adding the tax package:			
FTB Consolidation plus Single Income Tax Offset	+0.797	+0.694	+0.103
FTB Consolidation plus Single Income Tax Offset plus Low and Middle Income Tax Offset	+3.093	+2.723	+0.370
FTB Consolidation plus Single Income Tax Offset plus Low and Middle Income Tax Offset, plus an increase in the top tax threshold	+3.254	+2.833	+0.421

Adding the Low and Middle Income Tax Offset produces an estimated
package of about $3.093 billion (without behavioural effects), but a net cost
of about $2.723 billion if all the labour supply effects were converted into

employment and hours of work. The addition of raising the top income tax threshold adds slightly to the estimated potential behavioural savings, adding up to an amount of $421 million in total potential behavioural savings. Overall, if the full behavioural response is translated into an increase in employment and hours of work, the gross cost of the total package could be reduced by about 12.9 per cent.

11.4 The Time Path of Adjustment

To give an indication of the likely adjustment path following the proposed reforms, this section uses evidence from two sources. First, the budget savings from behavioural responses, reported in the supporting budget papers on the *Australians Working Together* package of reforms, were spread over the four years of the programme.[3] Second, evidence is used on the patterns of adjustment which have actually been observed following a substantial policy reform in the United Kingdom, the introduction of the Working Families' Tax Credit (WFTC) in October 1999. This evidence is then used to set out a time path of adjustment for the effects discussed in this chapter.

11.4.1 Previous Evidence on Time Paths of Adjustment

Turning to the budget measures announced in the 2001-02 *Australians Working Together* package, the budget papers (*Statement I: Fiscal Strategy and Budget Priorities, Table 3*) report that a total of $923.6 million of savings on the gross budget cost of $1.695 billion are claimed over a four-year period from 2001-02 to 2004-05. This is equivalent to a saving of 54 per cent on the initial gross cost. These savings are further divided into $587 million from behavioural responses to the policy measures over four years (which equates to 35 per cent of gross costs, or 63 per cent of total savings), and $304 million in savings from identification of incorrect payments (equivalent to 18 per cent of gross costs, or 33 per cent of total savings).

From answers to Parliamentary questions on the breakdown of total budget savings from the *Australians Working Together* package, the savings of $449.8 million accruing from reform to Parenting Payment are claimed to

---

[3] See http://www.budget.gov.au/2001-02/sitemap.htm for the budget papers.

be 'largely attributable to increased activity as a result of the Parents' Measure (approximately $270 million) and an increase in reported earnings as a result of the Working Credit (approximately $180 million)'.[4] The supporting budget documentation provides little explanation of the methods used to calculate these behavioural savings, or the estimates of their breakdown over the four-year budget period. These savings are reported to be distributed over a four-year budget period as in Table 11.5.[5]

Table 11.5 Annual behavioural savings from 2001-02 Parenting Payment reform

Budget period	2001-02	2002-03	2003-04	2004-05	Total
Annual behavioural savings	0.0	55.5	183.0	211.3	449.8
As a percentage of total savings:	0%	12%	41%	47%	

In addition, UK administrative data are available tracking the changes in costs and caseload following the introduction in October 1999 of the WFTC, which replaced the system of Family Credit.

Figures 11.1 and 11.2 below show how costs and caseloads for WFTC increased over the three years after its introduction. Costs increased as a substantial number of individuals entered employment. Simultaneous with the increase in WFTC cost, there were savings in other programmes (such as reductions in Income Support and unemployment payments, increases in income tax and National Insurance receipts).

The time profile of changes in WFTC costs and in caseload are shown in Figure 11.2. The caseload for WFTC increased by around 450,000 over three years, with around one half of the total caseload increase occurring by the end of year 1, one third in the second year, and one sixth in the third year. Much of this increase comes from families who were already employed before the change becoming entitled to in-work support under the more generous rules of entitlement to WFTC.[6] However, estimates from the

---

[4] See Question No. 53a, b, c and d, Hansard page CA314, and the answer.

[5] These changes were only implemented in July 2002, so presumably this was already taken into account when these numbers were released, which is why there are no savings in 2001-02.

[6] These increases will be front-loaded into the first half of the three-year period captured by the administrative data.

Figure 11.1 Total cost of Family Credit/Working Families' Tax Credit (July 2001 prices)

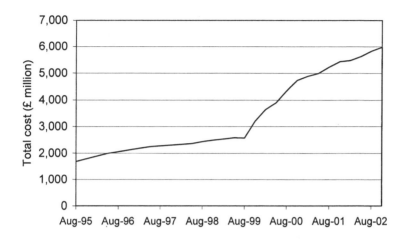

Figure 11.2 Caseload for Family Credit/Working Families' Tax Credit

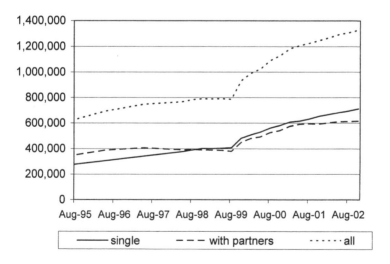

evaluation studies of the WFTC reform suggest that as many as 100,000 new recipients are labour market entrants, encouraged into work by the generosity of the WFTC reform. These are distributed more evenly over the three years following the introduction of the new tax credit, given lags in labour market adjustment. A reasonable estimate is for 20 per cent of total behavioural savings to have been secured by the end of year 1, an additional 40 per cent by end of year 2, an extra 35 per cent by the end of year 3, and the remaining additional 5 per cent still to be achieved.

11.4.2 Projected Savings From Policy Reform

Displacement effects and labour market inertia, fixed and search costs of employment, and difficulties in job matching might reduce the eventual employment effects of policy reform. On the positive side, wage progression for those attracted into employment, and further shifts in demand for labour following an increase in labour supply, might increase employment effects. For these reasons, high and low estimates are added to the central projection of the budget savings from estimated behavioural responses. The central estimates allow for 85 per cent of the behavioural savings to be translated into actual budget savings. The high estimates allow for 95 per cent of those savings to translate into actual savings, and further allows for wage progression in years 3 and 4 to inflate the savings by an additional 10 per cent. The low estimates factor labour market inertia and displacement effects into the behavioural projections, by suggesting a 65 per cent conversion of behavioural responses into actual savings. All projections are based on 20 per cent of the resulting total behavioural savings being secured by the end of year 1, an additional 40 per cent by end of year 2, an extra 35 per cent by the end of year 3, and the remaining additional 5 per cent still to be achieved.

The simulated potential saving of $421 million predicted by MITTS, from the introduction of the Labor package, can be divided into realised behavioural savings over a four-year period. Of the potential $421 million annual savings, the central estimate is that 85 per cent, or $358 million, would be saved after four years.

Table 11.6 Projected incremental behavioural savings ($m) and additional employment (persons) from total package

	Year 1	Year 2	Year 3	Year 4	Total
High-end:					
Savings	80	160	180	20	440
Employment	8401	16802	14702	2100	42005
Central:					
Savings	72	143	125	18	358
Employment	7517	15033	13154	1879	37584
Low-end:					
Savings	55	109	96	14	274
Employment	5748	11496	10059	1437	28740

Notes: a) The first year only includes savings from the first three components of the policy. The increase in the top tax threshold is only included from the second year onwards.
b) In the high-end projection of the behavioural savings, we allow for a 10 per cent increase in savings due to wage progression in the third and fourth year of the projection.

Table 11.6 shows these savings and the changes in employment on an incremental basis. Thus, the central estimate of the total annual savings to the budget due to the labour supply effect is $358 million after four years, which is 11 per cent of the non-behavioural annual cost of the package.

11.5 Conclusions

The estimates presented in this chapter show that all components of the Labor Party's tax package, except the Single Income Tax Offset, are expected to have a positive effect on labour supply and are expected to reduce the total number of jobless families. The Single Income Tax Offset encourages married women with children to withdraw from the labour market and transfer their free income tax area to their partners. This offset also makes nonparticipation more attractive for single parents, by an increase in net income for non-workers. The increase in the top income tax threshold only has a very small effect. The FTB Consolidation and the Low and Middle Income Tax Offset, which both target low- to middle-income households, have the largest effects.

After accounting for the labour supply effects, allowing for 85 per cent of the labour supply increase to be translated into actual changes in employment, the initial cost of about $3.3 billion is reduced by about $358 million or about 11 per cent.

12 Policy Reforms in New Zealand

This chapter presents the simulated labour supply, revenue and expenditure effects of recent policy changes in New Zealand.

From April 2005 to 2007-08, a range of proposed policy changes is to be implemented. The policy changes concerned the 2005 reforms of Family Assistance and the Accommodation Supplement (AS), in addition to proposed (then) future reforms as they were to be implemented between 2005 and 2008. The changes to the supplement are smaller than those to the Family Payments, and as a result, families with children are expected to be most affected by the changes. The chapter compares the labour supply responses resulting from going from the tax and social security system as it was in 2001 to the full reform in 2008. The recent development of TaxMod-B, a behavioural microsimulation model produced for the New Zealand Treasury by the Melbourne Institute of Applied Economic and Social Research, to be used alongside the already existing arithmetic model developed by the New Zealand Treasury, TaxMod-A, has made such an analysis possible.

Section 12.1 describes the policy changes analysed in this chapter. Section 12.2 briefly describes the behavioural microsimulation approach used in TaxMod-B. Sections 12.3 and 12.4 present a variety of simulation results for the different demographic groups.

12.1 The Policy Changes

This section briefly describes the policy changes that are simulated in this chapter. More details can be found in Kalb, Cai and Tuckwell (2005).

12.1.1 Family Assistance

The new policy was designed with the aim of encouraging benefit recipients into work and to address income adequacy issues for families with children. Benefit rates were changed so that families with children are paid the same rate of benefit regardless of the number of children. So couples with children receive the same amount of benefits as couples without children, and sole parents with more than one child receive the same amount as sole parents with two or more children. For example, couples with one child receive $280.96 per week in net unemployment benefits instead of the earlier $290.72 (couples without children experience an increase from $273.58 to $280.96). Sole parents with two or more children have experienced a decrease from $256.52 per week to $241.47 in Domestic Purposes Benefits. Sole parents with just one child had an increase in benefit from $235.12 to $241.47. This benefit cut is offset by an increase to Family Support, which is available to all beneficiaries with children, subject to an income test. An increase of $25 per week for the first child and $15 for the second and subsequent children more than compensates for the loss in benefit income. A further increase is planned in 2007 of $10 per child per week.

In addition, Family Assistance provided through the tax system consists of several components. First, the Child Tax Credit has been changed quite dramatically; it used to be $15 per week per child conditional on the family receiving no income-tested benefit. Under the new regime, there is an additional hours test, where couples must work at least 30 hours per week (combined) and sole parents must work at least 20 hours per week. The newly introduced hours test means that disposable income makes a discrete jump at those hours under the new system, providing an incentive to work at least at that level of labour supply. In addition, the rate has increased to $60 per week plus $15 per week extra for each child past the third. That is, $60 per week for one, two or three children, $75 per week for four children, $90 per week for five children etc. Note that it is not $60 per week per child for the first three. The payments are a hybrid between a flat rate and rates per child. As a result, families with one or two children are likely to gain the most from this change.

More families are eligible for the Parenting Tax Credit because this payment is linked to Family Support and Child Tax Credit receipt. With the increased rates and abatement thresholds for Family Support, more families have become eligible for the Parenting Tax Credit.

Finally, the Family Tax Credit is increased in 2006 to ensure that the take-home pay for a working family at least matches that for a working and abated benefit family. The Family Tax Credit guarantees the level of post-tax income from a wage/salary job, subject to an hours test, and is available only to families with dependent children.[1]

12.1.2 Accommodation Supplement

The amount of AS for which families are eligible is based on the amount of rent paid, region of residency and work status (working families are expected to spend 30 per cent of their net income on rent, compared with only 25 per cent for beneficiary families). The supplement is calculated as the minimum of the maximum supplement available and $0.7 \times$ (rent-fraction $\times$ benefit). The maximum supplement depends on the family type. Rent is the actual rent paid, and fraction $\times$ benefit is the 'reasonable rent' based on the sort of benefit for which the family would be eligible, with fraction = 0.30 for mortgage holders and fraction = 0.25 for renters. Maximum rates under the new system vary from $45 per week for a single person in a low-rent region to $225 per week for a family of three persons or more in the new very high rent region. Before the change, the lowest maximum rate was also $45 per week for a single person, but the highest maximum rate was only $150 per week. In addition to these maximum rate increases, the income thresholds at which the AS starts to be withdrawn (at a rate of 25 per cent) have increased as well by in between about $34 and $100 per week.

The policy reform involved an increase in the maxima of AS payable and an increase in the number of AS regions from three to four, introducing a new 'very high-rent region' in Auckland (Central and North Auckland), a subset of the previous high-rent region. In addition, some other locations move into a higher rent region. Unfortunately, the people living in this sub-region cannot be identified in the data on which the microsimulation modelling is based.[2] Therefore, it is assumed that rents will be high enough

---

[1] The full policy also includes some changes to early-childhood education which are not modelled in the New Zealand Treasury arithmetic model, TaxMod-A. In addition, more financial assistance is available for families who need to use childcare to enable them to participate in the labour force. Given the lack of information on hours and cost of childcare use in the data used in TaxMod-A, these changes are not analysed in the simulation presented in this chapter.

[2] The AS cannot be modelled accurately because the necessary regional information is not available. As a result, the arithmetic model, TaxMod-A, underpredicts the number of families who receive the supplement by about 60 per cent.

to be affected by the new maxima only if they both live in the very high rent area and lived in the earlier high rent area. In other words, the old region definitions are used with the top three new regions, to increase the maxima as appropriate. The increased maxima only increase payments for people who were previously receiving the maximum amounts.

12.1.3 Effects of the Policy Change

From the description in sections 12.1.1 and 12.1.2, it is clear that families with one child benefit most from the changes. Their benefit rate is not reduced and they receive $60 per week in Child Tax Credit instead of the previous $15 per week if the family fulfils the newly introduced hours test. Families with two children receive a lower benefit and, instead of a $45 increase in weekly Child Tax Credit, they receive a $30 increase from the previous level of $30 per week. Families with three or more children also receive a lower benefit and they receive only a $15 increase in Child Tax Credit from the previous levels. As a result, the gain from working the minimum amount required to pass the hours test is largest for families with one child.

Considering the new hours test, the potential for increased labour supply appears larger for sole parents than for couple families. The 2001 participation rate of sole parents is just below 50 per cent. A large increase in net income at the 20-hours level may induce nonparticipating sole parents into the labour market. The hours requirement of 30 hours for couple families is likely to have little impact given the participation rate of married men, which is already very high.[3] In addition, labour supply is usually at the full-time level of at least 40 hours. This means that providing higher net incomes at 30 hours may induce a reduction in labour supply of one or both partners. This is also true for some sole parents, who are already in the labour force. However, this negative effect is expected to be more than compensated by additional sole parents entering the labour force.

The effects of changes to the AS are more complicated. Increasing the maximum rates means more people are eligible, and withdrawal rates may

[3] In the sample containing observations in 2001, about 91 per cent of all married men in couple families with dependent children are already in the labour force, with around 87 per cent of all these men working at least 30 hours per week. Examining the combined labour supply of these families, only 8 per cent would not reach 30 hours per week.

start at a higher level of private income and continue up to a higher level before the complete supplement has been withdrawn. The changes in withdrawal rates result in an increase in effective marginal tax rates for some and a reduction for others. The additional income provides an incentive for people to reduce labour supply, particularly if withdrawal rates have increased the effective marginal tax rates. The effect on labour supply for those who are facing reduced effective marginal tax rates is ambiguous.

12.2 TaxMod-B

This section briefly describes the components of TaxMod-B.[4]

12.2.1 The Base Datasets

The microsimulation analyses can be based on the Household Economic Surveys (HES) 1991-92 to 2000-01, all released by Statistics New Zealand (NZSTATS). The arithmetic simulations in TaxMod-A are based on the same datasets. These surveys were released on a yearly basis from 1991/92 to 1997/98, but were subsequently undertaken only once every three years. The survey collects information on the sources and amounts of income received by persons resident in private dwellings throughout New Zealand, along with data on a range of characteristics for all individuals within the household. Individuals in each household are linked by a household number and family number, so that household characteristics such as income and the number and age of children can be derived by using information from other records in the same household.

12.2.2 Estimation of Labour Supply

The detailed information on income in the HES allows the budget constraint to keep its full complexity. In order to combine several years of data into input for one model, the monetary variables from the different years are converted to the December 2001 levels.[5] Furthermore, the observed nominal wages in these survey years are adjusted by the average wage increases for men or women as relevant.

---

[4] Buddelmeyer, Cai and Kalb (2005) provide a more extensive description of the programmes.
[5] For this, the quarterly Consumer Price Index as published by Statistics New Zealand is used.

The labour supply model is the same as that used in the MITTS model: estimation is described in Kalb and Scutella (2003), based on data from 1991 to 2001. However, the parameters on which the present behavioural responses is based were re-estimated using only the four most recent years of data, to avoid the extrapolation of time trends and ensure the behavioural response reflects the latest patterns of behaviour.[6]

12.2.3 The Link with TaxMod-A

The input for TaxMod-B is based on the HES datasets, but these need to be run through TaxMod-A, which calculates net incomes at a range of discrete labour supply levels before and after the reform. The details, along with a range of individual and household characteristics, are passed to TaxMod-B, which contains only the labour supply parameters on which the behavioural responses are based.

12.2.4 The Behavioural Simulation

In principle, the calibration should be carried out using the social security and tax system at the time of the survey that is used as the base dataset.[7] If a simulation of the effect of changes from a later year are required (with a different system in place), the preferred approach is to carry out two simulation runs. One to determine the effects of going from the social security and tax system in place at the time of the survey to the system of the later year and another to determine the effects of going from the social security and tax system in place at the time of the survey to the desired post-reform system. In both simulations, the base system is the one in place at the time of the survey. The difference in the change between the two simulations can be used to determine the effect of a change in the social security and tax system in the later year. Here, the HES 2000-01 is used as the base dataset. Incomes and wages have been inflated to 2008, the year in which the reform analysed will be fully implemented. Thus, the simulation compares the labour supply responses resulting from going from the tax and social security system in 2001 to the full reform in 2008.

---

[6] These alternative labour supply parameters can be found in Kalb, Cai and Tuckwell (2005). The effects of individuals' characteristics remain similar to those estimated in the earlier paper.

[7] For a description of calibration, see chapter 1.

Labour supply is held constant for the self-employed (383 cases), people over 65 years of age (677 cases), full-time students and disabled individuals (together 270 cases). This leaves 2177 out of the 3507 families in the HES sample for whom the effects of the policy reform on labour supply are simulated. That is, about 62 per cent of the total population or 77 per cent of the working-age population are allowed to change labour supply in the simulation.

12.3 Simulation Results Using TaxMod-A

Although there are some differences in the calculations as they are carried out in TaxMod-A compared with TaxMod-B, the results without labour supply responses as calculated in TaxMod-B are expected to be reasonably close to the results from TaxMod-A. Table 12.1 presents the predicted amounts of income from different sources and the amount of income tax paid before and after the policy change. In TaxMod-B, it is assumed that everyone who is eligible for benefits takes them up, whereas in TaxMod-A, information on actual take-up is used. This different approach is required to enable the calculation of labour supply responses. TaxMod-B also uses discrete hours levels rather than the actual hours used by TaxMod-A. As a result, the amounts are not exactly the same.

Table 12.2 gives an overview of the number of families gaining or losing from the reform by income unit type and benefit receipt. In addition, the average change in income is presented by the same categories. From the table, it can be seen that those with two or more children gain most on average. All families on benefit gain from the reform except for a few families receiving unemployment benefits. However, most of the families losing from this reform are those who receive no government payments at all. Table 12.2 only includes the Family Assistance changes. Therefore, families without children are not affected.

Table 12.1 Changes in tax and transfer costs (in million dollars)

	Base 0708	Future directions 0708	Change
Couple			
No. of families (1000s)	847	847	0
Private income	61908	61908	0
Benefits	803	767	-36
Family Payment	419	1161	742
NZ Superannuation	3204	3204	0
Rebate	222	221	-1
Tax	17245	17238	-7
Single men			
No. of families (1000s)	404	404	0
Private income	11836	11836	0
Benefits	651	651	0
Family Payment	0	0	0
NZ Superannuation	724	724	0
Rebate	69	69	0
Tax	3271	3271	0
Single women			
No. of families (1000s)	407	407	0
Private income	7602	7602	0
Benefits	752	752	0
Family Payment	0	0	0
NZ Superannuation	2167	2167	0
Rebate	90	90	0
Tax	2200	2200	0
Sole parents			
No. of families (1000s)	113	113	0
Private income	1661	1661	0
Benefits	1151	1057	-94
Family Payment	371	760	389
NZ Superannuation	5	5	0
Rebate	26	27	1
Tax	599	581	-18

Table 12.1 (continued)

	Base 0708	Future directions 0708	Change
All			
No. of families (1000s)	1771	1771	0
Private income	83007	83007	0
Benefits	3357	3225	-132
Family Payment	790	1921	1131
NZ Superannuation	6100	6100	0
Rebate	407	408	1
Tax	23315	23289	-26

12.4 Simulation Results Using TaxMod-B

This section presents the behavioural results from the policy changes described in section 12.1, including labour supply responses, the effect on the government's expenditure and revenue, and the distributional effects.

12.4.1 Labour Supply Responses

Summary labour supply responses are presented in Table 12.3 for the different demographic groups. The largest responses are for single parents. Nearly 2 per cent of single parents enter the labour force, with few sole parents wanting to leave the labour force. The number of sole parents who would like to increase their weekly working hours is smaller than the number who would like to decrease their hours. The overall effect is to increase average working hours by 0.63 hours per week. Single parents are the only group for whom a positive labour supply effect is expected. Small negative effects are found for the other four groups, with slightly larger groups leaving the labour force than entering and slightly larger groups reducing the number of hours worked.

The small negative effect for singles is not surprising because they are only affected by the change in the AS and a small change in the benefit level, which is not directly related to the individual's hours of work.[8]

---

8 Although the observed responses are fairly accurate, given the underestimation of the number of families taking up this supplement, the expectation is that there would be about 2.5 times more people responding in that manner in the full sample.

Table 12.2 Winners and losers from the policy change by income unit type and benefit receipt

Number of families per cell	Gainers	No change	Losers	Overall
Single, no children	0	1221704	0	1221704
Single, one child	71408	2765	0	74173
Single, two+ children	82272	812	0	83084
Couple, no children	0	468481	0	468481
Couple, one child	35106	68215	1542	104863
Couple, two+ children	103448	110831	1969	216248
Overall	292234	1872808	3511	2168553
Mean change in disposable annual income				
Single, no children	0	0	0	0
Single, one child	2217.43	0	0	2134.77
Single, two+ children	3271.59	0	0	3239.62
Couple, no children	0	0	0	0
Couple, one child	2549.74	0	-268.65	849.65
Couple, two+ children	4758.5	0	-140.43	2275.08
Overall	3453.64	0	-196.74	465.09
Benefit receipt (number of families per cell)				
Unemployment	23219	124701	399	148319
Domestic Purposes Benefit (DPB)	104934	6945	0	111879
Invalids' Benefit	6156	83955	0	90111
Sickness Benefit	8859	44029	0	52888
Widows' Benefit	509	7852	0	8361
NZ Superannuation	1644	389217	0	390861
None of the above	146913	1216109	3112	1366134
Overall	292234	1872808	3511	2168553
Mean change in disposable annual income				
Unemployment	2968.7	0	-184.12	464.25
DPB	2472.14	0	0	2318.68
Invalids' Benefit	2926.51	0	0	199.93
Sickness Benefit	2031.3	0	0	340.25
Widows' Benefit	2152.68	0	0	131.05
NZ Superannuation	6280.82	0	0	26.42
None of the above	4312.06	0	-198.36	463.26
Overall	3453.64	0	-196.74	465.09

Table 12.3 Simulated behavioural labour supply responses

	Married		Single		
	Men	Women	Men	Women	Parents
All workers (% before reform)	77.20	61.43	62.35	45.86	49.58
Salaried workers (% before reform)	62.21	53.24	54.94	43.75	45.70
Salaried workers (% after reform)	61.84	52.61	54.92	43.79	47.47
Behavioural response					
Non-work to work (%-points)	0.14	0.11	0.05	0.07	1.84
Work to non-work (%-points)	0.50	0.74	0.07	0.03	0.07
Workers working more (%-points)	0.07	0.06	0.00	0.00	1.93
Workers working less (%-points)	0.43	0.19	0.05	0.10	2.41
Average hours change (in hours)	-0.22	-0.23	-0.03	-0.02	0.63

The increase in the maximum rate means that for a small group of people their benefit income increases, thus slightly reducing the incentive to work. For example, of the group of single men who worked 35 hours per week before the change, 0.2 per cent no longer work after the change. These small changes are shown by the transition matrices of labour supply before and after the reform, in Tables 12.4 and 12.5.

The increase in work incentives for single parents is due to the 20-hour work requirement and the requirement not to be in receipt of income-tested benefits. At this hours level, income increases by at least $60 per week, making it more attractive to work at least 20 hours or more (depending on the level at which eligibility for benefits cuts out). This incentive is also reflected in the transition matrix presented in Table 12.6. Due to the extra income when working at least 20 hours, some sole parents may want to reduce their labour supply, but relatively few would reduce their labour supply below 20 hours. Increases in labour supply are mostly to 20 hours or more.

The results for married men and women are a combination of the change in family-related payments and the AS. The requirement for the household to work at least 30 hours per week does not have the same incentive effect as the 20-hours requirement for sole parents. This is explained by the fact that more than 50 per cent of all single parents are out of the labour force, whereas looking at married men with children alone, most in this group

Table 12.4 Single men's labour supply transitions (hours per week, row percentages)

	Post-reform											
Pre-reform	0	5	10	15	20	25	30	35	40	45	50	% of Pop.
0	99.9	0.0	0.0	0.0	0.0	0.0	0.0	0.0	0.0	0.0	-	45.1
5	-	100	-	-	-	-	-	-	-	-	-	1.1
10	-	-	100	-	-	-	-	-	-	-	-	1.2
15	-	-	-	100	-	-	-	-	-	-	-	2.4
20	-	-	-	-	100	-	-	-	-	-	-	1.0
25	-	-	-	-	-	100	-	-	-	-	-	2.0
30	0.1	-	-	-	-	-	99.9	-	-	-	-	1.2
35	0.2	-	-	0.0	-	-	-	99.7	-	-	-	2.5
40	0.1	-	-	-	0.0	-	0.0	-	99.9	-	-	19.0
45	0.1	-	0.0	-	0.0	0.0	0.0	-	-	99.8	-	6.8
50	0.2	0.0	0.0	0.0	-	0.0	0.0	0.0	0.0	0.1	99.6	17.7
% of Pop.	45.1	1.1	1.2	2.4	1.0	2.1	1.2	2.5	19.0	6.8	17.6	100.0

Table 12.5 Single women's labour supply transitions (hours per week, row percentages)

	Post-reform											
Pre-reform	0	5	10	15	20	25	30	35	40	45	50	% of Pop.
0	99.9	0.0	0.0	0.0	0.0	0.0	0.0	0.0	0.0	-	-	56.2
5	-	100	-	-	-	-	-	-	-	-	-	1.3
10	-	-	100	-	-	-	-	-	-	-	-	4.4
15	-	-	-	100	-	-	-	-	-	-	-	2.8
20	-	-	-	-	100	-	-	-	-	-	-	1.2
25	0.2	-	-	-	-	99.8	-	-	-	-	-	1.7
30	-	0.0	-	0.0	0.1	-	99.9	-	-	-	-	3.1
35	0.2	-	0.1	-	0.1	0.2	-	99.4	-	-	-	2.1
40	0.1	0.0	0.0	0.0	0.0	0.1	0.0	0.0	99.7	-	-	15.3
45	0.0	-	0.0	0.1	0.1	0.2	0.1	0.0	-	99.4	-	5.4
50	0.1	-	0.0	0.0	0.1	0.1	0.1	0.0	0.0	-	99.6	6.4
% of Pop.	56.2	1.3	4.4	2.8	1.3	1.8	3.1	2.1	15.2	5.4	6.4	100.0

Table 12.6 Single parents' labour supply transitions (row percentages)

	Post-reform											% of Pop.
Pre-reform	0	5	10	15	20	25	30	35	40	45	50	
0	96.6	0.3	0.3	0.1	0.4	0.3	0.4	0.4	0.6	0.4	0.2	54.3
5	-	99.2	-	-	-	-	-	-	-	0.8	-	0.5
10	-	-	88.8	0.5	0.6	0.5	0.9	1.2	3.5	2.4	1.5	7.9
15	-	-	-	88.5	0.2	0.1	0.5	2.2	2.8	3.3	2.4	4.2
20	-	-	-	-	92.8	0.1	0.4	0.7	2.9	1.3	1.8	3.2
25	-	-	-	-	0.2	95.8	-	0.5	1.8	1.0	0.8	1.9
30	-	-	-	-	0.2	0.0	93.0	1.7	2.2	1.7	1.2	3.8
35	-	-	-	-	0.2	0.2	0.5	99.2	-	-	-	2.2
40	0.0	0.0	0.0	-	0.4	1.5	2.4	1.7	93.9	-	-	13.1
45	0.1	0.1	-	-	-	0.4	0.8	2.3	2.1	94.1	-	1.8
50	0.9	0.5	0.4	0.3	1.2	2.0	5.2	4.7	4.1	2.3	78.5	7.1
% of Pop.	52.5	0.6	7.2	3.9	3.4	2.3	4.6	3.3	13.6	2.6	6.1	100.0

would already be in full-time employment. Instead, the income effect of the policy change may induce a tiny proportion of married men to reduce labour supply. Similarly, this change is unlikely to have a positive effect on married women's labour supply, given that the income effect is often dominant for married women.[9] In addition, the withdrawing of benefits as more income is earned continues up to a higher level. The transition matrices in Tables 12.7 and 12.8 are consistent with the above explanation, with a larger proportion of men reducing their labour supply to 30 or 40 hours. This is only partially counteracted by a small group of men entering the labour force. For married women, the most popular change is to reduce labour supply to zero. Exiting the labour force is much more common than entering the labour force or increasing labour supply.

The expected changes in the probability of working can be tabulated against individual and household characteristics. Table 12.9 presents these changes for the head of the income unit by income unit type, gender of the head of the household, number of children, age of the youngest child and by

---

[9] See for example, Hoynes (1996), Blundell and Hoynes (2004) and Blundell *et al.* (2000).

Table 12.7 Married men's labour supply transitions (hours per week, row percentages)

Pre-reform:	Post-reform						% of Pop.
	0	10	20	30	40	50	
0	99.6	0.0	0.0	0.1	0.2	0.1	37.8
10	0.0	99.8	-	0.1	-	0.0	1.5
20	0.2	-	99.0	0.1	0.4	0.3	1.8
30	0.1	-	0.0	99.6	0.2	0.0	2.7
40	0.8	-	0.1	0.3	98.7	0.2	31.1
50	1.0	0.0	0.1	0.5	0.7	97.8	25.2
% of Pop.	38.2	1.5	1.8	2.9	30.9	24.7	100.0

Table 12.8 Married women's labour supply transitions (hours per week, row percentages)

Pre-reform	Post-reform											% of Pop.
	0	5	10	15	20	25	30	35	40	45	50	
0	99.8	0.0	0.0	0.0	0.0	0.0	0.0	0.0	0.0	0.0	0.0	46.8
5	1.6	98.0	0.0	0.1	0.0	0.1	0.1	-	0.1	0.0	-	2.7
10	1.1	0.0	98.5	0.0	0.1	0.0	0.1	0.1	0.0	-	0.0	3.1
15	1.8	0.1	0.1	97.8	0.1	0.0	0.0	0.0	0.0	0.0	0.1	3.2
20	1.2	0.0	0.1	0.1	98.4	0.1	0.0	0.0	0.1	0.0	0.0	5.6
25	2.4	0.2	0.1	0.1	0.1	97.1	0.0	0.0	-	0.0	0.0	4.4
30	1.7	0.1	0.1	0.0	0.1	0.0	97.8	-	0.0	0.0	-	5.3
35	1.6	0.2	0.2	0.1	0.0	0.2	0.0	97.5	0.1	-	-	3.8
40	1.3	0.1	0.0	0.1	0.1	0.1	0.0	0.0	98.3	0.0	0.0	14.7
45	0.8	0.1	0.1	0.0	0.1	0.0	0.1	0.0	-	98.8	-	3.3
50	1.0	0.1	0.1	0.1	0.0	0.1	0.0	0.0	0.0	0.0	98.5	7.3
% of Pop.	47.4	2.7	3.1	3.2	5.6	4.3	5.2	3.7	14.4	3.3	7.2	100.0

region of residency. The table shows no change for a large proportion of the population. The largest category of change comprises those who experience a 2- to 10-percentage point decrease in the probability of working, followed by those experiencing a 2- to 50-percentage-point increase. Consistent with the previous results, single parents have the highest average increase in their probability, although the increases are mostly small. The gender of the head reflects single parenting, given that all couple households have the male assigned as the head. As expected, given the structure of the policy change, which provides an equal amount of Child Tax Credit for one child as for two or three children (resulting in a larger increase in this participation-dependent payment for families with one child), the increase in the probability of working is largest for one-child families. The decrease in the probability of working is largest for families with three or five children. There are few families with five or more children in the sample, so the results for this group should be treated with care. Smaller families receive the largest increase in Child Tax Credit comparing the pre-reform amount with the post-reform amount. For couple families, the expected effects are all negative, independent of the number of children, but the decrease is still largest for families with three and five children. The presence of younger children seems to increase the positive effect on labour supply, although the pattern is not very strong. There appears to be no clear pattern with regard to the region in which the income unit lives. Table 12.10 presents the expected changes in average working hours by the same characteristics as Table 12.9. The results are similar to those in Table 12.9.

Tables 12.11 and 12.12 present results on probability of labour force participation and hours of work for the spouse of the income unit by income unit type and age and number of children, which are similar to Tables 12.9 and 12.10. As expected, spouses in families without dependent children are less affected by the policy changes compared with spouses in families with dependent children. The change in the probability of working is larger for women than for men in income units with dependent children. All effects by the number of children are negative for spouses, but a similar pattern as for heads emerges, with the effect being smallest negative for women with one child only. The largest negative effects are expected for women with three-to five year olds, but otherwise no pattern is visible. The change in working hours in Table 12.12 displays similar patterns.

Table 12.9 Percentage point change in probability of income unit head working by individual and household characteristics (row percentages)

	Decrease				Increase			Avg	Count
	>50	10-50	2-10	None	2-10	10-50	>50		(×1000)
Income unit type									
Couple	-	-	3	97	-	-	-	-0.12	448.32
...With dependants	-	1	21	75	3	1	-	-0.64	398.54
Single	-	-	1	98	1	0	-	0.01	799.66
...With dependants	-	-	1	82	13	4	0	1.77	121.88
Gender of head									
Female	-	-	1	94	4	1	0	0.46	508.52
Male	-	0	8	90	1	0	-	-0.25	1259.88
Number of dependants									
None	-	-	2	98	1	0	-	-0.03	1247.97
One	-	0	8	81	8	2	0	0.67	202.87
Two	-	-	21	74	4	2	-	-0.35	199.35
Three	-	2	27	68	2	0	-	-1.13	84.88
Four	-	-	9	86	5	-	-	-0.31	25.27
Five	-	-	21	62	18	-	-	-0.45	5.52
Six	-	-	-	100	-	-	-	-0.23	2.53
Age of youngest child									
No dependants	-	-	2	98	1	0	-	-0.03	1247.97
<1 year	-	1	13	76	6	4	1	0.78	56.18
1 year	-	-	18	77	3	2	-	0.31	48.95
2 years	-	-	12	80	5	3	-	0.39	45.42
3 years	-	-	18	79	3	-	-	-0.65	32.24
4 years	-	3	15	75	6	1	-	-0.58	32.79
5 years	-	2	23	70	4	2	-	-0.38	26.28
6 to 9 years	-	-	19	73	7	1	-	-0.28	101.74
10 to 12 years	-	0	19	71	8	1	-	-0.07	68.37
13 to 15 years	-	-	19	75	5	1	-	-0.52	59.80
16 to 18 years	-	-	5	91	4	-	-	-0.08	48.64
Region of residency									
Auckland	-	0	5	91	3	0	-	-0.07	553.22
Canterbury	-	-	6	92	2	0	-	-0.15	231.51
Central North	-	-	5	94	1	-	-	-0.18	225.32
North North-Island	-	-	7	91	2	0	-	-0.14	352.17
South Island	-	0	7	89	2	2	0	0.55	192.95
Wellington	-	0	7	90	3	0	-	-0.13	213.22
Total	-	0.12	5.93	91.27	2.19	0.46	0.02	-0.05	-
Count (×1000)	-	2.21	104.9	1614.05	38.69	8.20	0.33	-	1768.40

Table 12.10 Absolute change in weekly working hours of income unit head by individual and household characteristics (row percentages)

	Decrease in hours				Increase in hours			Avg	Count
	>10	5-10	1-5	None	1-5	5-10	>10		(×1000)
Income unit type									
Couple	-	-	2	98	-	-	-	-0.06	448.32
…With dependants	0	1	18	77	3	0	0	-0.41	398.54
Single	-	-	1	98	0	-	-	-0.02	799.66
With dependants	-	2	6	72	14	2	3	0.63	121.88
Gender of head									
Female	-	0	2	93	4	0	1	0.16	508.52
Male	0	0	7	91	1	0	0	-0.17	1259.88
Number of dependants									
None	-	-	1	98	0	-	-	-0.03	1247.97
One	-	2	9	79	9	1	1	0.14	202.87
Two	-	0	19	74	5	1	1	-0.18	199.35
Three	1	2	25	70	2	-	0	-0.79	84.88
Four	-	1	6	93	-	-	-	-0.26	25.27
Five	-	4	32	64	-	-	-	-0.77	5.52
Six	-	-	-	100	-	-	-	-0.13	2.53
Age of youngest child									
No dependants	-	-	1	98	0	-	-	-0.03	1247.97
<1 year	-	1	15	76	4	1	2	0.11	56.18
1 year	-	-	13	81	4	-	2	0.07	48.95
2 years	-	1	14	78	3	3	-	-0.13	45.42
3 years	-	1	18	79	3	-	-	-0.49	32.24
4 years	-	3	14	79	4	-	1	-0.40	32.79
5 years	2	-	28	65	2	1	2	-0.44	26.28
6 to 9 years	-	0	16	74	9	0	-	-0.15	101.74
10 to 12 years	-	2	16	72	6	2	2	-0.04	68.37
13 to 15 years	-	3	18	70	9	-	-	-0.40	59.80
16 to 18 years	-	-	8	91	2	-	-	-0.13	48.64
Region of residency									
Auckland	0	1	5	92	2	0	-	-0.11	553.22
Canterbury	-	0	5	91	3	-	-	-0.07	231.51
Central North	-	0	4	94	2	0	-	-0.08	225.32
North North-Island	-	0	7	92	1	0	-	-0.12	352.17
South Island	-	0	6	90	1	1	2	0.15	192.95
Wellington	-	0	6	91	2	0	0	-0.08	213.22
Total	0.03	0.33	5.60	91.75	1.81	0.25	0.23	-0.07	-
Count (×1000)	0.51	5.91	99.07	1622.52	32.03	4.36	4.00	-	1768.40

Table 12.11 Percentage point change in the probability of working for the spouse of the income unit by individual and household characteristics (row percentages)

	Decrease				Increase			Avg	Count
	>50	10-50	2-10	None	2-10	10-50	>50		(×1000)
Income unit type									
Couple	-	-	2	98	0	-	-	-0.07	448.32
…With dependants	-	5	17	73	5	-	-	-1.28	398.54
Number of dependants									
None	-	-	2	98	0	-	-	-0.07	448.32
One	-	2	16	78	4	-	-	-0.74	135.24
Two	-	4	19	72	5	-	-	-1.22	163.78
Three	-	12	20	63	6	-	-	-2.41	72.03
Four	-	5	5	86	4	-	-	-0.89	21.50
Five	-	23	6	70	-	-	-	-4.18	3.84
Six	-	-	-	100	-	-	-	0.34	2.16
Age of youngest child									
No dependants	-	-	2	98	0	-	-	-0.07	448.32
<1 year	-	7	15	72	6	-	-	-1.46	45.82
1 year	-	5	18	72	5	-	-	-1.13	39.03
2 years	-	5	16	75	3	-	-	-1.22	35.88
3 years	-	16	15	64	5	-	-	-3.02	21.80
4 years	-	9	15	72	4	-	-	-1.98	25.58
5 years	-	9	21	67	3	-	-	-2.60	21.16
6 to9 years	-	5	16	71	8	-	-	-1.01	79.17
10 to 12 years	-	0	24	71	5	-	-	-0.81	50.64
13 to 15 years	-	2	23	72	3	-	-	-1.15	45.14
16 to 18 years	-	-	5	95	-	-	-	-0.27	34.33
Total	-	2.35	8.96	86.36	2.33	-	-	-0.64	-
Count (×1000)	-	19.87	75.87	731.35	19.77	-	-	-	846.86

Table 12.12 Absolute change in weekly working hours for the spouse in the income unit by individual and household characteristics (row percentages)

	Decrease in hours			None	Increase in hours		Avg	Count
	>10	5-10	1-5		1-5	5-10		(×1000)
Income unit type								
Couple	-	-	1	99	-	-	-0.04	448.32
…With dependants	0	2	12	85	1	-	-0.45	398.54
Number of dependants								
None	-	-	1	99	-	-	-0.04	448.32
One	-	2	9	87	2	-	-0.27	135.24
Two	-	2	12	86	1	-	-0.42	163.78
Three	1	5	16	77	2	-	-0.83	72.03
Four	-	1	9	90	-	-	-0.37	21.50
Five	-	-	30	70	-	-	-1.18	3.84
Six	-	-	-	100	-	-	0.04	2.16
Age of youngest child								
No dependants	-	-	1	99	-	-	-0.04	448.32
<1 year	-	2	13	85	-	-	-0.45	45.82
1 year	-	4	12	84	-	-	-0.38	39.03
2 years	-	2	10	86	2	-	-0.46	35.88
3 years	-	10	12	79	-	-	-0.94	21.80
4 years	1	5	10	84	-	-	-0.77	25.58
5 years	-	4	18	76	2	-	-0.87	21.16
6 to 9 years	0	1	11	85	2	-	-0.37	79.17
10 to 12 years	-	-	13	83	3	-	-0.27	50.64
13 to 15 years	-	1	17	81	1	-	-0.50	45.14
16 to 18 years	-	-	2	98	-	-	-0.07	34.33
Total	0.07	1.05	6.08	92.26	0.55	-	-0.23	-
Count (×1000)	0.56	8.91	51.45	781.3	4.64	-	-	846.86

12.4.2 The Effect on the Government's Budget

The labour supply responses affect changes in government expenditures and revenues. Table 12.13 shows expenditure and revenue changes with and without accounting for labour supply responses. After allowing for labour supply changes, the cost of the policy change increases for all groups except single parents, because labour supply decreases slightly for all groups. The decrease in the cost for sole parents after allowing for the increased effort in the labour market is modest. This is partly due to the increase in Family Payments as single parents choose optimal labour supply levels and partly due to the decrease in tax revenue. Tax revenue decreases because the single parents on higher incomes are likely to reduce labour supply while remaining eligible for the increased Family Payment whereas those increasing labour supply or entering the labour force are likely to be on low wages.[10] As a result, the reduction in taxes paid by the former group is not completely compensated by the increase in taxes paid by the latter group, even though the aggregate labour supply effect is positive. However, the reduction in benefit income is larger than the increase in Family Payments when accounting for labour supply responses. This results in a reduction in government expenditure, which more than compensates for the reduction in taxes paid.

---

[10] Table 12.6 shows that it is mostly women working 40 hours or more before the reform who are expected to reduce their labour supply, whereas it is women working 30 hours or less who are expected to increase labour supply. The women working 40 or more hours would be on higher incomes than the other groups not working or working low hours. In addition, given progressive taxes, an increase from 20 to 30 hours is expected to result in a lower average increase in tax revenue than an increase from 30 to 40 hours, even at the same hourly wage.

Table 12.13 The effect of labour supply responses: changes in tax and transfer cost

	Pre-reform ($m)	Allowing for labour supply responses		Keeping labour supply fixed	
		Abs. change ($m)	Rel. change (%)	Abs. change ($m)	Rel. change (%)
Couple					
Market/private income	59534.6	-421.6	-0.7	0.0	0.0
Government expenditure					
Benefit income	1029.2	36.4	3.5	-9.3	-0.9
Rebate	225.3	-2.1	-0.9	-2.8	-1.3
Family Payment	335.4	644.1	192.1	593.2	176.9
NZ Superannuation	3190.5	0.0	0.0	0.0	0.0
Total expenditure	4780.4	678.4	14.2	581.1	12.2
Government revenue					
Income tax paid	16338.3	-104.0	-0.6	-4.0	0.0
Total revenue	16338.3	-104.0	-0.6	-4.0	0.0
Net expenditure	-11557.9	782.3	-6.8	585.0	-5.1
Single men					
Market/private income	11510.8	-10.5	-0.1	0.0	0.0
Government expenditure					
Benefit income	852.7	14.4	1.7	11.9	1.4
Rebate	75.9	0.1	0.1	0.0	0.0
Family Payment	0.0	0.0	0.0	0.0	0.0
NZ Superannuation	723.6	0.0	0.0	0.0	0.0
Total expenditure	1652.1	14.5	0.9	11.9	0.7
Government revenue					
Income tax paid	3179.5	-1.8	-0.1	0.5	0.0
Total revenue	3179.5	-1.8	-0.1	0.5	0.0
Net expenditure	-1527.4	16.3	-1.1	11.4	-0.7

Actual and Proposed Reforms

Table 12.13 Continued

	Pre-reform ($m)	Allowing for labour supply responses		Keeping labour supply fixed	
		Abs. change ($m)	Rel. change (%)	Abs. change ($m)	Rel. change (%)
Single women					
Market/private income	7567.9	-8.0	-0.1	0.0	0.0
Government expenditure					
Benefit income	975.2	16.9	1.7	15.5	1.6
Rebate	92.0	0.1	0.1	0.0	0.0
Family payment	0.0	0.0	0.0	0.0	0.0
NZ Superannuation	2166.8	0.0	0.0	0.0	0.0
Total expenditure	3234.0	17.0	0.5	15.5	0.5
Government revenue					
Income tax paid	2210.6	-1.7	-0.1	0.1	0.0
Total revenue	2210.6	-1.7	-0.1	0.1	0.0
Net expenditure	1023.4	18.7	1.8	15.4	1.5
Sole parents					
Market/private income	1859.0	29.2	1.6	0.0	0.0
Government expenditure					
Benefit income	1347.0	-85.0	-6.3	-42.7	-3.2
Rebate	27.6	0.5	1.7	0.8	2.9
Family Payment	343.0	383.9	111.9	366.4	106.8
NZ Superannuation	5.5	0.0	0.0	0.0	0.0
Total expenditure	1723.0	299.4	17.4	324.5	18.8
Government revenue					
Income tax paid	664.4	-18.7	-2.8	-10.9	-1.6
Total revenue	664.4	-18.7	-2.8	-10.9	-1.6
Net expenditure	1058.6	318.1	30.0	335.4	31.7

12.4.3 Poverty and Inequality after the Reforms

Finally, the effect on poverty and inequality can be examined using TaxMod-B. The effect on the Lorenz curve is minimal, indicating that the effect of the policy reforms on inequality in the New Zealand population is minimal. Figure 12.1 shows the TIP curve, which reflects three characteristics of poverty (the 'Three "I"s of Poverty') - its incidence, intensity and inequality. Around 12.5 per cent of all income units fall below the poverty line after the reform, compared with 13.7 per cent before the reform. The poverty line is set at 50 per cent of the median equivalised income-unit income, which is $204.79 before the reform and $205.70 after the reform.[11] The incidence can be measured by reading the value on the horizontal axis at the points where the curves turn into horizontal lines. From a comparison of the poverty headcount before and after the policy reform by income unit type in Table 12.14, single parents have benefited most from the reform, followed by couples with dependent children. The change in AS has affected poverty rates only marginally for single persons.

Figure 12.1 TIP curves before and after the policy reform

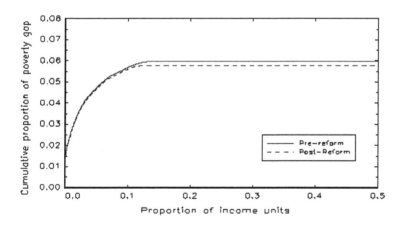

---

[11] Income is equivalised using the Whiteford equivalence scales (Whiteford, 1985).

Actual and Proposed Reforms

Table 12.14 Poverty headcount by income unit type

	Proportion in poverty		
	Before the policy change	After the policy change	Difference
Couple	0.0383	0.0383	0.0000
Couple + dependants	0.0795	0.0449	-0.0345
Single	0.2244	0.2252	0.0008
Single + dependants	0.1135	0.0459	-0.0676
All	0.1369	0.1248	-0.0121

The intensity of poverty is measured by the poverty gap, the extent to which the income-unit income falls below the poverty line. It is expressed as a proportion of the poverty line. The poverty gap is zero when income is above the poverty line. Income units are ranked in ascending order of their income. The TIP curve is obtained by plotting the total poverty gap per capita against the corresponding proportion of people. Overall, the poverty gap has decreased to a small extent, as shown by the lower level of the TIP curve. Inequality among those in poverty is reflected by the slope of the non-horizontal section of the curve at any point, which is the poverty gap at that point. This shows that there is quite a large difference between the poorest poor and the richest poor. This difference decreases somewhat after the reform (a straight line from the intersection of the TIP curve with the y-axis to the point where the curve turns into a horizontal line would indicate complete equality between all people below the poverty line).

12.5 Conclusions

This chapter has studied the effects of a recently introduced policy change in New Zealand. The changes involved decreased benefit rates; increased Family Assistance, which is partly made to depend on labour supply; and increased AS. The behavioural tax microsimulation model TaxMod-B was used to estimate the effects of the changes on average hours worked, participation rates, government expenditure on different payments, government revenue from direct income taxes and the implied effect on poverty and inequality in New Zealand.

Another important component of the policy change for families with children (in particular, children under school age) is the increased Childcare Assistance. Unfortunately, there are no data in the HES on the cost or use of childcare. As a result, the changes regarding Childcare Assistance could not be simulated. The expectation is that this additional payment for families with children would further increase the probability of labour force participation and the amount of labour supply in these families. This effect is probably largest for low-wage families, where the price of childcare might otherwise cancel out nearly all additional earnings to be obtained from additional working hours.

The effect of changes to the AS appears to be small. Although the effect is likely to be somewhat underestimated in the calculations presented here, they are not expected to increase to a large amount if they could be calculated more accurately. The changes to Family Assistance have had a positive effect on sole parents' labour supply and a small negative effect on married men and women's labour supply. For sole parents, independent of the number of children, the simulated effects are on average positive and the positive effects were generally largest for those with one child. However, the sample size is relatively small for this group when the number of children is three or more. For couple families, independent of the number of children, the simulated effect is negative but, similar to what is observed for sole parents, the negative effect is smaller for those with only one dependent child.

PART IV. FURTHER DEVELOPMENTS

13 Modelling Extensions

Previous chapters in this book have shown how a behavioural microsimulation model can be used to examine a wide range of hypothetical and actual policy changes to the direct tax and transfer system. The ability of behavioural models to give some indication of individuals' likely labour supply changes resulting from a tax change is clearly important, especially as many policy reforms are designed in an attempt to improve labour force participation and hours of work. Sometimes policies are aimed at specific demographic groups in the population, but in other contexts labour supply responses may be unintended consequences of reforms which have some other main objective, such as the alleviation of poverty or income redistribution, more widely considered. The implications, for total expenditure on benefits and for revenue from direct taxes, of allowing for potential labour supply responses have also been shown to be important.

Modelling labour supply behaviour in the context of a microsimulation model, where priority is placed on the need to include as much detail of the tax structure as possible, and handle the heterogeneity in the sample, presents a number of challenges. In addition, the production of useful summary information is itself far from straightforward. Although the discussion of technical aspects of specification, estimation and simulation has been kept to a minimum in this book, some indication has been given of the problems of evaluating redistribution in discrete hours labour supply models, and of adjusting population weights to allow for possible or actual demographic changes.[1]

The present chapter looks ahead to further modelling developments and challenges involved in trying to improve the practical value of microsimulation models for policy analysis. Section 13.1 discusses some aspects of policy evaluation, while section 13.2 examines some wider developments, in particular the need to allow for the demand side of the

---

[1] For a full-length treatment of technical aspects of microsimulation modelling see Creedy and Kalb (2006).

labour market. The models used in this book are based on cross-sectional datasets and consider individuals maximising utility in terms of current variables only. Section 13.3 turns to life cycle and dynamic issues.

13.1 Policy Evaluation

13.1.1 Welfare Measurement

Measures of inequality and their associated social welfare functions calculated by MITTS are based on a measure of income, using adult equivalence scales and alternative types of income unit. In a behavioural model, it might be suggested that allowance should be made for changes in individuals' leisure as a result of a tax change. This suggests the use of a 'money metric welfare measure' rather than simply an income measure in evaluating the impacts on individuals of tax changes. Furthermore, it would be useful to be able to compute standard measures of welfare change and marginal excess burdens for selected individual and household types (involving equivalent and compensating variations).

However, the computation of such measures in the context of income taxes and transfers is highly complex as a result of the nonlinearity of budget constraints and the role of corner solutions. In a discrete hours model, every position is effectively a corner solution. These problems are examined in detail in Creedy and Kalb (2005c), who suggested an algorithm for computing exact welfare changes. The application of the method to microsimulation models such as MITTS is not straightforward, but it is aimed to implement this in future versions.

13.1.2 Benefit Take-up

It has been mentioned that the MITTS model evaluates taxes and benefits for each individual using the detailed information provided by the Survey of Income and Housing Costs (SIHC), assuming that all benefits to which the individual is eligible are claimed (and no benefits are obtained to which the individual is not entitled). Ideally, it would be useful to model take-up rates for each of the types of benefit at the same time as labour supply behaviour is modelled. This is considerably complicated by the fact that take-up rates may depend on the levels and conditions applying to the benefits for which the individual is eligible, along with the income level and demographic structure of the household. The current (2006) version of MITTS allows for a very simple adjustment to take-up rates, whereby benefits below a small specified amount are not claimed. Further work is planned on this topic.

13.1.3 Policy Objectives

In practical tax policy design, there are always particular constraints and objectives, depending on the context. For example, an aim of policy-makers may be a desire to stimulate greater labour market participation by a particular demographic group, or to raise the net income levels of certain groups, or reduce overall inequality. Constraints may involve government expenditure, or a desire of governments to retain some features of an income tax schedule, such as top marginal rates or the existence of a tax-free threshold. It would therefore be useful to introduce into behavioural models the facility for users to produce policy changes that are, for example, revenue neutral. This would require iterative search methods in which certain tax parameters (chosen by the user) are automatically adjusted in response to some specified policy change. This represents another challenge for the future.

13.2 Wider Modelling Developments

Extensive work is needed to deal with general equilibrium issues, in order to avoid the restriction of the analysis to the supply side of the labour market. This restriction was in particular important for the analyses presented in Part III of this book. This section provides a tentative discussion of the development of new models that could potentially interact with MITTS.

13.2.1 General Equilibrium Adjustments

The emphasis on population heterogeneity has meant that the large-scale tax microsimulation models are partial equilibrium in nature. They focus on labour supplies and incomes of individuals and households, along with the associated taxes and transfer payments. Insofar as they deal with consumption, they only deal with the demand side, and insofar as they deal with labour supplies, they only handle the supply side of the labour market.

In practice, particularly for large tax changes, the resulting reallocation of resources may give rise to changes in factor prices. It has so far not been possible to construct general equilibrium models having extensive household components, though experiments have been made involving linkages between different types of model.

This aspect of partial equilibrium models always needs to be kept in mind when considering simulation results. They describe what, under specified situations, may happen to only one side of the relevant market; they cannot produce a new equilibrium resulting from economy-wide adjustments. The models are also static in the sense that there is usually no attempt to model a time sequence of changes.

However, chapter 11 calculated a time path for the expected employment increase resulting from an increase in labour supply. Three different possibilities were discussed, for a four-year period, based on evidence from another policy change. Nevertheless, this is necessarily a relatively ad hoc solution and a more formal process would be helpful to deal with this part of the simulation. The following two subsections suggest more formal procedures to incorporate general equilibrium adjustments into the simulated outcomes.

13.2.2 Third Round Effects of Tax Changes

In modelling terms there appears to be a dichotomy between large-scale tax microsimulation models and computable general equilibrium models. The former are partial equilibrium models, which replicate actual population heterogeneity and complex tax structures, while the latter typically have extremely simple tax structures and are based on a few representative household types.

It is useful to think in terms of a number of 'rounds' from a policy change. The 'first round' effects of a tax reform arise in an arithmetic model in which labour supplies are fixed. The 'second round' effects, produced by a behavioural model, allow for labour supply responses, with wage rates held constant. The challenge is to take behavioural microsimulation analysis one step further, by modelling possible effects on individuals' wages of a tax policy reform.

Given a method of producing changes to the wage rate distribution arising from labour market effects, such changes could be fed back into the behavioural microsimulation model in order to obtain adjusted labour supply responses and government expenditure estimates: this gives what may be called the 'third round' effects. Creedy and Duncan (2005) explored the use of a multi-stage procedure in which the simulated labour supply effects of a policy change are aggregated and combined with extraneous information about the demand side of the labour market. Their approach involves the concept of a 'supply response schedule'. This is a numerical construction, based on simulated labour supply responses to wage changes, conditional on a given tax and transfer structure.

MITTS is used to obtain individuals' hours responses to a proportionate change in all observed wage rates for individuals in a specified occupational or demographic group. That is, the full wage distribution is perturbed, and the aggregate labour supply response to that perturbation is obtained. The advantage of this type of supply response schedule is that each point on the schedule is consistent with a distribution of wages, together with the underlying tax and transfer scheme and population characteristics. Movement along the supply response schedule arises from a shift in the entire wage distribution. While Creedy and Duncan demonstrated the potential usefulness of this extension to standard microsimulation, its practical application requires substantial disaggregated information about demand conditions. This extreme, in which wages must fully adjust to an unchanged demand for labour, provides a useful contrast to the opposite extreme, currently implied by MITTS, of no adjustment; and it can be modelled using the supply response schedule. This appears to be an area where links, rather than full integration, between general equilibrium models and behavioural microsimulation models could be exploited.

13.2.3 Alternative General Equilibrium Extensions

Another area of potential extensions involves complementing the microeconomic approach of MITTS with analyses from recently developed macroeconomic models in which households have differing employment histories, levels of wealth, education, access to credit, or in general exhibit realistic degrees of heterogeneity. The Applied Macroeconomics research programme of the Melbourne Institute is in the process of adapting several of these models to the Australian context. It is anticipated that the interaction between MITTS and this class of macroeconomic models would be two way: MITTS can provide guidance on the appropriate methods of calibrating existing models to be representative of Australian households, while the macroeconomic models can be used to provide a broader context in which to view the results of MITTS.

This strand of research could examine ways in which the capabilities of the MITTS model can be used in conjunction with a class of dynamic, stochastic general equilibrium (DSGE) macroeconomic models. Of particular interest are DSGE models which incorporate heterogeneity among consumers. These models have not been as widely used as the benchmark 'representative agent' DSGE models, but are growing in popularity. A key feature of heterogeneous agent models, which makes them particularly attractive for use in this research, is that they generate equilibrium outcomes with non-trivial distributions of income, wealth, hours worked and other variables of interest.

Early versions of heterogeneous agent models focused on environments in which consumers could not perfectly insure themselves against all idiosyncratic risk, because of liquidity constraints, incomplete markets or other features. Examples include Imrohoroglu (1989, 1990), Hansen and Imrohoroglu (1992), and Aiyagari (1994); an overview of these models is in Ríos-Rull (1995).

More recently, models have been developed that incorporate a much richer degree of heterogeneity among households. Imrohoroglu, Imrohoroglu and Joines (1999a, b) present a model with overlapping generations of people who face both mortality risk and individual income risk. These agents also differ in their employment status and asset holdings. The authors use this model to examine the implications of an unfunded social security system and the optimal replacement ratio. Gourinchas and Parker (2002) analyse consumption decisions over consumers' life cycles in a model that features heterogeneity in occupation and education as well as income. Regalia and Ríos-Rull (2001) construct a model with both male and female agents, who make decisions about marriage and childbearing and invest in their children's human capital. They find that this model accounts very well for observed increases in the number of both single women and single mothers in the United States.

Using heterogeneous agent DSGE models in conjunction with MITTS has several other attractions. First, MITTS is calibrated to the Australian economy (with respect to wage and income distributions, for example), and so could provide guidance in how best to modify existing DSGE models in order to examine issues specific to Australia. Second, the general equilibrium nature of heterogeneous agent DSGE models may provide useful guidance on how best to incorporate dynamic features into MITTS. Third, heterogeneous agent DSGE models allow for more sources of uncertainty than does MITTS. For example, macro models could be used to incorporate business cycle shocks, monetary policy and productivity shocks into MITTS-based analyses.

13.3 Life-cycle Dynamics and Population Dynamics

Both the behavioural and arithmetic components of MITTS are concerned with a cross-section of individuals at a single point in time. Behaviour is based on estimated utility functions that are defined in terms of current (single-period) levels of net income and leisure. This places an obvious restriction on the nature, or interpretation, of the types of counterfactual examined. MITTS-B provides the probabilities that individuals work a range of alternative hours levels, under the assumption that only net incomes at those hours are different from the net incomes in the sample period. Behaviour may in practice change because people get older or they anticipate future tax changes, perhaps as a result of government responses to expected population ageing.

This means that MITTS does not look at changes over the lifetime of individuals or at the aggregate situation in future years. A number of features of the tax and transfer system are nevertheless designed specifically with a longer period perspective in mind, so that concern is not so much with income redistribution in cross-sectional data but with redistribution over the lifetime. An obvious example relates to pension or superannuation schemes, but sickness and unemployment benefits, and many family-related transfer payments, are received by individuals at various stages of the life cycle rather than reflecting permanent features.

Longer period considerations are also relevant in designing policies to encourage labour force participation. For example, it is well known that mothers with young children reduce their hours of work or completely cease to participate in paid employment. To determine what influences this decision and investigate how it may be affected by tax policy, the full impact of this decision needs to be taken into account; not only the effect on the income level in the same period but also on future income levels. Individuals' decisions are likely to be influenced by long-term plans as well as single-year impacts. Similarly, when studying retirement decisions, it is important to take into account the long-term nature of retirement planning. To study these issues, it is necessary to model individuals' life cycles.

As indicated earlier, population changes over calendar time are also important, in addition to life-cycle changes, which take place for a variety of cohorts in a population over the same time period. Changes in population structure can be projected under particular assumptions regarding fertility, death and migration rates. Such projections can be used in conjunction with microsimulation models to provide a limited number of counterfactual analyses.

The construction of life-cycle models is obviously much more demanding than that of cross-sectional models, in terms of conceptual, computational and data demands. It is therefore not surprising that earlier life-cycle tax models tended to concentrate on specific issues such as superannuation, using a single cohort and little heterogeneity in terms of household structures.[2]   However, developments in computing facilities, data availability and an increased willingness to fund the teamwork necessary for the production and maintenance of large-scale models has led to recent fruitful developments in dynamic simulation modelling; for a survey of a range of dynamic models, see O'Donoghue (2001). There is therefore scope for combining some of the benefits of dynamic models with the advantages of a microsimulation model such as MITTS.

Unlike cross-sectional tax microsimulation models, a dynamic model requires some kind of demographic component to deal with life-cycle events such as marriage, fertility, divorce and death. The ability to model

---

[2] Australian examples are the cohort model of the complex Superannuation and Age Pension scheme in Atkinson, Creedy and Knox (1996) and the analysis of indirect taxes and lifetime inequality in Cameron and Creedy (1995).

these features is needed even if they are not endogenised, that is, made to depend on incomes and relevant characteristics of the tax and transfer system. It may be possible to use such a demographic model to age a cross-sectional dataset artificially, using details of, for example, marriage and fertility patterns in relation to a range of individual characteristics (in addition to age). If all the relevant characteristics of a person at a future point in time (that is, at a future age) were predicted in this way, then the amount of social security benefits or tax given a particular tax and transfer system could be calculated using MITTS. This could perhaps be done for a sequence of years up to an individual's entire lifetime and for different tax and transfer systems. The 'ageing' of the individuals in the dataset must necessarily relate to a specific calendar-time period, over which exogenous changes, not only in the tax structure but for example also in inflation, real wage growth and nominal interest rates, need to be made explicit.

In this way, a person's lifetime income from different income sources could be projected under different tax and transfer systems. Similarly, the accumulation of net worth over a person's life cycle could be simulated, assuming a particular saving rate or profile of saving rates. This type of approach also requires explicit assumptions to be made regarding differences between cohorts as they age over the same calendar-time period. Such differences may be particularly important regarding fertility, for example. Naturally, estimation of models regarding the decisions of individuals over the life cycle ideally requires longitudinal data over a long period of time. These are not available for Australia but even with relatively few 'waves' of survey data or using a pseudo cohort constructed from a sequence of cross-sectional surveys, models could be estimated for a prototype, which could be improved and extended in the future as more data become available.

The majority of dynamic models are discrete-time models given the large computational requirements of continuous time models. One type of modelling approach uses an annual transition matrix for the different lifetime transitions. Shortening the time period between transitions obviously increases the amount of information required and the time needed to calculate all variables in the model, and it is unlikely to provide significant benefits. It may be possible to combine this type of model with

MITTS, particularly if the dynamic model produces data that are consistent with the form of input used within MITTS.

However, the use of transition matrices as the basic information on which life-cycle changes are generated makes it difficult to examine counterfactuals, given the large number of elements involved, which need to be changed. For example, it would be of interest to consider the implications of various changes in the age of marriage, or of associated fertility patterns. An alternative, more parsimonious, approach was adopted by Creedy and van de Ven (1999, 2001), where functional relationships were estimated and the parameters had clear economic or demographic interpretations, so that counterfactuals could easily be specified. Simulated life-cycle changes were based on random drawings from the estimated distributions underlying the functional relationships. Nevertheless, the Creedy and van de Ven approach was limited in the degree of heterogeneity modelled and, in addition, it did not model optimising behaviour (though a certain amount of endogeneity was built into the simulations).

Allowing for optimising behaviour in dynamic models may perhaps more easily be incorporated if it is assumed that only past outcomes and the current time period's set of outcomes are relevant for the different decisions to be made, and the order of decision making is known (whereby some types of decision take priority or must necessarily occur before others). Simple assumptions about expectations formation would be needed. More interesting, but also more complicated and computationally demanding, would be to allow for behavioural responses to policy changes, allowing a long-term view when households make a particular decision, for example whether or not they want to be in paid employment. The complication arises from having to calculate the effect of taking each possible path at each decision moment. There are many possible paths with different outcomes; one of these has the highest utility and is expected to be chosen. Solving this type of model requires the optimisation of intertemporal equations at each point in time where a decision is made; see Sefton (2000) for further discussion of this problem.

13.4 Conclusions

This book has illustrated the value of a microsimulation model in examining the potential implications of a range of tax policy changes. The focus has been on behavioural tax microsimulation modelling, which takes individuals' labour supply responses into account. Microsimulation models are particularly useful in tax policy analysis and design as they are built to replicate closely the considerable degree of heterogeneity observed in the population.

After illustrating a range of uses of microsimulation in this book, this final chapter considered several opportunities for further extensions. This opportunity, and need, is due to the relatively recent development of this type of model, which requires powerful computers to allow simulations to be run in a reasonable amount of time. Many of the proposed extensions would require a considerable amount of additional running time to carry out a simulation. Examples of valuable extensions are to allow for the demand side of labour, indicating whether new labour force participants are likely to find work; or to allow for life-cycle dynamics, which are important to deal with population ageing issues or with female labour force participation.

All models have their limitations and these must be recognised when producing policy simulations. Indeed, the use of formal models helps to make the assumptions explicit. Reminders must regularly be issued regarding the need to treat models as providing, at best, tentative guidance about the possible implications of tax changes in well-specified circumstances. In addition, it can be important to run several simulations based on different assumptions. This allows an examination of the sensitivity of outcomes to alternative assumptions.

An important component of every microsimulation model is the dataset on which it is based and which has been used to estimate behavioural relationships. It is particularly important that the data are up to date, and that detailed information on income and hours of work is available. Without this, obtaining reliable results would be extremely complicated or perhaps even impossible.

Every tax policy change involves losers and gainers. Hence distributional value judgements are unavoidable. It is argued here that the most useful role of models is in supporting 'rational policy analysis'. By this is meant the examination and reporting of the implications of alternative policies, so that policy-makers can form their own judgements. It also involves the determination of the appropriate policies that are implied by the adoption of a range of clearly specified value judgements.

As always, given that no model is without its limitations, it is necessary to treat the output from microsimulation models with caution. Nevertheless, given the importance of the issues examined, such models can provide a valuable element of policy analysis and can thereby help to provide a counterweight against the rhetoric and special pleading that otherwise play a major role in tax policy debates.

References

Aiyagari, S.R. (1994) Uninsured idiosyncratic risk and aggregate saving. *Quarterly Journal of Economics*, 109, pp. 659-684.

Alvarado, J. and Creedy, J. (1998) *Population Ageing, Migration and Social Expenditure*. Cheltenham: Edward Elgar.

Apps, P. and Savage, E. (1989) Labour supply, welfare rankings and the measurement of inequality. *Journal of Public Economics*, 47, pp. 336-364.

Atkinson, A.B. (1995) *Public Economics in Action*. Oxford: Clarendon Press.

Atkinson, M., Creedy, J. and Knox, D. (1996) Alternative retirement income strategies: a cohort analysis of lifetime redistribution. *Economic Record*, 72, pp. 97-106.

Australian Bureau of Statistics (1999) *Employee Earnings and Hours*. ABS catalogue no. 6306.0.

Australian Bureau of Statistics (2000) *2000 Yearbook Australia*. ABS catalogue no. 1301.0.

Australian Bureau of Statistics (2002) *2001 Census Community Profile Series: Basic Community Profile*. ABS catalogue no. 2001.0.

Australian Bureau of Statistics (2003a) *Population by Age and Sex, Australian States and Territories*. ABS catalogue no. 3201.0.

Australian Bureau of Statistics (2003b) *Population Projection Australia 2002-2101*. ABS catalogue no. 3222.0.

Australian Labor Party (2004) *Labor's Tax and Better Family Payment Plan; Rewarding Hard Work*. Campaign 2004 Policy Document.

Banks, J., Blundell, R. and Lewbel, A. (1996) Tax reform and welfare measurement: do we need demand system estimation? *Economic Journal*, 106, pp. 1227-1241.

Beckerman, W. (1979) The impact of income maintenance programmes on poverty in Britain. *Economic Journal*, 89, pp. 261-279.

Blundell, R. and Hoynes, H. (2004) Has 'in-work' benefit helped the labour market? In *Seeking a Premier League Economy* (ed. by R. Blundell, D. Card and R. Freeman), pp. 411-459. Chicago: University of Chicago Press.

Blundell, R. and MaCurdy, T. (1999) Labor supply: a review of alternative approaches. In *Handbook of Labor Economics*, Vol. 3 (ed. by O.C. Ashenfelter and D. Card), pp. 1559-1695. Amsterdam: North-Holland.

Blundell, R.W., Meghir, C., Symons, E. and Walker, I. (1986) A labour supply model for the simulation of tax and benefit reforms. In *Unemployment, Search and Labour Supply* (ed. by R.W. Blundell and I. Walker), pp. 267-293. Cambridge: Cambridge University Press.

Blundell, R., Duncan, A., McCrae, J. and Meghir, C. (2000) The labour market impact of the Working Families' Tax Credit. *Fiscal Studies*, 21, pp. 75-104.

Blundell, R., Brewer, M., Duncan, A., Reed, H. and Shephard, A. (2004) *The Employment Impact of Labour Market Reforms: A Bank of England Report*. London: Institute for Fiscal Studies.

Buddelmeyer, H., Cai, L. and Kalb, G. (2005) Documentation for TaxMod-B; a behavioural microsimulation model. Report for New Zealand Treasury, Wellington.

Buddelmeyer, H., Dawkins, P., Duncan, A., Kalb, G. and Scutella, R. (2004a) An analysis of the Australian Labor Party's tax and family benefits package: using the Melbourne Institute Tax and Transfer Simulator (MITTS). Report to the Australian Labor Party, September 2004.

Buddelmeyer, H., Dawkins, P., Freebairn, J. and Kalb, G. (2004b) Bracket creep, effective marginal tax rates and alternative tax packages. *Mercer–Melbourne Institute Quarterly Bulletin of Economic Trends*, 1.04, pp. 17-28.

Buddelmeyer, H., Dawkins, P. and Kalb, G. (2004) The Melbourne Institute report on the 2004 Federal Budget. *Mercer–Melbourne Institute Quarterly Bulletin of Economic Trends*, 2.04, pp. 19-23.

Cai, L., Creedy, J. and Kalb, G. (2004) Accounting for population ageing in tax microsimulation modelling by survey reweighting. Melbourne Institute Working Paper No. 26/04.

Cai, L., Creedy, J. and Kalb, G. (2006) Accounting for population ageing in tax microsimulation modelling by survey reweighting. *Australian Economic Papers*, 45(1), pp. 18-37.

Cai, L., Kalb, G., Tseng, Y.-P. and Vu, H.H. (2005) The effect of financial incentives on labour supply: evidence for sole parents from microsimulation and quasi-experimental evaluation. Melbourne Institute Working Paper No. 10/05.

Callan, T. and Van Soest, A. (1996) Family labour supply and taxes in Ireland. ESRI Working Paper No. 78, Dublin: The Economic & Social Research Institute.

Cameron, L. and Creedy, J. (1995) Indirect tax exemptions and the distribution of lifetime income: a simulation analysis. *Economic Record*, 71, pp. 77-87.

Commonwealth Department of Family and Community Services, and the Department of Education, Science and Training (several issues between 2000 and 2004) *A Guide to Commonwealth Government Payments*, http://www.centrelink.gov.au/internet/internet.nsf/publications/co029.htm.

Commonwealth Treasury of Australia (2003a) *Mid-Year Economic and Fiscal Outlook 2003-04*. Canberra: Commonwealth of Australia.

Commonwealth Treasury of Australia (2003b) Preliminary assessment of the impact of The New Tax System. *Economic Roundup*, Autumn, pp. 1-49.

Creedy, J. (1994) Taxes and transfers with endogenous earnings: some basic analytics. *Bulletin of Economic Research*, 46, pp. 97-130.

Creedy, J. (1995) Taxes and transfers: target efficiency and social welfare. *Economica*, 63, pp. S163-74.

Creedy, J. (1997a) Evaluating alternative tax and transfer schemes with endogenous earnings. *Oxford Economic Papers*, 49, pp. 43-56.

Creedy, J. (1997b) Means-tested versus universal transfers: alternative models and value judgements. *Manchester School*, 66, pp. 100-117.

Creedy, J. (1998) The welfare effect on different income groups of indirect tax changes and inflation in New Zealand. *Economic Record*, 74, pp. 373-383.

Creedy, J. (1999) *Modelling Indirect Taxes and Tax Reform*. Cheltenham: Edward Elgar.

Creedy, J. and Dawkins, P. (1999) Modelling the incentive effects of alternative tax and transfer systems. *Australian Social Policy*, 1, pp. 61-73.

Creedy, J. and Duncan, A.S. (2002) Behavioural microsimulation with labour supply responses. *Journal of Economic Surveys*, 16, pp. 1-39.

Creedy, J. and Duncan, A.S. (2005) Aggregating labour supply and feedback effects in microsimulation. *Australian Journal of Labour Economics*, 8(3), pp. 277-290.

Creedy, J. and Kalb, G. (2005a) Behavioural microsimulation modelling with the Melbourne Institute Tax and Transfer Simulator (MITTS): uses and extensions. In *Quantitative Tools for Microeconomic Policy Analysis* (ed. by the Productivity Commission), pp. 247-292. Canberra: AGPS.

Creedy, J. and Kalb, G. (2005b) Discrete hours labour supply modelling: specification, estimation and simulation. *Journal of Economic Surveys*, 19, pp. 697-734.

Creedy, J. and Kalb, G. (2005c) Measuring welfare changes with nonlinear budget constraints in continuous and discrete hours labour supply models. *Manchester School*, 73, pp. 664-685.

Creedy, J. and Kalb, G. (2006) *Labour Supply and Microsimulation: The Evaluation of Tax Policy Reforms*. Cheltenham: Edward Elgar.

Creedy, J. and van de Ven, J. (1999) The effects of selected Australian taxes and transfers on annual and lifetime inequality. *Australian Journal of Labour Economics*, 3, pp. 1-22.

Creedy, J. and van de Ven, J. (2001) Decomposing redistributive effects of taxes and transfers in Australia: annual and lifetime measures. *Australian Economic Papers*, 40, pp. 185-198.

Creedy, J., Duncan, A.S., Harris, M. and Scutella, R. (2002) *Microsimulation Modelling of Taxation and the Labour Market: The Melbourne Institute Tax and Transfer Simulator*. Cheltenham: Edward Elgar.

Creedy, J., Kalb, G. and Kew, H. (2003) Flattening the effective marginal tax rate structure in Australia: policy simulations using the Melbourne Institute Tax and Transfer Simulator. *Australian Economic Review*, 36, pp. 156-172.

Creedy, J., Kalb, G. and Scutella, R. (2004) Evaluating the income redistribution effects of tax reforms in discrete hours models. In *Studies on Economic Well-Being: Essays in Honor of John P. Formby* (ed. by Y. Amiel and J.A. Bishop), pp. 201-228. New York: Elsevier.

Creedy, J., Kalb, G. and Scutella, R. (2006) Income distribution in discrete hours behavioural microsimulation models: an illustration. *Journal of Economic Inequality*, 4, pp. 57-76.

Department of Family and Community Services (FaCS) (2001) *Department of Family and Community Services Annual Report 2000-01*. Canberra.

Department of Family and Community Services (FaCS) (2003) Income support customers: a statistical overview 2001. *Occasional Paper*, no. 7.

Department of Veterans' Affairs (2004). DVA FACTS, DP 43, IS 21, IS 22, IS 30.

Department of Veterans' Affairs: *Annual Report 1999-2000, 2000-2001, 2002-2003.*

Deville, J.-F. and Särndal, C.-E. (1992) Calibration estimators in survey sampling. *Journal of the American Statistical Association*, 87, pp. 376-382.

Doiron, D.J. (2004) Welfare reform and the labour supply of lone parents in Australia: a natural experiment approach. *Economic Record*, 80, pp. 157-176.

Duncan, A.S. (1993) Labour supply decisions and non-convex budget sets: the case of National Insurance contributions in the UK. In *Empirical Approaches to Fiscal Policy* (ed. by A. Heimler and D. Meulders), pp. 137-162. London: Chapman & Hall.

Duncan, A.S. and Giles, C. (1996) Labour supply incentives and recent family credit reforms. *Economic Journal*, 106, pp. 142-155.

Duncan, A. and Harris, M.N. (2002) Simulating the behavioural effects of welfare reforms among sole parents in Australia. *Economic Record*, 78, pp. 264-276.

Duncan, A., Giles, C. and MacCrae, J. (1999) Household labour supply, childcare costs and in-work benefits: modelling the impact of the working families tax credit in the UK. Institute for Fiscal Studies, London.

Ebert, U. (1997) Social welfare when needs differ: an axiomatic approach. *Economica*, 64, pp. 233-244.

Eissa, N. and Hoynes, H.W. (1999) The earned Income Tax Credit and the labor supply of married couples. *University of Wisconsin-Madison Institute for Research on Poverty Discussion Paper*, no. 1194-99.

Folsom, R.E. Jr and Singh, A.C. (2000) The generalized exponential model for sampling weight calibration for extreme values, non-response and post-stratification. In *Proceedings of the Survey Research Methods Section: American Statistical Association* (pp. 598–603). Alexandria, VA: American Statistical Association.

Foster, J., Greer, J. and Thorbecke, E. (1984) A class of decomposable poverty measures. *Econometrica*, 52, pp. 761-762.

Gerfin, M. and Leu, R.E. (2003) The impact of in-work benefits on poverty and household labour supply: a simulation study for Switzerland. Institute for the Study of Labor, IZA Discussion Paper no. 762.

Gourinchas, P.O. and Parker, A.J. (2002) Consumption over the life cycle. *Econometrica*, 70, pp. 47-89.

Hansen, G. and Imrohoroglu, A. (1992) The role of unemployment insurance in an economy with liquidity constraints and moral hazard. *Journal of Political Economy*, 100, pp. 118-142.

Harding, A., Warren, N., Robinson, M. and Lambert, S. (2000) The distributional impact of year 2000 tax reforms in Australia. *Agenda*, 7, pp. 17-32.

Hotz, V.J. and Scholz, J.K. (2003) The earned income tax credit. In *Means-Tested Transfer Programs in the United States* (ed. by R. Moffitt), pp. 141-197. Chicago: The University of Chicago Press.

Hoynes, H.W. (1996) Welfare transfers in two-parent families: labor supply and welfare participation under AFDC-UP. *Econometrica*, 64, pp. 295-332.

Imrohoroglu, A. (1989) Cost of business cycles with indivisibilities and liquidity constraints. *Journal of Political Economy*, 97, pp. 1364-1383.

Imrohoroglu, A. (1990) The welfare cost of inflation under imperfect insurance. *Journal of Economic Dynamics and Control*, 16, pp. 79-91.

Imrohoroglu, A., Imrohoroglu, S. and Joines, D.H. (1999a) A dynamic stochastic general equilibrium analysis of social security. In *The Discipline of Applied General Equilibrium* (ed. by T. Kehoe and E. Prescott). Berlin: Springer-Verlag.

Imrohoroglu, A., Imrohoroglu, S. and Joines, D.H. (1999b) Computing models of social security. In *Computational Methods for the Study of Dynamic Economies* (ed. by R. Marimon and A. Scott), pp. 221-237. Oxford: Oxford University Press.

Johnson, D., Creedy, J., Freebairn, J., Scutella, R., Cowling, S. and Harding, G. (1998) *Evaluation of Tax Reform With Producer and Consumer Responses.* Melbourne: MIAESR.

Kalb, G. (2002a) Estimation of labour supply models for four separate groups in the Australian population. *Melbourne Institute Working Paper*, no. 24/02.

Kalb, G. (2002b) Estimation of alternative labour supply model specifications for the Australian population. Final report prepared for the Department of Family and Community Services.

Kalb, G. and Kew, H. (2002) The effect of a reduced allowance and pension taper rate: policy simulations using the Melbourne Institute Tax and Transfer Simulator. *Melbourne Institute Working Paper*, no. 25/02.

Kalb, G. and Scutella, R. (2002) Estimation of wage equations in Australia: allowing for censored observations of labour supply. *Melbourne Institute Working Paper*, no. 8/2002.

Kalb, G. and Scutella, R. (2003) New Zealand labour supply from 1991-2001: an analysis based on a discrete choice structural utility model. *New Zealand Treasury Working Paper*, no. 03/23.

Kalb, G. and Scutella, R. (2004) Wage and employment rates in New Zealand from 1991 to 2001. *New Zealand Economic Papers*, 38, pp. 21-47.

Kalb, G., Cai, L. and Tuckwell, I. (2005) The effect of changes in Family Assistance: allowing for labour supply responses. Mimeo, Melbourne Institute of Applied Economic and Social Research, University of Melbourne.

Kalb, G., Cai, L. and Vu, H. (2004) Updating the input for the Melbourne Institute Tax and Transfer Simulator. Report for the Department of Family and Community Services.

Kalb, G., Kew, H. and Scutella, R. (2002) The effect of a reduced Family Payment taper rate: policy simulations using the Melbourne Institute Tax and Transfer Simulator. *Melbourne Institute Working Paper*, no. 26/2002.

Kalb, G., Kew, H. and Scutella, R. (2005) Effects of the Australian New Tax System on income tax and benefits: with and without labour supply responses. *Australian Economic Review*, 38, pp. 137-158.

Keane, M. and Moffitt, R. (1998) A structural model of multiple welfare program participation and labor supply. *International Economic Review*, 39(3), pp. 553-589.

Killingsworth, M.R. (1983) *Labor Supply*. New York: Cambridge University Press.

Killingsworth, M.R. and Heckman, J.J. (1986) Female labor supply. In *Handbook of Labor Economics*, Vol. 1 (ed. by O.C. Ashenfelter and R. Layard), pp. 103-204. Amsterdam: North-Holland.

Klevmarken, N.A. (1997) Modelling behavioural response in EUROMOD. University of Cambridge *Department of Applied Economics Working Paper*, no. 9720.

Lambert, P.J. (1985) Endogenising the income distribution: the redistributive effect, and Laffer effects, of a progressive tax-benefit system. *European Journal of Political Economy*, 1, pp. 3-20.

Lambert, P.J. (1988) The equity-efficiency trade-off: Breit reconsidered. *Oxford Economic Papers*, 42, pp. 91-104.

Maddala, G.S. (1983) *Limited Dependent and Qualitative Variables in Econometrics*. New York: Cambridge University Press.

Mitchell, D. (1991) *Income Transfers in Ten Welfare States*. Newcastle: Avebury.

Moffitt, R. (1992) Incentive effects of the U.S. welfare system: a review. *Journal of Economic Literature*, 30, pp. 1-61.

Moffitt, R. (2000) Simulating transfer programmes and labour supply. In *Taxes, Transfers and Labour Market Responses: What Can Microsimulation Tell Us?* (ed. by T. Callan), pp. 1-22. Dublin: The Economic and Social Research Institute.

Murray, J. (1996) Modelling the labour supply behaviour of sole parents in Australia. In *Proceedings of the Econometric Society Australasian Meeting 1996, Volume 4: Microeconometrics* (ed. by M. McAleer, P. Miller and C. Ong), pp. 507-546. Perth: Uniprint, University of Western Australia.

O'Donoghue, C. (2001) Dynamic microsimulation: a methodological survey. *Brazilian Electronic Journal of Economics*, 4(2), http://www.beje.decon.ufpe.br/v4n2/cathal.pdf.

Pencavel, J. (1986) Labor supply of men. In *Handbook of Labor Economics*, Vol. 1 (ed. by O.C. Ashenfelter and R. Layard), pp. 3-102. Amsterdam: North-Holland.

Reference Group on Welfare Reform (2000) *Participation Support for a More Equitable Society*. Canberra.

Regalia, F. and Ríos-Rull, J.V. (2001) What accounts for the increase in the number of single households? University of Pennsylvania Department of Economics.

Ríos-Rull, J.V. (1995) Models with heterogeneous agents. In *Frontiers of Business Cycle Research* (ed. by T.F. Cooley), pp. 98-125. Princeton: Princeton University Press.

Scholz, J.K. (1996) In-work benefits in the United States: the Earned Income Tax Credit. *Economic Journal*, 106, pp. 156-169.

Sefton, J. (2000) A solution method for consumption decisions in a dynamic stochastic general equilibrium model. *Journal of Economic Dynamics and Control*, 24, pp. 1097-1119.

Singh, A.C. and Mohl, C.A. (1996) Understanding calibration estimators in survey sampling. *Survey Methodology*, 22, pp. 107-115.

Stern, N.H. (1986) On the specification of labour supply functions. In *Unemployment, Search and Labour Supply* (ed. by R.W. Blundell and I. Walker), pp. 143-189. Cambridge: Cambridge University Press.

The Treasurer (2000) Consumer price index – September quarter. Press release No. 100.

Van Soest, A. (1995) Structural models of family labor supply: a discrete choice approach. *Journal of Human Resources*, 30, pp. 63-88.

Warren, N., Harding, A., Robinson, M., Lambert, S. and Beer, G. (1999a) Distributional impact of possible tax reform packages. Report to Senate Select Committee on a New Tax System.

Warren, N., Harding, A., Lambert, S. and Robinson, M. (1999b) Distributional impact on households of the Australian Y2k tax and transfer reforms. Paper presented at a conference on 'Reform of Tax and Tax Transfers in Germany and Australia – and Ralph', UNSW, Sydney, 1-3 September.

Whiteford, P. (1985) A family's needs: equivalence scales, poverty and social security. *Department of Social Security Research Paper*, no. 27.

Index

Accommodation Supplement (AS)
(New Zealand) 207–9, 215, 227,
229
see also New Zealand tax and social
security system reforms 2005-8
microsimulation
accounting microsimulation models
see non-behavioural
microsimulation models
AFDC program 106
age groups
and Family Payment taper rate
reduction 77, 78
and New Zealand tax and social
security system reforms 2005-8
220–223, 229
and survey weights 115, 116, 132
and taper rate reduction 51, 52, 57,
58, 59, 60, 61
(*see also* survey reweighting for
population ageing)
Age Pension
and Australian New Tax and Social
Security System 148, 156
in survey reweighting 116, 117, 118,
123, 125, 128
and taper rate reduction 51, 52, 54
Age Pensioners 55, 156, 157, 185
see also over 65s
allowances 52–5, 65–6, 162
see also individual allowances
annual transition matrix 241–2
Applied Macroeconomics 237–9
arithmetic microsimulation models *see*
non-behavioural microsimulation
models
assets 14, 103
Atkinson, A.B. 36
Atkinson measure of inequality 102,
104, 105–6
Australian Bureau of Statistics (ABS)
6, 99

see also Census (Australia); Survey
of Income and Housing Costs
(SIHC) (Australia); survey
reweighting; survey reweighting
for population ageing; survey
weights
Australian Labor Party's tax and
Family Payments package 2004
and Australians Working Together
package 199–200
Family Tax Benefit Consolidation
191, 192, 193, 194, 195–6, 197,
198, 203
government expenditure and
revenue 192–3, 198–203
labour supply effects 193–7, 198–9,
200, 202, 203
Low and Middle Income Tax Offset
192, 193, 194, 196, 197, 198–9,
203
Single Income Tax Offset 192, 193,
194, 195–6, 197, 198, 203
top income tax threshold increases
192, 193, 195, 196, 197, 198,
199, 203
and Working Family Tax Credit
(UK) 200–202
Australian New Tax and Social
Security System 24, 137, 141–2,
159–63, 167–8
see also bracket creep in Australian
New Tax System
Australian New Tax and Social
Security System evaluation
dataset, sample and simulation
procedure 139–41
government expenditure and
revenue 141–2, 145–50, 151,
152, 153, 154, 158
labour supply 139, 140, 144, 145–6,
148, 149–52, 153, 154, 155,
156–8